Praise for Managing Your Career For Dummies

"From successful job interviewing to navigating office politics to dealing with difficult bosses, Messmer's book has something for every business professional who wants to build a great career."

— Anne Fisher, "Ask Annie" columnist, *Fortune* Magazine

"Max Messmer gives maximum value in career advice, whether you are just starting out or looking for a new path to pursue."

— Mr. Steve Forbes, President and CEO, Forbes Inc., Editor in Chief,
Forbes Magazine

"Messmer has crammed into this book an enormous amount of career advice that in most cases one only acquires over a lifetime. It's so much better to have all of this when you start your career!"

— David S. Pottruck, President and Co-CEO, Charles Schwab Corp.

"Once again, Max Messmer has created an entertaining and highly useful tool that's filled with practical advice. This career book includes not only what to do, but also what *not* to do when climbing the corporate ladder."

—David H. Komansky, Chairman & CEO of Merrill Lynch & Co., Inc.

Praise for Job Hunting For Dummies, 2nd Edition

"Comprehensive and easy-to-understand, this street-smart reference is a must read! *Job Hunting For Dummies* helps you take control of the process in finding the best job possible, regardless of your chosen field or level or experience. It's like navigating through your search with a knowledgeable partner."

— Tony Lee, Editor in Chief, *The Wall Street Journal* Interactive Edition's
Career Site (careers.wsj.com)

"Max Messmer is a renowned authority on finding the right job. His cutting-edge job-hunting guide taps the expertise of his company, which places thousands of job seekers every year."

— George T. Shaheen, President and CEO, Webvan Group, Inc.

"Max talks today, not yesterday. His advice can make the difference in putting you on top."

— Joyce Lain Kennedy, Syndicated Career Columnist and Author

Praise for Human Resources Kit For Dummies

"Amazing! HR today is more likely to induce eye-rolling, teeth-gnashing, and even tears than any other business function. Somehow, Max Messmer manages to get past the confusion and contradictions to make it all seem perfectly reasonable. Anyone with HR responsibilities, especially in small or mid-size organizations, should take a deep breath and read; this book could become the most well-thumbed volume in the office."

— Allan Halcrow, Publisher/Editor in Chief, *Workforce* Magazine

"One of the most comprehensive human resources reference tools on the market, this book walks you through everything from hiring, retention, and training to performance appraisals and disciplinary practices. Pragmatic and reassuring, Messmer covers it all within the framework of today's business realities."

— Dr. George B. Weathersby, President and CEO,
American Management Association

"Max Messmer, with the help of the national law firm, O'Melveny & Myers, LLP, addresses hot-button HR issues and illustrates that the proverbial ounce of prevention is worth a pound of litigious cure. The book points out the problems that arise from inconsistent and ill-executed policies and provides tips for avoiding legal minefields."

— Michael R. Losey, SPHR, CAE, President and CEO,
Society for Human Resource Management

"An effective HR department is the primary determinant of a successful company — its expansion, profitability, and future. This book offers proven practices to help you succeed. It contains the unbeatable combination of Max Messmer's expertise as head of the world's largest specialized staffing firm with the sage counsel of law firm O'Melveny & Myers, LLP, a nationally renowned authority on employment law."

— Ned Spieker, Chairman and Chief Executive Officer,
Spieker Properties

Managing Your Career For Dummies®

Cheat Sheet

Tips for Finding (And Being Hired for) the Right Job for You

The fundamentals of successful job searching are much the same today as they've always been — albeit with certain modifications that take into account the changing business environment. Here's a list of reminders:

- **Instead of viewing the objective as simply finding a new job, consider each search an opportunity to move one step closer to your long-term goals.** Target your efforts to job opportunities that will ultimately advance your career.

- **Make the most of every source of job leads.** This includes online job boards, recruiters, advertisements, and of course, your own network.

- **Use the Internet and other sources to find out as much as you can about any company in which you're interested.** Research the company's mission and its strategic priorities and speak with your professional network of contacts to gain insight on the corporate culture.

- **When preparing your resume, do more than describe your qualifications.** Make the strongest case possible for how you can help the organization accomplish its mission and achieve its strategic goals.

- **Put your best self forward during a job interview.** Remember that in many companies, positive energy, enthusiasm, and people skills count as much as technical skills.

Factors to Consider When Weighing a Job Offer

When evaluating a job offer, always consider your long-term career objectives. Here's a list of topics to take into account:

- **Salary and benefits:** Do they equal or exceed the market value for the job? Do they meet the basic requirements of your lifestyle?

- **Career implications:** Will successful performance in this job bring you closer to achieving ultimate career goals?

- **Financial and competitive health of the company:** How financially sound is the company? Is it gaining or losing market share? Where does it rank with competitors in the industry?

- **The culture:** Are the mission, values, and operating practices of the company consistent with your career goals?

- **Development opportunities:** Will the job and its responsibilities provide opportunities for professional development?

- **Your lifestyle:** How will the job affect your personal life, in such areas as commute time and work/life balance?

For Dummies™: Bestselling Book Series for Beginners

Managing Your Career For Dummies®

Cheat Sheet

Strategies for Expanding Your Circle of Personal Contacts

Whether they're your mentors, potential employers, or information resources, people are your link to professional success. The following are some ideas to help you develop and maintain your network of contacts:

- ✔ **Make networking an ongoing priority.** Set monthly goals for increasing your number of professional contacts and enhancing the quality of those relationships.
- ✔ **Join and become active in professional associations.** Attend conferences, seminars, and conventions where you're likely to meet people who can help you in your career.
- ✔ **Volunteer.** Sign up for projects in your company that will bring you into contact with people with whom you don't normally interact in the course your daily job.
- ✔ **Remember that networking is a two-way street.** Be responsive when people come to you for assistance in their professional development.

Keys to Successful Job Performance

Doing your best each day that you're on the job is the key to long-term career success. Here are a few tips:

- ✔ **At the start of a new job, take time to meet with your manager and review your responsibilities and performance standards.** Make sure you have a clear understanding of your role and his or her expectations.
- ✔ **Take a big picture view of your job.** Look for the links between your responsibilities and the strategic objectives of your company. Establish your priorities based on these larger goals.
- ✔ **Be a team player.** Share your expertise with coworkers, pitch in when possible, and strive to work collaboratively.
- ✔ **Look for ways to more effectively assist your supervisor.** With each new assignment, expand your knowledge, offer to accept more responsibility, and increase your understanding of the company's policies and procedures.
- ✔ **Commit to professional growth.** Be willing to set goals that stretch your experience and skills.
- ✔ **Focus on quality.** Regardless of how successful you may have been in the past, always look for opportunities to do things more productively and more creatively.

IDG BOOKS WORLDWIDE

For Dummies™: Bestselling Book Series for Beginners

™

References for the Rest of Us!™

Managing
Your Career
FOR
DUMMIES®

Managing Your Career

FOR

DUMMIES®

by Max Messmer

IDG Books Worldwide, Inc.
An International Data Group Company

Foster City, CA ◆ Chicago, IL ◆ Indianapolis, IN ◆ New York, NY

Managing Your Career For Dummies®

Published by
IDG Books Worldwide, Inc.
An International Data Group Company
919 E. Hillsdale Blvd.
Suite 400
Foster City, CA 94404
www.idgbooks.com (IDG Books Worldwide Web site)
www.dummies.com (Dummies Press Web site)

Library of Congress Control Number: 00-104214

ISBN: 0-7645-5253-8

Printed in the United States of America

10 9 8 7 6 5 4 3 2 1

1O/QZ/QY/QQ/IN

Distributed in the United States by IDG Books Worldwide, Inc.

Distributed by CDG Books Canada Inc. for Canada; by Transworld Publishers Limited in the United Kingdom; by IDG Norge Books for Norway; by IDG Sweden Books for Sweden; by IDG Books Australia Publishing Corporation Pty. Ltd. for Australia and New Zealand; by TransQuest Publishers Pte Ltd. for Singapore, Malaysia, Thailand, Indonesia, and Hong Kong; by Gotop Information Inc. for Taiwan; by ICG Muse, Inc. for Japan; by Intersoft for South Africa; by Eyrolles for France; by International Thomson Publishing for Germany, Austria and Switzerland; by Distribuidora Cuspide for Argentina; by LR International for Brazil; by Galileo Libros for Chile; by Ediciones ZETA S.C.R. Ltda. for Peru; by WS Computer Publishing Corporation, Inc., for the Philippines; by Contemporanea de Ediciones for Venezuela; by Express Computer Distributors for the Caribbean and West Indies; by Micronesia Media Distributor, Inc. for Micronesia; by Chips Computadoras S.A. de C.V. for Mexico; by Editorial Norma de Panama S.A. for Panama; by American Bookshops for Finland.

For general information on IDG Books Worldwide's books in the U.S., please call our Consumer Customer Service department at 800-762-2974. For reseller information, including discounts and premium sales, please call our Reseller Customer Service department at 800-434-3422.

For information on where to purchase IDG Books Worldwide's books outside the U.S., please contact our International Sales department at 317-596-5530 or fax 317-572-4002.

For consumer information on foreign language translations, please contact our Customer Service department at 800-434-3422, fax 317-572-4002, or e-mail rights@idgbooks.com.

For information on licensing foreign or domestic rights, please phone 650-653-7098.

For sales inquiries and special prices for bulk quantities, please contact our Order Services department at 800-434-3422 or write to the address above.

For information on using IDG Books Worldwide's books in the classroom or for ordering examination copies, please contact our Educational Sales department at 800-434-2086 or fax 317-572-4005.

For press review copies, author interviews, or other publicity information, please contact our Public Relations department at 650-653-7000 or fax 650-653-7500.

For authorization to photocopy items for corporate, personal, or educational use, please contact Copyright Clearance Center, 222 Rosewood Drive, Danvers, MA 01923, or fax 978-750-4470.

About the Author

Max Messmer's business is devoted to career success. As the chairman and CEO of Robert Half International Inc. (RHI), the world's largest specialized staffing firm, he is a widely recognized expert on employment and management issues. His company helps hundreds of thousands of people pursue, secure, and advance meaningful careers in which success is determined by each individual's values and goals.

Messmer's previous titles for IDG Books Worldwide, Inc. include *Human Resources Kit For Dummies* (1999), *Job Hunting For Dummies* (1995), and *Job Hunting For Dummies, 2nd Edition* (1999). In addition, he's authored several other critically acclaimed books, such as *The Fast Forward MBA in Hiring* (John Wiley & Sons, Inc., 1998), *50 Ways to Get Hired* (William Morrow & Co., Inc., 1994), and *Staffing Europe* (Acropolis Books Ltd., 1991). Messmer has written hundreds of articles and columns on job seeking, employment, and management topics, and his expertise has been featured in major business publications, including *Fortune, Forbes,* and *The Wall Street Journal.*

Robert Half International (NYSE symbol. RHI), a Fortune 1000 firm, is ranked among the top performers on the New York Stock Exchange, based on returns to investors for the five- and ten-year periods ending April 20, 2000. For two years in a row, *Fortune* Magazine included the company on its roster of "America's Most Admired Companies," ranking it number one among all staffing services firms. The company also appeared for the past two consecutive years on the *Forbes* "Platinum List" of top business services firms for investor returns and growth.

Founded in 1948, the firm's specialized staffing services include Accountemps, Robert Half, and RHI Management Resources, for temporary, full-time, and project professionals, respectively, in the fields of accounting and finance; OfficeTeam, for highly skilled temporary administrative support; RHI Consulting, for information technology professionals; The Affiliates, for temporary, project, and full-time staffing of attorneys and specialized support personnel within law firms and corporate legal departments; and The Creative Group, for creative, advertising, marketing, and Web design professionals on a project basis. The company serves its clients and candidates through more than 275 offices in North America, Europe, and Australia and through online job search services for each division, accessible through www.rhii.com.

Messmer is a member of the board of directors of a number of major corporations, including Airborne Freight Corporation, Health Care Property Investors, Inc., and Spieker Properties, Inc. Previously, he served on the boards of First Interstate Bancorp, NationsBank (of North Carolina), Pacific Enterprises, and Southern California Gas Company, among others. During the administration of President Ronald Reagan, he was appointed to the President's Advisory Committee on Trade Negotiations, on which he served for two years. Messmer was valedictorian of his graduating class at Loyola University and also grauated cum laude from the New York University School of Law.

ABOUT IDG BOOKS WORLDWIDE

Welcome to the world of IDG Books Worldwide.

IDG Books Worldwide, Inc., is a subsidiary of International Data Group, the world's largest publisher of computer-related information and the leading global provider of information services on information technology. IDG was founded more than 30 years ago by Patrick J. McGovern and now employs more than 9,000 people worldwide. IDG publishes more than 290 computer publications in over 75 countries. More than 90 million people read one or more IDG publications each month.

Launched in 1990, IDG Books Worldwide is today the #1 publisher of best-selling computer books in the United States. We are proud to have received eight awards from the Computer Press Association in recognition of editorial excellence and three from Computer Currents' First Annual Readers' Choice Awards. Our best-selling ...*For Dummies*® series has more than 50 million copies in print with translations in 31 languages. IDG Books Worldwide, through a joint venture with IDG's Hi-Tech Beijing, became the first U.S. publisher to publish a computer book in the People's Republic of China. In record time, IDG Books Worldwide has become the first choice for millions of readers around the world who want to learn how to better manage their businesses.

Our mission is simple: Every one of our books is designed to bring extra value and skill-building instructions to the reader. Our books are written by experts who understand and care about our readers. The knowledge base of our editorial staff comes from years of experience in publishing, education, and journalism — experience we use to produce books to carry us into the new millennium. In short, we care about books, so we attract the best people. We devote special attention to details such as audience, interior design, use of icons, and illustrations. And because we use an efficient process of authoring, editing, and desktop publishing our books electronically, we can spend more time ensuring superior content and less time on the technicalities of making books.

You can count on our commitment to deliver high-quality books at competitive prices on topics you want to read about. At IDG Books Worldwide, we continue in the IDG tradition of delivering quality for more than 30 years. You'll find no better book on a subject than one from IDG Books Worldwide.

John Kilcullen
Chairman and CEO
IDG Books Worldwide, Inc.

Eighth Annual Computer Press Awards ≥ 1992

Ninth Annual Computer Press Awards ≥ 1993

Tenth Annual Computer Press Awards ≥ 1994

Eleventh Annual Computer Press Awards ≥ 1995

IDG is the world's leading IT media, research and exposition company. Founded in 1964, IDG had 1997 revenues of $2.05 billion and has more than 9,000 employees worldwide. IDG offers the widest range of media options that reach IT buyers in 75 countries representing 95% of worldwide IT spending. IDG's diverse product and services portfolio spans six key areas including print publishing, online publishing, expositions and conferences, market research, education and training, and global marketing services. More than 90 million people read one or more of IDG's 290 magazines and newspapers, including IDG's leading global brands — Computerworld, PC World, Network World, Macworld and the Channel World family of publications. IDG Books Worldwide is one of the fastest-growing computer book publishers in the world, with more than 700 titles in 36 languages. The "...For Dummies®" series alone has more than 50 million copies in print. IDG offers online users the largest network of technology-specific Web sites around the world through IDG.net (http://www.idg.net), which comprises more than 225 targeted Web sites in 55 countries worldwide. International Data Corporation (IDC) is the world's largest provider of information technology data, analysis and consulting, with research centers in over 41 countries and more than 400 research analysts worldwide. IDG World Expo is a leading producer of more than 168 globally branded conferences and expositions in 35 countries including E3 (Electronic Entertainment Expo), Macworld Expo, ComNet, Windows World Expo, ICE (Internet Commerce Expo), Agenda, DEMO, and Spotlight. IDG's training subsidiary, ExecuTrain, is the world's largest computer training company, with more than 230 locations worldwide and 785 training courses. IDG Marketing Services helps industry-leading IT companies build international brand recognition by developing global integrated marketing programs via IDG's print, online and exposition products worldwide. Further information about the company can be found at www.idg.com.   1/26/00

Dedication

To Marcia, Michael, and Matthew: Your support has been the foundation for success throughout my career.

Author's Acknowledgments

As in any successful endeavor, *Managing Your Career For Dummies* was made possible by the talents, efforts, and advice of numerous people. Thank you to Barry Tarshis, for his insights, research, and assistance. I'd also like to thank Lynn Taylor, vice president of strategic marketing and director of research at Robert Half International Inc., and Lynn Marie Glaiser, group manager of editorial services, for their ongoing contributions and counsel throughout the writing of this book, as well as Reesa McCoy Staten, Natalie Coleman, and Amanda Jo Beck.

Special recognition goes to Kathy Welton, vice president and publisher, and Mark Butler, senior acquisitions editor, at IDG Books Worldwide, Inc. who saw the need for this book, and Tere Drenth, project editor, for her editorial expertise.

Finally, I'd like to acknowledge Mr. Robert Half, the founder of our company and a close friend. His career in specialized staffing, begun in 1948, laid the foundation for our firm's success and has served as a model for all in our industry.

Publisher's Acknowledgments

We're proud of this book; please register your comments through our IDG Books Worldwide Online Registration Form located at `http://my2cents.dummies.com`.

Some of the people who helped bring this book to market include the following:

Acquisitions, Editorial, and Media Development

Project Editor: Tere Drenth

Acquisitions Editors: Mark Butler, Karen J. Doran

Acquisitions Coordinator: Lisa Roule

Editorial Administrator: Michelle Hacker

General Reviewer: Marilyn Maze

Editorial Manager: Pamela Mourouzis

Production

Project Coordinator: Maridee Ennis

Layout and Graphics: Jason Guy, Clint Lahnen, Tracy K. Oliver, Jill Piscitelli, Brent Savage, Jacque Schneider, Julie Trippetti

Proofreaders: Corey Bowen, John Greenough, Betty Kish, Susan Moritz, Marianne Santy, Charles Spencer

Indexer: Lynnzee Elze

General and Administrative

IDG Books Worldwide, Inc.: John Kilcullen, CEO

IDG Books Technology Publishing Group: Richard Swadley, Senior Vice President and Publisher; Walter R. Bruce III, Vice President and Publisher; Joseph Wikert, Vice President and Publisher; Mary Bednarek, Vice President and Director, Product Development; Andy Cummings, Publishing Director, General User Group; Mary C. Corder, Editorial Director; Barry Pruett, Publishing Director

IDG Books Consumer Publishing Group: Roland Elgey, Senior Vice President and Publisher; Kathleen A. Welton, Vice President and Publisher; Kevin Thornton, Acquisitions Manager; Kristin A. Cocks, Editorial Director

IDG Books Internet Publishing Group: Brenda McLaughlin, Senior Vice President and Publisher; Sofia Marchant, Online Marketing Manager

IDG Books Production for Branded Press: Debbie Stailey, Director of Production; Cindy L. Phipps, Manager of Project Coordination, Production Proofreading, and Indexing; Tony Augsburger, Manager of Prepress, Reprints, and Systems; Shelley Lea, Supervisor of Graphics and Design; Debbie J. Gates, Production Systems Specialist; Steve Arany, Associate Automation Supervisor; Robert Springer, Supervisor of Proofreading; Trudy Coler, Page Layout Manager; Janet Seib, Associate Page Layout Supervisor, Kathie Schutte, Senior Page Layout Supervisor; Michael Sullivan, Production Supervisor

Packaging and Book Design: Patty Page, Manager, Promotions Marketing

◆

The publisher would like to give special thanks to Patrick J. McGovern, without whom this book would not have been possible.

◆

Contents at a Glance

Cartoons at a Glance

By Rich Tennant

page 5

page 55

page 153

page 245

page 277

Fax: 978-546-7747
E-mail: richtennant@the5thwave.com
World Wide Web: www.the5thwave.com

Table of Contents

Introduction

● ●

*T*he world of work has undergone remarkable changes over the past ten years, so it's no surprise that the ground rules for getting ahead and managing your career have also changed.

Of course, the basics still count. If you want to be successful in today's workplace — regardless of where your career ambitions lie — you still have to be good at what you do, work hard, and make a difference in your organization. But in today's workplace, you have many opportunities to create and pursue a career path that meets both your business and personal goals. And the purpose of this book, in short, is to explain how to get the most out of these opportunities.

About This Book

Managing Your Career For Dummies is a valuable resource for anyone who is seeking timely, real-world guidance on how to achieve not only career, but also personal, satisfaction. You'll find this book especially helpful if you identify with any of the following statements:

- ✔ "I've worked for a few years in several different jobs, but I don't have an actual career plan. I want to gain a better understanding of my interests and develop specific career goals."

- ✔ "I'm reasonably happy with my job and company, but I'm looking for ideas to advance my career."

- ✔ "I've been in the workforce for many years but I'm not thrilled with either my job or career progress. I want to pursue and develop a career that's meaningful to me."

The Table of Contents of this book outlines the topics and issues addressed. Here's a brief look at what this information will do for you:

- ✔ Help you clarify your values, interests, and professional aspirations as the basis for your strategic career plan.

- ✔ Guide you in targeting job opportunities that support your career goals and outline strategies to pursue the jobs you want.

- ✔ Provide you with an enlightening — and real-world — picture of what's happening in today's rapidly changing workplace, highlighting important opportunities and the strategies to capitalize on them.

✔ Explain how to adapt your career goals and strategies to meet the changing demands of the marketplace and workplace.

✔ Offer valuable insights into the sometimes tricky and intimidating political aspects of career management and explain how to deal with these issues without compromising your ethics.

✔ Help you maximize every job situation or consulting assignment.

✔ Help you determine whether it's in your best interest — professionally and personally — to become self-employed.

How This Book Is Organized

Managing Your Career For Dummies consists of 23 chapters, broken down into five broad areas. Here's a closer look at those parts.

Part I: Managing Your Career in the 21st Century

The first four chapters of this book help you build the foundation of a successful career in today's world. Chapter 1 spells out the new career management imperative: You're in control of your own success. Chapter 2 helps you determine (with the help of others) which career options make the most sense, based on your interests, passions, and aptitudes. Chapter 3 shows you how to research your options. And Chapter 4 offers step-by-step advice on setting up your own strategic career plan.

Part II: Succeeding in the Corporate Culture

Part II provides practical advice on making your mark in today's workplace, regardless of your organization's size or industry. This part begins with a crash-course in landing the job you want (and, as you'll note, the rules of successful job searching have changed). It's followed by a chapter that focuses on how to successfully begin a new job. In Chapter 7, you gain valuable insights into what it means these days to climb the corporate ladder (and here, too, you'll find that the ground rules have changed). Chapter 8 deals with one of the most important trends in corporate life today — alternative work arrangements, such as flextime and telecommuting. Chapter 9 explores what it takes to join the ranks of elite performers in business. And Chapter 10 provides inspiring yet practical advice to get back on track when things don't go as planned.

Part III: Working Well with Others

Part III focuses on the soft skills that have solid implications for career success. In Chapter 11, you discover the ins and outs of effectively working with any supervisor — even in different situations. Chapter 12 brings you up to speed on the managerial techniques you need to coach your team, while Chapter 13 focuses on the flip side: enhancing your team-player skills. Chapter 14 covers the art of communication — how to use both the spoken and written word more effectively in all aspects of your job. And Chapter 15 provides key advice on developing and maintaining a circle of professional contacts as you advance in your career.

Part IV: Taking a Non-Corporate Approach

The two chapters in this part are designed for readers whose career goals may lie outside the traditional corporate path. Chapter 16 outlines the basics of self-employment and helps you assess your readiness to pursue various opportunities. Chapter 17 focuses on how to market and promote yourself after you've gone out on your own.

Part V: The Part of Tens

The final six chapters of this book give you some valuable supplementary information, including top career management Web sites to access, books to read, and savvy ways to handle some of the most common quandaries in office politics. You also get a review of the key principles of career management and a list of questions to ask yourself before you make the plunge into self-employment.

Icons Used in This Book

Whenever I want you to pay close attention to a specific piece of information or a particular passage in this book, I place little pictures, called *icons,* next to the text in the margin. Here's what the icons mean:

Timely information that can make an immediate difference in your ability to solve a problem or achieve a goal. (***Note:*** You may want to set up a separate file on your computer for these tips or jot them down on a sticky-back note and attach it to your computer or bulletin board.)

Information that, if not heeded, may create problems for you.

Tips for avoiding clashes with people and companies that have a different approach to work than you do.

Real-life stories — from famous and not-so-famous people — for insight and inspiration. These individuals don't necessarily have *your* dream job, but through careful career management, they are finally working in the jobs that are ideally suited to them.

Activities and step-by-step instructions that you can put to use right away.

Ideas or insights that have special relevance to the topic being discussed in each chapter or the overall challenges of career management.

Where to Go from Here

Even though every chapter in this book covers a topic with important implications for managing your career, some chapters may have more relevance to your particular situation. You don't have to read this book from start to finish to get the most out of it. I recommend that you look through the Table of Contents and Index and begin with those chapters or sections that address issues currently on your mind, regardless of where the chapters may lie in the book. And keep in mind at all times that career management is a journey, not a process carved in stone. This book will help you find the path that's right for you.

Good luck!

Part I
Managing Your Career in the 21st Century

The 5th Wave   By Rich Tennant

"This is a 'dot-com' company, Stacey. Risk-taking is a given. If you're not comfortable running with scissors, cleaning your ear with a darning needle, or swimming right after a big meal, this might not be the place for you."

In this part . . .

*B*efore you can chart your course to career success, you need to figure out which direction to choose. This part helps you define your goals and values and then guides you through the career-planning process.

Chapter 1

Becoming the CEO of Your Career

- -

- -

This is an unusually eventful time for career-minded professionals. The competitive challenges for organizations of all sizes and in virtually every industry have never been more intense nor more varied. And these challenges have created new and unprecedented levels of opportunity for people who possess the skills and attributes that firms are actively seeking. There is, however, one catch to this otherwise rosy career scenario: You have to know how to get the most career mileage out of the skills and attributes you possess.

This chapter gives you an overall picture of career management in today's workplace. You get a brief look at how the basic rules of the game have changed and what that means to you.

The New Rules of Career Management

The unwritten contract in organizational life used to be that as long as you worked hard and stayed out of trouble — and if the company was operating profitably — you didn't have to worry about job security (see Table 1-1). You also knew that, based on your length of service and your position, you'd be entitled to periodic pay raises and promotions. That unwritten contract has pretty much gone the way of typewriters and the executive washroom. Even in countries like Japan, where firms have long been known for their cradle-to-grave employment philosophies, companies no longer guarantee their employees lifetime jobs, regardless of how well the company is doing. Today, what you're offered instead is an opportunity to prove yourself, learn, and advance. You also have the opportunity to earn more money on the basis of your job performance, as opposed to your time in rank.

Table 1-1	How Business Was and How It Is Today
Then	*Now*
Job security depends on the success of the company you work for	Job security depends on you — and whether your skills and attributes are keeping pace with the changing requirements of the global marketplace
Keep your nose to the grindstone	Keep your eye on your career
A gold watch after 25 years	Stock options after you've proven yourself
Cradle-to-grave employment	The multifaceted career
Corporate loyalty	Individual opportunity
Chain of command	Self-managed teams
Do your "job"	Do whatever it takes to make your company more competitive
The Man in the Gray Flannel Suit	Dress-down Fridays
Catching the 6:45 a.m. train	Walking from your kitchen to your home office
Working 9 to 5	Flexible work hours
Do it "by the book"	Make sure the client is happy
Temporary work as a stop-gap measure when you're "between jobs"	Project consulting as a viable and attractive career option
Once trained, forever educated	Continuing and constant learning
The organization knows what is best for you	You control your own future
Move up or stay where you are	Explore all opportunities to develop new skills and increase your marketability in your profession or industry

In light of this overall paradigm shift, the following sections share some of the trends and issues you can factor into your career-management strategies.

Who's in charge of your career? You are

Today, more than ever, it's not your supervisor or the company you work for who has the most control over where you go in your career and how long it takes you to get there. That control lies primarily with you. And the first — and most critical — step in successful career management is recognizing and embracing this fundamental principle.

The old notion of climbing the corporate ladder has undergone a profound change. The ladder is no longer a sequence of promotions in a single company but rather, a sequence of strategic career moves (from one company to another or one specialty to another) that are part of a plan that you create.

The people responsible for making hiring decisions are no longer as wary as they once were of hiring job candidates who've moved from one company to the next. What's important is not so much where you've been or how long you've been there, but specific skills and attributes you can offer right now.

The task is boss

Some organizational experts argue that the very concept of a *job* — as that term has traditionally been understood — is obsolete. While that assessment may be an exaggeration, the nature of work has changed radically over the past two decades. Job descriptions are increasingly focused on responsibilities and objectives, as opposed to specific tasks. More than ever, responsibilities overlap between specific departments and the individual employees within those departments. What matters most to senior managers in progressive companies is not so much who's doing what, but whether the collective effort of everyone involved in a particular project is meeting the needs of customers and enhancing the company's ability to achieve its corporate objectives.

Going soft

Logic would dictate that the proliferation of technology in the workplace reduces the need for people to interact with one another on a personal level, thus lessening the importance of so-called *soft skills* — the ability to communicate, listen, and work collaboratively. But guess what? The opposite is true. In one of the surveys commissioned by Robert Half International, some 77 percent of chief information officers polled said that the increased use of technology will require workers to communicate more effectively and accurately in coming years. The reason? With information technology accelerating the frequency of communication, any deficiencies in diplomacy, negotiation, and oral and written skills are increasingly obvious to others.

So how does this affect you? Your career success in the workplace of today — independent of technical expertise — depends on the quality of your people skills. Recognizing this priority and taking steps to enhance your communication abilities may accelerate your career progress (see Chapter 14).

Balancing act: Resolving the work-family conflict

As part of a study conducted by Robert Half International, working men and women were asked to list their primary career concerns. The answer that turned up most frequently wasn't salary, job security, or getting a corner office. It was finding the proper balance between the responsibilities of work and home.

The response isn't entirely surprising. As more and more parents work outside the home, they feel the need to fulfill responsibilities of both work and family. As a result, many companies have instituted policies and practices (flextime, job sharing, telecommuting, company-subsidized concierge services, and so on) that are expressly designed to help employees balance work/life responsibilities. These policies have helped the companies, too — in their ability to recruit and retain highly skilled talent, as either full-time employees or project consultants.

This new emphasis on work-family balance has important ramifications for career management. For one thing, family-friendly policies are helping to take some of the either/or element out of the choices people make between their jobs and their personal lives. If you're qualified and you work for a progressive company, modifying your work arrangement can help you achieve the career — or careers — you've always wanted.

A flip-side exists: If you're a manager, you're no longer able to personally oversee everything your staff members do because not everyone may be available or in the office at the same time. Your effectiveness may be measured not only by the results you achieve, but also by your ability to enhance the productivity and job satisfaction of the people who work for you.

Teamwork: Ten heads are better than one

Teamwork has always been a valuable component in most corporations, but more recently the concept has taken on considerable operational significance. The most important development in this trend has been the work practice known as *self-managed work teams* — groups of individuals representing different departments and functions who work collectively on a specific project. In a study commissioned by Robert Half International, 79 percent of executives polled said that self-managed teams will increase productivity. Driving this trend is the pressure for companies to compete in global markets and respond more promptly and strategically to changes in the market. When operating at peak efficiency, self-managed, cross-functional teams reduce the communication bottlenecks that typically slow productivity in traditionally structured companies. But self-managed teams aren't a panacea, and many companies have struggled in their efforts to develop processes that foster better team efforts.

As part of your career development, you must work effectively as part of a team while still pursuing your individual career goals, find a way to share credit with others without letting your contributions be overlooked, and communicate well with people at various levels of seniority and in different departments to achieve a common objective. Check out Chapter 13 for more on teamwork.

Blurring boundaries

The boundaries of responsibility and function that once separated different workers in an organization aren't as sharply drawn today as they once were. Consequently, it's not unusual in many companies to find a strategically calibrated mix of full-time employees, part-time staff, consultants, and independent contractors who have been hired for a particular project. See Chapters 8 and 16 for more on taking advantage of changing work arrangements.

This trend has vastly broadened the opportunities now open to independent project consultants (see Chapter 16). And it has created new challenges for managers as they strive to communicate effectively with a diverse group of people and bring a process-oriented, problem-solving mind-set to each project.

By the numbers

Survey results from OfficeTeam's *Office of Future: 2005* study underscore how rapidly things are changing in the workplace. Here's a look at some of the key findings.

✔ **Talking heads:** 77 percent of chief information officers believe that increased use of technology by 2005 will make it more important for employees to be able to communicate effectively and articulately.

✔ **You've got mail!** 73 percent of executives believe that e-mail will be the leading form of business communication for employees in 2005.

✔ **It's your call:** 91 percent of *Fortune* 1000 executives believe that managers today are giving employees more authority to make their own decisions or take their own actions, as compared to five years ago.

✔ **Loosening up:** 82 percent of executives say that their companies now promote casual dress as a benefit to attract new candidates.

✔ **Balancing act:** A higher proportion of working men and women in the United States (26 percent) now describe the ability to balance work and family demands as a more important career-related concern than earning a competitive salary.

Taking Control of Your Career

In today's rapidly changing workplace, only one person is qualified to make important decisions: you. It is up to you — not your boss, coworkers, senior management, or astrologer — to formulate objectives, develop a plan, and follow through with the necessary steps to realize your career goals.

Think of it this way. You're the CEO of your career. Like any CEO, of course, you need to solicit advice from others and, in many instances, rely on the expertise of people who have additional knowledge and experience. Ultimately, though, you have to make the big decisions.

You can get plenty of specific advice on how to be a successful CEO of your career throughout this book. In the meantime, however, here are some guidelines worth considering:

✔ **Know where you're going.** Successful CEOs invariably have a clear vision or direction for their companies. As the CEO of your career, you also need a vision — an overall goal of what you want to achieve with your career. You don't have to cross every "t" and dot every "i" in the vision you formulate, especially early on in your career, when you may be exploring various options. But you need a general sense of what's important to you; that is, how successful you want to be and what form that success should take. How you measure your success — by financial gain, rank, peer recognition, or personal satisfaction — is up to you. What's important is that you have a target that's more than a dream.

✔ **Develop a plan.** A common pitfall in career management (and in running a company, as well) is getting sidetracked — getting so bogged down with the priorities and pressures of a single day or situation that you lose sight of the big picture — from where you eventually want to go in your career. One way to guard against this pitfall is to create a *strategic career plan:* a broad outline of the steps to take to achieve your career goals. Every few months, set aside some time — two or three days, at least — to reflect on where you've been, what you've been doing, and where you're headed. Make sure you're still on target with respect to long-term career goals. If not, make the appropriate adjustments.

✔ **Make every job count.** Every job you take as you progress in your career should be logically keyed to the goals you've established. This way, when you uncover new opportunities, you're able to capitalize on them and run a success-driven job-hunt strategy (see Chapter 5). And as an employee, this means working effectively within that company's culture and dealing wisely with the political dynamics without getting too caught up in all of the negative aspects of office politics.

✔ **Keep your life well balanced.** Due to today's alternate work arrangements, you may have an easier time than ever before staying actively involved in a career and still devoting time and energy to your family, your leisure pursuits, or your personal priorities in general. Investigate opportunities for alternate work arrangements, such as flextime, part-time employment, job sharing, and telecommuting. These arrangements — when they're compatible with your job duties — give you more control of your time and help to ease the pressures that arise when the responsibilities of your career and your personal life coincide. They may also allow you to pursue a new career or juggle two careers simultaneously.

✔ **Find ways to manage yourself.** The typical CEO in a large company almost always operates in overload mode. Only those who have discovered how to set priorities and manage their time effectively are able to meet their responsibilities. Managing a career is, in many respects, a job unto itself (granted, a part-time job), and so it lends itself to many of the principles that apply to time management:

- You set goals.

- You reevaluate priorities on an ongoing basis.

- You recognize when you're taking on more tasks and responsibilities than you can possibly manage.

Tools such as project-management software or day-planning notebooks can help. More importantly, work on developing a commitment to organization and a sense of discipline — see Chapter 9.

✔ **Become a better communicator.** Effective communication has always been an important skill in organizational life. But it's a critical skill for anyone who wants to make any sort of mark for him-or herself in today's virtual workplace. The most important aspect of communication is the ability to listen — not only to hear the words that people are saying but also to understand the concerns and motivations that lie beneath the words. And it's especially important, in this era of e-mail, to communicate as clearly, concisely, and persuasively on paper (or on-screen) as you do when dealing with people in person or over the phone. See the chapters in Part III.

✔ **Expand your network.** For most — if not all — high-level executives, networking has played an important part in their career advancement. True, staying in touch with people takes time and effort — two precious commodities in today's workplace. But if you organize your schedule well, you can usually fit in one or two days per month to mingle with colleagues at an association meeting, trade show, or similar venue. Think of it as an investment. A network of colleagues and associates is not only a resource for advice and help (as you are for them), but also enriches your life on a personal level. Keep in mind that networking isn't something you do only when you're looking for a job; it needs to be an ongoing element of career development.

✓ **Stay on the cutting edge.** No CEO can possibly know every aspect of his or her company. And it's unrealistic for you to think that you can keep your finger on the pulse of everything going on that may relate to your career. Even so, take reasonable steps to stay abreast of new developments in your field — especially if you're in an industry that's changing at warp speed, such as a high-tech business. A recent survey commissioned by Robert Half International showed that 65 percent of the men and women polled spend less than an hour each day scanning newspapers, industry publications, and/or Web sites for information on business and technology trends. The Internet is a powerful tool to help you access important information and find out more about recent events. Most major organizations and publications have their own Web sites, making it easier and more convenient than ever to gather and organize the information — assuming you know what you're looking for and where to find it. And if you're a technical professional, stay as current as possible with new systems and software applications.

✓ **Conduct yourself with absolute integrity.** One of the most interesting ironies in business life is that while competition has become more intense (many would say cut-throat), ethics have assumed unprecedented importance. The main reason for this apparent paradox is that organizational alliances, which are fundamental to business life today, require unqualified trust among all parties. Integrity isn't something practiced now and then, when it's convenient. It is a core value that governs everything you do and say.

✓ **Be visible.** Without clamoring for constant attention, be sure that your supervisor is aware of your hard work and accomplishments. Contribute ideas during meetings, doing your best to offer suggestions for improving business practices. Arrive early to the office. And, most important, don't hesitate to stretch your abilities. While you don't want to take on tasks you can't do, stay open to opportunities that may fall outside of your job description — they could serve as springboards to career advancement.

Chapter 2

Getting Started on a Strategic Career Plan

Career planning has traditionally meant deciding how you would earn your living. After that decision was made — sometime before college graduation — the actual career path typically consisted of achieving certain milestones — more precisely, promotions or salary raises. Getting ahead was synonymous with rising through the ranks or climbing the corporate ladder.

This traditional concept of a career path — getting slotted into the ranks of a single profession, industry, or company and moving up one step at a time — hasn't died out completely. But for most business professionals today, the career planning process is more fluid and dynamic than it used to be. Yes, it's still important to do well at whatever job you happen to be in at a given time, but your next step isn't as scripted as it once was. Companies no longer promote the notion of cradle-to-grave employment, and business professionals in their 20s and early 30s are less concerned about remaining in a single occupation, industry, or company for extended periods of time. That's because hiring managers in most companies aren't as quick to automatically rule out for consideration so-called *job-hoppers* (people who stay in their jobs for approximately two years or less) — not if they've been successful in the jobs they've held.

Similarly, no one is shocked any longer if someone who has been highly successful in a single occupation for 20 years wakes up one morning and decides to discard that career (and all the trappings it may include) to go back to school, take a few months off, or jump to an entirely different occupation.

True, many of the literally millions of people who have changed careers within the past decade have done so as a result of mergers, acquisitions, and restructurings. But more professionals than ever are switching careers not because they're being forced to but because they want to — they're looking for opportunities for professional growth and challenges.

What do these changes mean to you? In short, more opportunities and, at the same time, more decisions. The next milestone in your career isn't necessarily going to be a promotion with your current employer. It may be a job with another company, a lateral move designed to position you for a career shift in a year or two, a decision to go out on your own as a business owner or consultant, or a move to another field entirely. This is why you need to develop and be guided by an overall idea of where you want to go. According to a recent survey commissioned by Robert Half International, 82 percent of men and women in the U.S. who were polled believe that people who develop a career plan are more successful than those who don't develop such a plan. Without a sense of direction, you'll be in a reactive mode much of the time, and your success will be determined not by you but by the events and forces around you. You need to take charge of your career.

This chapter gives you an overview of the strategic career planning process as it applies to today's changing workplace, and it zeroes in on the critical first steps you need to take to gain insights into your most important career asset: you. You get a chance to think through your values and your interests and to gain a better understanding of your personality characteristics and how they impact your career choices. This chapter isn't so much about the real world of business — it's about the "real world of you."

Strategic Career Planning: The Basics

There's nothing exotic or unusually complicated about strategic career planning. It's a logical process that can be broken down into three pieces:

- ✔ **Finding out about yourself:** Gathering insight into the things that really matter to you — your values, interests, and (this is important!) your passions.

- ✔ **Scoping the market:** Finding out as much as you can about what it takes to get launched and succeed in careers, jobs, or industries that are appealing to you.

- ✔ **Tooling up:** Creating a reasonably structured plan designed to close the gap between the assets you currently possess and the assets you need in order to pursue certain careers.

Here are some additional considerations before going any further:

- ✓ **It's not a science.** You won't find any cookie-cutter formulas to strategic career planning. It's not simply a matter of going through a battery of tests to identify your interests, skills, and strengths and then playing mix and match with the available career path choices. Every decision you make in this process needs to take into account a variety of factors, not the least of which are your own lifestyle needs (whether you can earn the kind of living you require to support the lifestyle you want).

- ✓ **It's not only about your career.** One of the hidden benefits of strategic career planning is that, if done properly, you gain insights into not only your career but also what makes you tick as a human being. As you determine what's important to you in a career, you're examining what's important to your life.

- ✓ **It doesn't require drastic changes in your life.** Even if you discover early in your strategic planning process that you are (yikes!) clearly in the worst job you could possibly hold in light of your values, talents, and interests, the process doesn't oblige you to make radical changes in your life — not immediately, anyway. Strategic career planning, especially in the initial stage, is primarily an exercise in introspection. You're looking for insight and clarity. Your goal is to get to know yourself better and to develop an awareness that will shape the decisions you make in the future. After you commit yourself to change, strategic career planning helps you implement that transition in logical, prudent baby steps, not big leaps into unfamiliar territory.

Starting with What You Value

Shortly after Andrea Jung was named the president and chief operating officer (COO) of Avon, the cosmetics firm, *Fortune* magazine asked her if she could explain why she was chosen over several other veterans in the company. She said it wasn't her education or experience but her passion. And now Ms. Jung is the president and CEO of Avon.

Point well taken. If you're not really passionate about your work, you're probably not going to give 100 percent and you'll have difficultly excelling in your field. You won't be motivated to do all the little things — networking, developing your skills, handling day-to-day frustrations with patience and grace — that you have to do to be successful in today's highly competitive world. And even if you manage to become a leader in your chosen field, you're not going to derive much pleasure from that achievement — not unless you truly relish what you do. And where does passion originate? It starts with your values.

Why values matter

Values can best be described as the things you consider important. Think of values as the guides that govern your day-to-day life, whether at business or at home. They're the points on your moral compass. Your values define your character: how ethical and caring you are in your dealings with others and the criteria you use when you're making key decisions. Values are the driving (and often hidden) force behind your priorities.

One of the cardinal principles of strategic career planning is that your career choices must be consistent with your values. You pay a high price when you flout this principle: Serious conflicts between what you value and what you actually do in your job will almost invariably prevent you from performing well and enjoying your work. If one of your values is that human beings must live in harmony with nature, for example, you're not likely to draw fulfillment working for a company whose products pollute the environment — never mind your salary or level of prestige. If you have a strong ethical sense, you're not going to be comfortable working for a fly-by-night telemarketing company that dupes unsuspecting retirees into investing their life savings in swampland.

One well-known business authority who recognized the importance of values early in his career was Peter Drucker, who began his business career as an investment banker during the mid 1930s. As he described in an article written for the *Harvard Business Review,* he was doing very well for himself. He recognized, however, that he would never be happy unless he felt that he was making a contribution. So even though it was the height of the depression and he had no other job to go to, he quit — and never regretted his decision. Values should be the ultimate test of whether you're well suited to a particular career.

Zeroing in on your values

Numerous methods have been developed to help people align their career choices with their values. Most of these approaches are variations on the same theme, but all help you identify your *core values* — those that transcend what you do for a living.

Some career counselors, for example, have clients write their own obituaries. This sounds depressing, but there's logic to it. The idea is to get you to think about and write down on paper what you would like to be remembered for. If, after completing this exercise, you see very little in the obituary that has any bearing on what you are currently doing for a living, you may not be on a career path that's destined to bring you fulfillment.

If you find the idea of writing out your own obituary too depressing, here is a simple exercise that should yield some equally useful insights. To get the most from this activity, you must keep an open mind. Don't judge your responses. And don't try to reconcile your answers with your current work situation; that tendency will corrupt the process. Listen to your instincts.

1. **Read each of the value statements below and assign a number to each based on the following scale:**

   • Very important: 4

   • Somewhat important: 3

   • Little importance: 2

   • Not important at all: 1

   ___ Doing something worthwhile for society

   ___ Providing for my family

   ___ Making a great deal of money

   ___ Getting ahead quickly in my profession

   ___ Working with people that I like and admire

   ___ Following the tenets of my religion

   ___ Becoming famous

   ___ Spending quality time with my family

   ___ Enjoying time with friends or in leisure activities

   ___ Expressing myself artistically

   ___ Making my own decisions

   ___ Influencing a lot of people

   ___ Participating in something bigger than myself that I can believe in

   ___ Learning, growing, and experiencing new things

   ___ Belonging to an organization where my contributions are valued

   ___ Other _____

2. **Look at only those values in Step 1 that you've rated as a "4" and try to rank them in their order of priority.**

   Focus on those values that are at the top of your list and ask yourself whether your current career direction is consistent with those values. If it isn't, you may want to consider a career change.

Think about recent projects or events (in your job or in your private life) that brought you a great deal of satisfaction. Take some time to reflect and then try to identify the aspects of the project that contributed most to your sense of satisfaction. (Use the list in the previous exercise to give you some ideas.) For example, you may write:

- ✔ "Was able to make my own decisions."
- ✔ "Worked with people I admired and respected."
- ✔ "Participated in something bigger than myself that I could believe in."

Look for patterns. Are the answers in this exercise consistent with the insights you gained from the previous exercise? If your responses differ significantly, take some additional time to reflect on your experiences and pinpoint the key aspects. Talk it over with a friend to help clarify your thoughts.

Let Your Interests Be Your Guide

Suppose you're on an airplane, and the pilot has just informed you and your fellow passengers that the plane is going to be in the air two hours longer than expected. You've finished whatever work you've had, but you don't have anything to read. Luckily, though, you're sitting next to the magazine rack. So the question is, which magazine do you pick? Or to be more precise, what is the focus of the magazine you would choose — fashion, sports, religion, gardening, decorating, politics, finance, computing, hang gliding, show business, art, opera, alligator wrestling? Would the focus of the magazine you select coincide with what you do for a living?

This is one of any number of simple exercises you can do to gain some sense of what you're really interested in. Most people have been conditioned to think of their interests as activities they pursue when they're not actually working — hobbies, in other words. But who's to say that you can't be intensely interested in the things you do for a living? Granted, you may not have the skills or talents necessary to make the grade in those fields that interest you the most. Not everyone, after all, has the wherewithal to star on Broadway or play center field for the New York Yankees. For now, though, don't worry about the practical aspects of finding out what interests you.

The following exercise offers a more reflective consideration of your interests.

1. **With pen and paper, set aside a few hours of quiet time in a peaceful spot (and while you're at it, pour a cup of your favorite beverage) and think back on the activities you enjoyed most during your childhood.**

   For example, write down your favorite subjects in school — the classes you didn't have to keep pinching yourself to stay awake in. What extra-curricular activities did you enjoy the most (as opposed to those that came easily to you)? When were you the happiest? Was it being out-doors, close to nature? Did it have anything to do with the arts? Was it making things with your hands? Sure, you're different today: a grown-up. But interests can transcend age. This exercise is designed to reacquaint you with whom you used to be before people started to tell you whom you ought to be.

2. **Think back over the last two or three years and try to come up with at least five school- or work-related experiences that brought you a great deal of enjoyment — regardless of success.**

   Look for common denominators. Are the activities mostly adventure-related or intellectual? Do they all relate to the same interest? And the big question: How many of those activities correspond with what you now do for a living?

3. **Consider the setting or environment of each experience.**

   What were your "working" conditions in these situations? Were you inside, outdoors, constantly on the go, or primarily stationary? Did you interact with many people or work independently? Your environment can play a significant role in your assessment of whether something was interesting or satisfying.

This and similar exercises aren't meant to reveal to you in a flash of blinding light the one and only occupation or career path ideally suited to your inter-ests. The purpose instead, as in the value exercises, is to steer you toward those career options that are well suited to your interests. Numerous other testing instruments — commonly used by career counselors and guidance counselors — can give you similar insights, but if you do nothing else but give yourself permission to think about the things that interest you, you may not need to take those tests.

And don't feel bad if you have trouble immediately identifying key events or related interests. Not many people have burning, innate interests. You may need some time over a period of weeks or months to reflect and gather your thoughts.

And Now a Look at Your Personality

The role that personality characteristics play in career success (and for that matter, which jobs you should be pursuing) is a hotly debated issue in busi-ness today. The debate isn't over whether temperament has a bearing on job performance — it clearly does. The issue is whether it's possible, in light of the complexity of most mid- to high-level jobs, to identify specific personality characteristics that are reliable predictors of job success in a given profes-sion. Many people seem to think it is possible.

One of the key staffing trends in hiring today is a practice known as *competency modeling*. Companies identify their most successful performers, put them through a battery of tests, and on the basis of the results, develop a *success profile* that becomes the basis of hiring criteria. Still other companies have developed testing instruments and strategies designed to identify those candidates who, based on their personality traits, are likely to flourish in that company's corporate culture.

Chances are, you already have a fairly accurate idea of your basic personality traits. You probably know, for example, whether you're an extrovert or an introvert, whether you're action-oriented or thought-oriented, whether you're a detail or a big-picture person, or whether you're slow or quick to burn when you're under stress.

In other words, you probably know as much about your personality as necessary to avoid really disastrous career choices. If you're not a people person at heart, you're not likely to find fame and fortune (not to mention career satisfaction) in the hospitality industry. If you lose your cool whenever your phone rings twice in ten minutes, you may reconsider any ambitions you have about becoming a commodities trader or a hostage negotiator.

If you'd like to get additional insight into your personality, though, you have several options. Probably the best-known and most widely used personality assessment tool today is Myers-Briggs Type Indicator (MBTI), which many organizations routinely use as a guide in staffing decisions. What the MBTI indicates, at root, is where people register on the personality continuum in four particular aspects: extroversion or introversion, intuition or thinking, sensing or feeling, and perceiving or judging.

In case you're not familiar with the MBTI, you should know that the test doesn't label you as a specific type. It simply measures tendencies. As such, though, it can be very helpful to you in your strategic career planning. If the test shows, for example, that you tend to be more process-oriented than results-oriented, you're probably not going to be at your best when you're constantly trying to meet short-term deadlines.

If you'd like to take MBTI, you can request it through most career centers and, in many cases, your company's HR department. There's also a great deal of information about MBTI on the Internet: companies and individuals that administer and interpret the test, lists of books and articles that help you interpret the findings, and in some instances, self-assessment exercises that are similar to MBTI.

Another self-assessment test, which can be found online, is called the Keirsey Temperament Sorter (www.keirsey.com). There are two versions: one with 36 questions and one with 70 questions, each designed to give you a rough indicator of your temperament. The test, including the scoring, is free. But to get a full understanding of the results you'll probably want to buy David Keirsey's book, *Please Understand Me II: Temperament Character Intelligence* (Promethius Nemesis Book Company).

Getting feedback from others

Few people know themselves as well as they may think — or as well as the people closest to them do. Consequently, consider getting some feedback on your personality traits from friends, family members, colleagues, and former associates. You have to be careful here, of course. Most people (most *nice* people, at any rate) are understandably reluctant to tell you negative things about yourself, even when you've given them *carte blanche* to do so. To get around this problem, make sure that those you approach understand why you're doing it. And make sure, too, that you don't get too grumpy if people you've been close to tell you things you don't really want to hear. For this strategy to work, try to gain insights from as many people as you can — and if possible, from those who've seen you operate in a variety of environments. The following are some questions you may want to ask them:

- ✔ How assertive do you think I am?
- ✔ Do you think of me as a pessimist or an optimist?
- ✔ Do you consider me an extrovert or an introvert?
- ✔ Do you think I'm sensitive to other people's feelings?
- ✔ How would you describe my ability to deal with stress and frustration?
- ✔ Do you think I'm flexible or uncooperative?
- ✔ Would you describe me a team player or a loner?
- ✔ Do you consider me a risk taker?

Keeping a daily log

One of the simplest things you can do to gain insight into your professional personality is to keep a log for at least two weeks. It doesn't have to be a work of art; you're not going to publish it. At the end of each work day for the next two weeks, think back on the various interactions you had with other people or review in your mind a problem that arose. Then, without judging, record how you responded. Consider the following questions:

> ✔ Did the situation make you feel unusually uncomfortable — if so, why? In other words, what you were being asked to accept or do that made you feel uncomfortable?
>
> ✔ If you had another chance to repeat this situation, what would you do differently? Would you listen more attentively? Would you try not to jump too quickly to a conclusion? Would you voice your concerns more confidently?

Keep in mind that the fundamental purpose of this exercise is not necessarily to help you reinvent your personality. It's simply to give you some additional insights into your tendencies and help you make more informed career decisions.

Fred Kirshenmann, Ph.D.

Dr. Fred Kirshenmann spent the first seven years of his professional career as a professor and the head of the religion department at a small liberal arts college. After several years in a successful academic role, he decided to pursue what his friends and colleagues considered a career reversal: He moved back home to manage the family farm and convert it to an organic operation.

As manager of Kirshenmann Family Farms, a North Dakota-based company that grows and markets organically grown produce, Kirshenmann meets people all over the world, addresses important conferences in the U.S. and abroad, and wrestles with critical problems facing society. He says he could not have imagined — or crafted — a more exciting career. While he never really "planned" his future, Dr. Kirshenmann believes that his preparation was in developing a set of skills that could be adapted for a variety of careers:

✔ **On skills:** "By far, the most important attributes and skills in my career are imagination, flexibility, and listening abilities. And by 'listening,' I don't mean passive 'hearing,' but 'engaged listening.' For me this means listening to not only other people but also all of nature."

✔ **On the importance of mentors:** "My training has always been on the job. I always had the good fortune of working with colleagues who served as constant mentors."

✔ **On planning your career:** "My advice is to be open to the future. Don't get locked in to a specific career path, especially if you find yourself in one you don't really enjoy. Develop yourself — your person, your spirit, your interpersonal and thinking skills."

✔ **On office politics:** "One of the wonderful aspects of managing your own farm is that you are absolutely free to be and do what you want — within the natural boundaries nature provides. But there were, of course, politics in my academic career. Mostly, I tried to get people to keep an ongoing dialogue to better understand one another's positions. I tried to create space for people to teach and learn in the ways they were most comfortable while still moving the institution in a common direction."

What Makes You So Talented?

Common sense tells you that you're much more likely to enjoy — and be successful at — jobs or careers that are well matched to your strengths. Here are three of the many the questions frequently asked by people who are undecided about their professional lives:

> ✔ How do you find out what you do well until you've had an opportunity to try your hand at different things?
>
> ✔ After you discover that you're good at something, how do you get a chance to prove yourself in real-life situations?
>
> ✔ How good do you need to be at something you enjoy in order to be able to earn a decent living doing it (forgetting for the moment how successful you want to be)?

None of these questions lends itself to an easy answer. Most people have the potential, assuming they're motivated enough, to pursue careers in any number of occupations or industries. And if you're willing to work hard and long enough, you can become reasonably proficient at skills that may not come to you naturally. You don't have to be born with the genes of an Einstein to get good grades in your science classes — not if you're willing to dedicate extra hours to studying. But these extra hours don't guarantee that you'll rewrite his theory of relativity.

Yes, but . . .

Two quick points are worth stressing:

✔ **Being good at something doesn't automatically mean that you're going to love doing it and vice versa.** When Michael Jordan decided to retire from professional basketball (for the first time) in 1993 so that he could begin a new career in baseball, he was still at the top of his game. But as Jordan explained on the day he announced his retirement, he simply wasn't interested in basketball anymore. Jordan, of course, returned to basketball two seasons later, but only after he'd reconciled himself to the fact that as much as he loved baseball, he didn't have the talent or skills to play baseball in the major leagues.

✔ **Being good or even extraordinary at something doesn't necessarily mean that you'll be able to support yourself in the lifestyle you want.** One of the most celebrated American poets of the 20th century, Wallace Stevens, lived a comfortable, upper-middle-class life in Hartford, but not because he was getting rich from his poetry. Stevens spent the major portion of his life working as an executive for the Hartford Accident and Indemnity Company.

So, in addition to focusing on your values, interests, and temperament, you also need to factor in the skills and talents you bring to the table.

Testing one, two, three

On the surface, skills tests may appear to be a useful way to get some objective feedback on not only what you're already good at, but also on what you could be good at if you applied yourself. The problem with most of these tests, though, is what they don't do. The fact that you're currently proficient at a particular activity doesn't take into account the time and effort it took to reach that level of proficiency. That's an important consideration if you're exploring an occupation that requires an ability to acquire new skills quickly. And the results from tests that measure your aptitude for various *occupation-related skills* (how readily you can learn and develop proficiency in that skill) don't necessarily point you in any specific career direction.

So the best thing to do is look at the "big picture." Take what you've learned from skills tests and compare it to your own personal experience. For instance, maybe a skills test says you're very proficient in written communication. Great! Now, think back to high school: Were you a quick study in writing quality assignments? Or was it a slow and difficult process that has improved over time? Above all, remember that assessing your skills, abilities, and interests is often more art than science!

Differentiating hard and soft skills

Most occupations require proficiency in not just one but in several skills. The abilities to think sequentially and logically, for example, are critical skills if you want to succeed in law, but they're also fundamental skills in fields as widely diverse as computer programming, hospital administration, and event planning. Whatever strategy you pursue in your efforts to gain insight into your abilities, make sure you draw a distinction between hard skills and soft skills.

- *Hard skills,* broadly speaking, tend to be technical. They also tend to be occupation specific. Being able to write HTML code is a hard skill — so is knowing how to operate a fork lift, cook a soufflé, edit a movie, and hit a golf ball 250 yards without shanking it.

  Make no mistake about it, hard skills still matter: They're a fundamental requirement in most fields. But the problem with many hard skills is that they're not readily transferable. The fact that you can tear down a computer and put it back together in 20 minutes is a solid, hard skill, but its career relevance is limited to those occupations that involve mechanical or electronic devices. So if your skill set is too specialized, your career options may be limited.

✔ *Soft skills,* unlike most hard skills, are highly transferable. Okay, you know how to tear down and put together a computer in 20 minutes. But can you explain over the phone how to do this? That skill — being able to communicate complicated directions in a simple, easy-to-follow manner — is a skill that will hold you in good stead in dozens of occupations.

You may never have thought of them as career assets, but it's possible that many of the things you're good at right now represent the very kind of soft skills that are in high demand in most occupations. Many skills fall into this category, but all relate in one way or another to how you deal with people and how you manage yourself when you're in pressure situations.

Assuming you possess the hard skills that are fundamental for a position, the options you can pursue and the progress you can make in your career depend more than ever on the softer side of your skill set. OfficeTeam developed the PEOPLE Skills Index to indicate those soft skills that will be important for career success in the years ahead. Table 2-1 gives you a look at these skills.

Table 2-1	Soft Skills for Success
Skill	*What it affects*
P: Problem-solving abilities	How adept you are at using logic, judgment, and creativity in dealing with the day-to-day business problems — particularly as those problems relate to interpersonal conflicts.
E: Ethics	Your ability to conduct business and fulfill your responsibility in an ethical way, with fixed (rather than situational) values, determining the difference between right and wrong.
O: Open-mindedness	Keeping an open mind to new ideas and adapting your own practices to the changing realities of the business — but without compromising your integrity or your values.
P: Persuasiveness	How well you listen to others and articulate your point of view without pulling rank or raising your temper.
L: Leadership	Your ability to assume accountability for the tasks you undertake — and to motivate those with whom you work to do the same. Providing your staff with the support and resources they need to do their jobs.
E: Educational interests	Your commitment to lifelong learning — how committed you are to steady growth in your knowledge and skills development.

Bringing It All Together

Whether you intend to do it on your own or with the help of a career planning specialist, creating a strategic career plan means you need to ask yourself dozens of questions that relate to your interests, values, working habits, personality traits, and skills. Figure 2-1 addresses key areas for you to explore. While it doesn't lay out an actual process, it can help you outline your career goals. Feel free to add any personal comments or observations in the right-hand column to customize this tool.

After you complete the exercise in Figure 2-1, you can use Figure 2-2 to document your tailored career plan.

Your passions and interests:

Use the space on the right to jot down all the activities and subject areas you can think of that you find interesting, enjoyable, and exciting. Examples include classical music, running, cooking, bicycling, and reading about current events.

Note: Many of these activities may be hobbies or avocations, but the fact that you enjoy them can provide insights to help you find a career you consider equally enjoyable.

_____

_____

_____

_____

_____

_____

_____

_____

_____

_____

Your values:

On a scale of one to five (five = very important), indicate the importance of each personal goal listed on the right. When you've finished this, reorganize the list according to numerical rating, with the most important ratings at the top.

___ **Material desires:** Making a great deal of money

___ **Creative drive:** Expressing myself artistically

___ **Self-development:** Constantly learning new things and expanding my mind

___ **Autonomy:** Being independent — making my own long-term strategic decisions as well as short-term decisions

___ **Spirituality:** Living a life consistent with my religious or moral beliefs

___ **Community:** Being an integral part of a group of people who share a common interest

___ **Altruism:** Making a contribution to society

___ **Balance:** Having enough time during the week to devote to family or personal interests

Figure 2-1:
A strategic career-planning tool.

(continued)

(continued)

Your working style: On a scale of one to five (five = very important), indicate the importance of the qualities on the right in your day-to-day work.	____ **Variety:** Assignments are very diverse and require many different skill sets (interpersonal, analytical, creative, and so on). ____ **Challenge and excitement:** Job presents frequent challenges (either mental or physical). I'm constantly being tested but rewarded on the basis of performance. ____ **Creativity:** Work offers numerous opportunities to solve problems and develop innovative ideas. ____ **Stability:** Job tasks are predictable and easily handled. I have little need to worry about performance issues that could affect earnings or job security.
Your strengths and weaknesses: Based on what you know about yourself through past on-the-job performance, indicate on a scale of one to five (five = strongest performance) how well you typically do in the conditions described. After you're finished, reorganize the list according to your ratings, with your strongest accomplishments listed at the top.	____ The project I'm involved with requires strong organizational skills and great attention to detail. ____ I'm coordinating the efforts of many people. ____ I'm working very independently, developing long-term strategies and making short-term decisions. ____ I'm part of a close-knit team. ____ I'm juggling a variety of projects at the same time. ____ I'm working on one project from start to finish. ____ I'm in a situation in which other people make the key decisions. ____ I'm interacting frequently with people who have a different style of work. ____ I'm under pressure constantly and need to maintain a calm demeanor.

Figure 2-1:
A strategic career-planning tool.

Goal:_____ Deadline: _____   Interests:

                                                _____

Objective:_____ Deadline: _____   _____

Action items: _____

_____ Deadline: _____   Values:

_____ Deadline: _____   _____

_____ Deadline: _____   _____

_____ Deadline: _____   Work style:

                                                _____

                                                _____

Objective:_____ Deadline: _____   _____

Action items: Strengths:

_____ Deadline: _____   _____

_____ Deadline: _____   _____

_____ Deadline: _____   Weaknesses:

_____ Deadline: _____   _____

_____ Deadline: _____   _____

Figure 2-2:
A career-
planning
document.

Chapter 3

Researching Career Options

. . . .

In This Chapter

▶ Researching career options, made easy

▶ Using the *Occupational Outlook Handbook*

▶ Accessing the Internet as a career information resource

▶ Interviewing for information

▶ Broadening your perspective with other resources

▶ Considering career counselors: Should you or shouldn't you?

. . . .

*I*n a perfect world (or, better still, if you were the prince or princess in an absolute monarchy), setting up a strategic career plan would be a piece of cake. Your biggest challenge would be deciding which career you wanted to pursue, based, of course, on what looked like the most fun. Whether you were particularly skilled in your chosen field wouldn't matter. Your level of proficiency would be the benchmark of excellence throughout the entire kingdom. Whether you could earn a good (or even decent) living in your chosen field wouldn't matter because, when the bills started to pile up, you could simply dip into the Royal Treasury. And the last thing you'd have to worry about would be other people — nobles or commoners, that is — competing for the same job. You could get Mom or Dad to pass a royal decree and send your would-be competitors off into exile.

Okay, but in the real world of career planning, it isn't enough simply to know thyself. You also need a general idea of your options and the job possibilities in those industries. You also have to consider the practical aspects of that field, especially when it comes to the two big C's of career planning: cash flow (the amount of money you need to support your lifestyle) and competition (the number of people who are pursuing the same jobs that you're trying to land).

In this chapter, I help you bring a real-world perspective to your strategic career plan. You find out how to take an inventory of your skills (and it may be trickier than you think). You're introduced to research processes that will give you an insider's view of what it's like to work in the fields or careers that seem interesting to you. You also get a chance to see how marketable you are as a job candidate in those fields.

Albert Wertheim, Ph.D.

Although Albert Wertheim has spent more than 35 years in the same field, his career has grown in directions he never expected. As an assistant professor of English at Princeton University, he was persuaded by a friend to teach at Indiana University for a year — and has remained there for three decades. Ten years after his relocation, Wertheim decided to offer a new and progressive course in international English literature — just for the fun of it. Ultimately the class was so successful that it led to his specialization and recognized expertise in that area. And a few years later, he pursued another learning experience. He was asked to take on the role of associate dean and — although he admits having had no prior administrative experience — he accepted the challenge and realized his talent for management.

Wertheim currently holds three positions at Indiana University: professor of English, professor of theater and drama, and associate dean for research. Speaking from experience, he advises professionals to be open to new directions in their careers and pursue satisfying work.

✔ **On office politics:** "My simple piece of wisdom is that most people want Valentine cards more than salary increases. In other words, they need to hear someone say, 'I read your article and thought it was so perceptive,' or 'Thanks so much for taking care of that — I don't know how I'd manage without you.'" He believes that a little present or kind word goes a long way to make people feel appreciated and smooth working relationships.

✔ **On management:** Wertheim notes that it's key to recognize that each person is different. "If you see your customers, clients, patients, or students as a monolith, you will not serve them well or be successful. If you recognize their individuality and treat them as individuals, you cannot fail."

✔ **On pursuing career success:** "My parents wisely said that what is important is not how much money you make, but whether you are happy in your work. Teaching in America is genteel poverty. I had the brains to enter a profession in which I might well have made a lot of money. I chose instead a life in which my career has brought me great pleasure and satisfaction. And that is worth more than a seven-figure stock portfolio, a huge house, or a vacation home on Hilton Head."

Finding Out about the Marketplace

Chances are, you already know a little bit about a lot of different careers. That knowledge may have come from any number of sources: your own job experience, the careers of friends or family, movies or television shows that depict people working in various careers (does anyone not know what it's like to be a police detective?), job fairs you may have attended, or information from recruiters with whom you've spoken. In other words, you probably have a general idea of what a typical workday would be like if you were a forest ranger, political campaign worker, graphic designer, computer programmer, or hotel manager. Ideally, it would be in your best interest to spend several months actually working in a national forest, local political organization, advertising agency, computer services department, or resort. This is why internships can be such a valuable experience for college students.

The trouble is, there is a limit to the number of careers you can actually sample before you make a choice. So you need to narrow your options. You need a strategy for exploring opportunities without actually working in every occupation that may conceivably bring you satisfaction. Fortunately, you have many resources available to you. You simply have to take advantage of them. (The following sections can help.)

Getting information direct from Uncle Sam

Probably the best place to begin is a U.S. government publication called the *Occupational Outlook Handbook*. Published every other year by the Bureau of Labor Statistics — a branch of the Department of Labor — the *Occupational Outlook Handbook* can be found in the reference section of virtually every library in the U.S. A more user-friendly compilation of this information can be found on the Internet at a related government site, America's Career InfoNet (www.acinet.org/acinet/).

What makes this reference guide so valuable is its scope and depth of detail. It provides an in-depth profile of more than 250 occupations, grouped by 11 broad clusters. Each occupation profile begins with a summary of the key trends in that field — for example, whether the number of openings is on the rise or on the decline. That overview is followed by information designed to answer questions such as

- What is the nature of the work?
- What sort of credentials (if any) do you need to get started?
- What skills and attributes do you need to be successful in the field?
- How much can you expect to earn, and how long before you earn it?
- How competitive is the field?

Searching the Internet

Is it possible to have too much of a good thing? When it comes to the volume of career-related information now available on the Internet, the answer may be "yes." The challenge you face when you use the Internet to research careers isn't a lack of availability of information. It's figuring out which of the thousands of career- related sites you should be relying upon.

The majority of career-related sites are sponsored by individuals and firms that offer career counseling or outplacement services. Other sites operate primarily as job posting sites but offer career planning advice as part of the overall mix. Nearly all the major Internet service providers (AOL, CompuServe, Earthlink, and so on), for example, have sections devoted exclusively to careers and jobs.

Some sites are better than others when it comes to career and industry descriptions. Here's a look at some of the sites you may want to check out first:

- ✔ **BestJobsUSA.com:** On this site you can find Employment Review Online — the Web version of a monthly magazine by the same name. An interesting feature, the 'Pro' files section, provides the opportunity to listen in on interview sessions with professionals who work in a wide range of fields. The list of fields covered in these Q&A sessions changes periodically, but the focus of each interview is generally the same: Questions relate to what makes a particular career unique, and what it takes to be successful in that profession or occupation.

- ✔ **About:** This well-designed, easy-to-navigate information source includes a section called Career Planning. Among its many features is the Occupations area, which provides hyperlinks to dozens of other Internet sources for a given industry, including associations, periodicals, and books. In short, this is a good one-stop resource.

- ✔ **Quintessential Careers:** This popular site at www.quintcareers.com has been around since 1996 and is a robust source of information about every aspect of career management, including occupational descriptions. Like Career Planning (see the previous bullet), this site has an unusually extensive array of hyperlinks to other career- and job-related sites on the Internet.

- ✔ **WetFeet.com:** This multi-dimensional site at www.wetfeet.com is primarily in the business of selling you its "Insider Guides," which are candid snapshots of what it's really like to work for specific companies. But one of the free — and extremely useful — features is called Real People Profiles. Questions asked in these profiles replicate what you may ask of employees:

    - "How did you get your job?"

    - "Describe a typical day"

    - "What do you like the most (or least) about this job?"

    - "What kind of people do well in this field?"

  The site is attractively designed, easy to navigate, and enjoyable to read.

Q and A: Arranging informational interviews

One of the best — and often, most reliable — ways to get an idea of what it's like in the trenches of any given field or industry is to get the information straight from the source — someone who is currently employed in that field. This type of conversation is typically known as an *informational interview* or *informational meeting* (as opposed to a job interview).

When speaking with potential contacts, you may want to use the word "meeting" rather than "interview." Some people may misunderstand your purpose and think you're looking for a job interview.

Here's some advice on how to put this valuable tool to work for you.

- **Network to those in the know.** When scouting around for possible contacts, seek out people who've been actively involved for at least three or four years in the career you're researching. Preferably (but not necessarily) that person should be your age or someone with whom you can identify. If you don't know anyone who meets these qualifications, get names from friends, relatives, classmates, or even your alumni association.

- **Ask and you shall receive.** Assuming their schedule permits it and you approach them properly, most professionals will agree to meet you. You'll be pleasantly surprised at how many people — even strangers — will agree to help you when you're not too embarrassed to ask for their insights. Occasionally, you may meet with someone who provides you with little more than name, rank, and serial number, but most people who like what they do enjoy telling other people about it.

- **Be prepared.** The more research you do prior to the session, the more you're going to derive from the experience. Familiarize yourself — through reading or surfing the Net — with the real basics. That way, you'll be better equipped to ask intelligent questions. It's also a good idea to go into the meeting with questions already written out. The following are some questions you may want to consider:

    - "What made you decide to go into this field?"
    - "How did you get your first job?"
    - "Can you describe a typical work day?"
    - "How many hours, on average, do you work per week?"
    - "If you had it to do over again, would you choose the same field?"
    - "What kind of pressures are you under?"

- "What do you like most about this field?"
- "What do you like the least?"
- "What qualities, above all, does it take to be successful in this field?"

✔ **Dress appropriately and observe etiquette.** Informational meetings can be conducted just as easily over the phone as in person. But face-to-face sessions are preferable, assuming you don't have to fly across the country to meet with the person. If you're going to interview someone personally, look your best, especially if the meeting is taking place in the person's place of work. (Word to the wise: Dress as though you were actually applying for a job.) Even though you're not looking for employment at the moment, the person you meet may be in a position to give you some job leads in the future, so you want to make the most positive impression.

✔ **Send a word of thanks.** Always take time — no later than the next day — to send a brief note (it's okay to send an e-mail) thanking the person for his or her time.

Taking temporary work

Assuming you're able to do so (in other words, that you're not already employed full-time), working as a temporary or project consultant is one of the best ways to gain some good insights into different career possibilities. True, no staffing agency is going to put you in a job you're not qualified to handle. But on a project basis, you may get a chance to work in different occupations, companies, and industries. You get an opportunity to meet, work with, and get to know professionals you may not otherwise get a chance to know. The best way to find temporary work is to look for a staffing firm that specializes in the fields you're interested in. Quality staffing firms or recruiting services — particularly those that specialize in a particular field — are well positioned to know the skills and qualities that employers in various fields are looking for when evaluating candidates. Savvy recruiters can provide candid feedback about how marketable you are as a candidate and can offer sound advice to make you even more marketable.

Looking at job boards

Classified ads in newspapers, professional publications, and online job boards are geared primarily toward job seekers, but if the ads are detailed and well written, they can be a fruitful source of information about the basic requirements and attributes that employers in different fields are seeking in today's employment market. After you've read a dozen or so ads that relate to a specific occupation, you should begin to notice that certain terms ("good communication skills," for example) keep cropping up — a reliable sign that you're going to need that quality or attribute yourself if you hope to make any headway in the field.

Career Counselors: Should You or Shouldn't You?

Before you can decide whether consulting a *career counselor* (also known as a *career coach* or a *career development professional*) is worth your time and money, ask yourself a simple question: How well are you doing in your career-planning process? If you already have a pretty good idea of who you are, what you value (see Chapter 2), and what type of work you want to pursue, and if you've started to research specific careers, the average career counselor may not have too much to offer. On the other hand, if you're having trouble clarifying your goals and interests, an experienced career counselor can help navigate the process in a logical, systematic way. More important, a good career coach can help you take a more objective view of yourself. You won't be able to get away with simply saying, for example, that one of your strengths is your ability to remain cool in a crisis. The counselor will want to hear about specific events in your life that give credence to that perception.

Keep in mind what career counselors aren't. They're not therapists (although many career counselors are, in fact, licensed psychologists). Nor are they specialists in job placement or sources of actual job leads. Their mission is to help you gain a better understanding of your values, interests, strengths, and weaknesses.

Most career coaches offer the same general mix of services.

✔ They administer and interpret assessment tests.

✔ They probe to get a clearer picture of your goals and aspirations.

✔ They present you with a range of career possibilities that seem well-suited to your interests.

✔ They help you put together short-term and long-term career plans.

If the process is successful, you emerge with a better understanding of your values and goals, a broad strategy for managing your career, and some skills (how to write a better cover letter, for example) that will hold you in good stead after you launch your job search.

Figuring out how much it'll cost

Career counseling can cost anywhere from $40 to $150 an hour, depending on which region of the country you live in or whether you go to a not-for-profit organization (the YMCA, for example, or a government-funded agency), a private practitioner, or a company that specializes in career counseling. Most career coaches prefer that you sign up for a package of five or six sessions, with total fees ranging from a few hundred dollars at a not-for-profit agency to as much as thousands of dollars at the largest, high-end private career counseling companies. (What you get in return for the higher fee is not only the standard mix of career counseling services but a personal career coach who works closely with you throughout the job search.)

Making a good choice

The most reliable way to choose a career counselor is to get a recommendation from someone who has good things to say about a particular professional. Many career advisors have degrees in psychology, counseling, social work, or education and typically have a license or some other state certification. Several organizations have established accreditation guidelines, but accredited counselors represent only a small fraction of the people working in the field.

Regardless of how much a career counselor charges, how he or she likes to work, and how many degrees you find after his or her name, it's essential that you have confidence in the counselor you work with and that you feel comfortable speaking with that individual. Here are some guidelines designed to help you make a good choice:

- ✔ Take the time to interview any counselor you're considering — before you sign up. Be wary of anyone who balks at your questions or makes you feel uncomfortable in any way. Ask about his or her background and experience.

- ✔ Don't hesitate to ask about the process. Ask the counselor to describe the process and try to get a sense of what you can reasonably expect to gain from the experience.

- ✔ Steer clear of any career counselor who uses high-pressure tactics, who guarantees you a good job if you sign up, or who insists on a hefty up-front fee.

- ✔ Always ask for references. Look elsewhere if the counselor doesn't want to comply with the request.

Chapter 4

Tooling Up for the Future

● ●

In This Chapter

▶ Assessing your marketability

▶ Positioning yourself for your next move

▶ Reengineering your current job

▶ Going back to school

▶ Considering project work

● ●

*W*hile you may have a reasonably clear idea what you want to do with your life and which career opportunities represent the most logical routes to those goals, making it happen is something else altogether. What you need is a plan of attack — an action plan.

The timetable and actual steps you need to take are determined primarily by two factors: what needs to be done and how much time it is likely to take, in light of your other responsibilities and your financial needs. You may already be well positioned to find a good job in the occupation that appeals to you or you may need to make some interim moves first. You may need some additional coursework or you may need to gain broader experience in certain specialties. You may even need to beef up certain skills. But there is no one-size-fits-all approach to this aspect of strategic career planning. Whatever plan you develop needs to be customized to you, which means that it needs to be in sync with not only your professional goals but also with the priorities in your personal life.

This chapter includes tips, techniques, and real-world strategies. You find out how to assess your marketability in light of the jobs you'd like to get. Equally important, you discover how to identify gaps in your education, background, and skill set that you need to bridge before making the transition. Perhaps you've been dreaming and reflecting for awhile. Now it's time to take action.

How Marketable Are You?

Before venturing down any new career path, you must assess your marketability. *Marketability* means the same thing in career planning as it does in commerce: It's the number of potential buyers, relatively speaking, for what you're selling, keeping in mind that plenty of other sellers are in the marketplace, as well. And what, exactly, are you selling? In short, you're offering your particular mix of skills, attributes, experience, and credentials. Your marketability is a measure of how much you have in relation to what an employer wants. Think of your marketability in terms of your assets (those aspects of your background, education, and skills that make you an attractive candidate for a particular job) and your liabilities (those aspects that could work against you — until, of course, you eliminate them).

A force unto itself

The job market is a force that marches to its own drum. Job market conditions can change from year to year and can differ from one field to the next, as well as from one region to another. Although the hiring environment is shaped by forces and trends you can't control, you can understand it and adapt to it. The following sections give you a brief look at some factors that can affect your marketability in any given field. (Be ready — there's a test afterward!)

Gaining credentials

Credentials refer to degrees, licenses, certificates, and accreditations that document your completion of courses, training, experience, or test scores. Credentials carry more weight in some fields than in others. For instance, you don't need an MBA or Ph.D. to become a Hollywood producer, an entrepreneur, or a personal trainer. But if you want to practice law, you can't simply buy an Armani suit, put an ad in the yellow pages, and print up business cards with the letters "Esq." after your name. You need a degree from an accredited law school, and you also need to pass the bar in the state you hope to practice. Sorry, watching reruns of *Law & Order* and *Ally McBeal* doesn't count.

Because credentials represent, in effect, the entrance fee to many professions and careers, you need to find out early on what certification is required to get started and, equally important, what's required if you hope to advance. Here are some questions to ask when assessing your career goals:

> ✔ Are requirements for certification uniform or do they vary from state to state?
>
> ✔ How long does it typically take to get certified or licensed or to complete the educational requirements, and what's involved?
>
> ✔ How much does it cost to get the credentials?

After you gather this information, you may decide that the hoops you have to jump through aren't worth it. Or, if you're still interested in pursuing a career that requires particular credentials, you need to build into your plan a realistic timetable for acquiring them.

Reviewing your previous experience and track record

Your track record is an account of your experience and accomplishments: It encompasses the organizations you worked for, the jobs you held, what you actually did in those jobs, and what you accomplished.

As it happens, your track record — what you've done in the past — is not quite as critical a factor in most hiring situations as it once was. That's the case at least in certain fields — information technology, for example — in which the rapid pace of change has made many employers less interested in what positions or job titles you've held in the past, and more interested in what skills you possess now. But assuming you can meet those skill requirements, your track record provides tangible evidence that you're up-to-speed in the skills employers want. In that respect, an impressive history of accomplishments gives you an edge over less experienced candidates who may be competing for the same position. Bottom line: The more your track record matches the hiring criteria of a would-be employer, the more marketable you are.

Even if your accomplishments aren't as imposing as you would like them to be, you can make moves right now and over the next several months — possibly in your current job — that will provide you with the kinds of work experiences that make you a more marketable candidate for jobs in the future.

Understanding the importance of skills

Skills play an important role in your marketability, and no matter what sort of a career you're pursuing, you're going to have to meet the performance requirements. Keep in mind, however, that in most professions today, your marketability is no longer determined solely by your technical skills — how quickly you can write computer code or put together a profit-and-loss statement. Soft skills (discussed in Chapter 2) count more than ever — and may well be more important in the jobs you're aiming for than in the jobs you've held in the past.

If you're an information technology specialist, for example, and you want to move into consulting, you need to convince a would-be consulting firm (through your accomplishments) that you have the communication, leadership, and problem-solving skills that are in such high demand. You should know, too, that more and more companies employ sophisticated tests and other methods to identify whether candidates have the required people skills. Being able to eloquently expound on your achievements during an interview may not be enough to get you past the first round.

Taking your lifestyle requirements into account

If you're wondering what lifestyle requirements have to do with your marketability, the answer is this: more than you might think. If, for example, your career ambitions lie in any of the glamour professions — broadcasting, Hollywood entertainment, or music, for example — you could have trouble making ends meet on the meager entry level salaries that are the norm in these industries. If you can get by on a shoestring budget or have an outside source of income (a trust fund or generous parents), you have a distinct advantage over people who have to support themselves on the salaries they're paid.

The same principle holds true for any other special requirements you may have. If, because of family responsibilities, you're obliged to live in one specific region of the country, you may be less marketable than someone who can pick up and move wherever he or she chooses. Other lifestyle factors that could affect your marketability include how important it is for you to stay involved in the leisure pursuits you love. If you're a dedicated marathoner, you could have trouble balancing your 20-hour-per-week training schedule with a job that keeps you in the office 60 or 70 hours a week.

If your lifestyle factors aren't compatible with the demands of a specific career, you aren't automatically ruled out as a viable candidate. But the more competition for the job — and the more pressure you feel to pay the rent on time — the more flexible your lifestyle requirements need to be. You may want to reevaluate your priorities for the meantime and try to pursue your original goals when opportunities are more readily available.

Evaluating the fit

If you've done your homework on starting and advancing in a given career, you can now identify the gaps that may exist between what the marketplace is looking for and what you have to offer.

Table 4-1 helps you take inventory of your career assets and liabilities and compare them with what the market requires. You can use this form for any job or occupation. If you have trouble answering the questions in either column, don't worry — you just have to do a little more homework.

Table 4-1	Evaluating Your Assets and Liabilities
What the Job Requires	***What You Possess***
List the credentials (degrees, licenses, and so on) that are required for entering or for advancing in a given field.	List the credentials, if any, that you currently possess.
_____	_____
_____	_____
_____	_____
_____	_____
Describe the kinds of work experience or track record that represent key hiring criteria for the job you want.	Describe your own work experience.
_____	_____
_____	_____
_____	_____

(continued)

Table 4-1 *(continued)*

What the Job Requires	*What You Possess*
List at least four hard, technical skills that you must possess to take the next step in your career plan. _____ _____ _____ _____	Rate yourself on a scale of 1 to 10 (10 the highest) on each of the skills listed in the left column. _____ _____ _____ _____
Write down at least five soft skills that, based on your research, are needed to succeed in the jobs you want. _____ _____ _____ _____	Rate yourself on a scale of 1 to 10 (10 the highest) in each of these skills. _____ _____ _____ _____
What is the typical salary for the kind of position you want?	How much do you need to live on right now?
What is the average starting salary of people who have been at the job or career five years?	How much money do you either need or want to be making in five years?
How many hours per week do successful people in this job typically work?	How many hours a week are you willing (or able) to work in order to be successful in that job?
Which cities or regions of the country or world offer the best opportunities for your job targets?	How convenient is it for you to relocate to the cities in the left column?
Are there any unusual demands (being able to work under stress, for example) that differentiate this field from most fields?	How easily will it be for you to meet the demands in the left column, in light of your responsibilities of outside interests?

Bridging the Gap

A careful analysis of the evaluation in Table 4-1 should provide you enough insight to determine whether you have a realistic shot at getting the kinds of jobs you want. If there's little or no difference between the two sets of answers, there's no reason to procrastinate — you're ready to make your move. If, however, a gap is substantial, or if you have more than four or five gaps, you may want to rethink your career goals — or, at the very least, establish a longer timetable for your progress. But assuming the discrepancies are not that significant, your next step is to find ways to bridge these gaps. The timetable is up to you. It may take a year. It may take three years. Remember: You tailor it to your needs.

Reengineering your current job

The first — and best — place to increase you're marketability is right where you are. While your current job may be so demanding and limited in its focus that there's simply no opportunity to change it, you can still explore the possibility. By staying in your current position while you're gearing up for your next career move, you avoid the disruption and pressure that may result if you were to simply quit your job to make a new start somewhere else.

Here are some suggestions for building career bridges while on the job:

- ✔ Request a meeting with your manager and explore opportunities to expand your current responsibilities to help fill in some of your experience gaps.

- ✔ Take advantage of any training resources that your company offers — seminars, a learning center, audio tapes, and so on — to strengthen your skills.

- ✔ Volunteer for special projects or task forces that give you an opportunity to develop your soft skills. If, for example, you haven't participated on a self-managed team — a critical skill in today's workplace — your involvement with such a team could prove extremely valuable.

Finding a mentor

Mentors have been traditionally thought of as people who help you learn the ropes of a company or an industry. But you can just as easily seek out mentors to help you bridge the gaps that may exist in your soft skills. If you have good reason to suspect that you don't relate as well with your coworkers as you should (hint: you're the only person in your department who doesn't get a cake on your birthday), find someone who knows you reasonably well and who possesses the people skills you lack. You're not looking necessarily for someone to teach you how to get along better with people; instead, you want someone to observe your interaction with others and sit down with you from time to time to give you some constructive feedback. Ultimately, of course, you have to teach yourself.

Should you go public?

How public you can afford to be when considering a career change can be a tough call, especially if you can't afford to lose your job. You do run a slight risk that if you communicate your intentions, the company may want to find a replacement for you. You have to know your customer (or, in this case, your employer). Explain to your manager the types of responsibilities and skills you'd like to have and ask if there's a way to make that transition in your current position. What could well happen, after you begin to take some initiative and try to reengineer your current job, is that your new responsibilities have rekindled your excitement about the job. You may discover that the best way to get to where you want to be in five years is to stay right where you are.

Taking on temporary or project assignments

If you're in a job that you don't like, isn't paying very much, or isn't in sync with your career goals, it may make sense for you to think about working as a temporary and enhance your marketability. True, you're not going to get too much opportunity on your temporary assignments to develop new skills because you're expected to bring the necessary qualifications to each assignment. But you'll probably have more flexibility than you now have, with more time to take classes or work on the skills you're trying to develop. One suggestion: As long as you're going to be working with a temporary firm, look for assignments in companies that are part of your career plans. A good place to start your quest for these jobs is with a staffing firm that specializes in your field of interest.

Going back to school

To really advance your career, education needs to be a consistent priority. And sometimes on-the-job training is no substitute for a little dedicated coursework. Here are some options to consider as you strive to make the grade at your workplace.

Seminars

Seminars are one-, two-, or three-day courses that focus on a single skill, such as business writing, supervision, customer service, Internet searching, or time management. You don't earn any heavy-duty credentials from a seminar, but they give you an opportunity to focus on a particular skill or knowledge area in a concentrated time period. A good seminar also gives you insights into what you need to do to continue your own self-improvement campaign.

Most companies that offer seminars promote their offerings through direct mail (there's probably a brochure for an upcoming public seminar in your business mailbox right now), and the costs range from next-to-nothing to thousands of dollars. The organization best known throughout the United States for its management-level seminar programs is the American Management Association (www.amanet.org), which offers a variety of topics. A quick tour of their Web site gives you an idea of what's available and whether the courses are a good match for your needs.

Paula Lambert

From teacher to gourmet mozzarella cheesemaker, Paula Lambert has strolled down a career path suited to her own personal tastes (pardon the pun). After teaching school for a few years, she moved to Italy to study art history and Italian — and developed a love for fresh mozzarella cheese. When she returned home to Dallas, she decided to be an entrepreneur. Building her business around the two things she loves — Italy and food — seemed only natural.

Understanding the value of firsthand instruction, Lambert took a trip back to Italy to visit a small cheese factory where she was able to study her craft. After leasing and remodeling a small site of her own in Dallas, she sharpened her skills further by learning at the side of a visiting cheese professor from Italy.

Since its beginnings in 1982, The Mozzarella Company has grown from a small, local business to a million-dollar operation serving customers in the U.S. and abroad. Lambert's award-winning cheeses have been served to presidents and royalty, as well as at the Academy Awards, and have been featured in prestigious publications such as *Gourmet, Food & Wine, Bon Appetit,* and *The New York Times.* She credits her success to her ability to set a goal and stick with it no matter how tough things may have seemed.

✔ **On her most important career decisions:** "Teaching school was invaluable, because I learned how to teach and motivate people. And I use that knowledge in teaching my employees all sorts of skills, from cheesemaking to customer service. Another important career decision involved volunteerism. I learned many skills that came in handy, from bookkeeping to public relations to public speaking, through my involvement in various volunteer jobs."

✔ **On office politics:** "Office politics involves personalities — so it's an inevitable part of business. The most important thing you can do is hire good, highly motivated people who are there to work and concentrate on doing their jobs effectively and efficiently."

✔ **On entrepreneurialism:** "There are a million details involved in running a successful company. Patience and organization are constantly required, as well as perseverence. And last, but certainly not least, is a positive attitude."

✔ **On pursuing career success:** "Work hard and concentrate on your job. Try to anticipate problems so you can be prepared for them. Persevere, have patience, and don't give up — it will get easier. But the most important thing of all is to love your job and what you're doing. If you are happy, you will be successful and will inspire others."

Adult education courses

No matter where you live, you're probably within commuting distance (maybe even shouting distance) of a least one college, high school, or community organization that offers *continuing-education classes* or, as they're usually called, *adult-education classes*. These courses are almost always noncredit, which means that you can't apply them to an undergraduate or graduate degree, and they're generally held once a week for a period of 4 to 12 weeks. Prices are generally well below what you would pay for a college course. The quality of these courses, as you may expect, depends almost entirely on the organization offering them or, more specifically, on the skill, knowledge, and commitment of the instructor. But don't sell short adult education courses.

They can be excellent places to shore up your basic skills, such as reading, writing, and public speaking and can also help you brush up on your computer skills. You may also find classes to earn credentials (such as a real estate license) or enhance your knowledge prior to a career change (with vocational classes, for example). For many people, not being under pressure to get a good grade enhances the learning process.

Graduate school

Few people dispute the fact that earning a graduate degree gives you an added edge in whatever field you're pursuing. And, from all accounts, a graduate degree can considerably enhance your earning power. According to the U.S. Census Bureau in 1998 — the most recent year for which data is available — a person with a master's degree earns, on average, $10,000 more per year than someone with a bachelor's degree. And the gap widens when workers with bachelor's degrees are compared to those with Ph.D.s.

But the question you need to ask yourself with respect to graduate school is: Does this make sense for me? Consider where you want to go with your career and take into account the heavy-duty commitment that graduate school requires. You want to be particularly careful that you don't fall into the all-too-common trap of using two years of graduate school as a way of helping you decide where you want to go in your career. Graduate school should be a tool in your plan, not the plan itself.

It may well be that you need graduate school. In certain lines of work — library science, college teaching, social work, and psychology, to name just a few — an advanced degree is an essential credential. In other fields, however, the advantages of an advanced degree are not as clear-cut. And even the strongest advocates of graduate school concede that what you learn in graduate school doesn't automatically produce the necessary growth and improvement for success in your field. You don't, for example, find out how to become an effective manager in most graduate schools. Nor do you gain mental toughness, flexibility, resourcefulness, persistence or all the other intangible skills that have become fundamental to career success today.

Six really bad reasons for going back to school

People actually have given these reasons for attending graduate school!

- ✔ Increases your chances of meeting someone whom you'll eventually marry.

- ✔ Impresses all the teachers in high school who said you would never amount to anything.

- ✔ Helps you decide what you want to be when you grow up.

- ✔ Postpones the need to get a full-time job for at least two years — even longer if you go for your doctorate.

- ✔ If you don't go, you'll be the first person in your family, dating back to your great Uncle Cedric, who didn't earn at least one advanced degree.

- ✔ You've seen all the reruns of *Law & Order,* and you don't know what else to do with your afternoons.

So before you make this important decision, you need to ask some hard questions. Here are a few to get you started:

- ✔ **How much good will it really do?** Advanced degrees are more instrumental to career advancement in certain companies and fields. To find out how valuable a degree will be for you in light of your career goals, take a look at the people in those jobs or companies you want to pursue, and determine what percentage of them have advanced degrees. Also find out what the trend is: Is it becoming more or less likely that the most successful people in that field will have advanced degrees?

- ✔ **Can you afford it?** The cost of an advanced degree these days can range anywhere from $5,000 to $100,000, depending upon where you go and how many credits you have to earn to get the degree. Tuition at state schools is almost always less expensive than tuition at private schools, but the additional costs — textbooks, lab fees, and so on — add up quickly no matter where you go. If someone else — your company, for example — can invest in your education, great. Otherwise, you may have to do what most graduate students do: Take out a student loan. Before financing your own education, meet with a financial planner to figure out how long it's going to take to recoup your investment.

- ✔ **Can you qualify for admission?** Before you get admitted to any reputable graduate school, you may have to do a little work — or, as they like to put it, "meet their entrance requirements." You may discover, for example, that some of the really boring courses you decided to drop when you were an undergraduate are prerequisites for the graduate program you're interested in. You may also have to take a standardized test that's similar to the SATs you took when you were applying for college. And if you have your sights set on one of the more prestigious graduate schools, you need to rack up some fairly high scores. You also have to prepare a stellar essay. If you've made up your mind to go to graduate school, give yourself at least six months to navigate the admission process — longer if you have your eye on highly prestigious schools.

✔ **Is now the best time to do it?** The answer to this question depends on what "now" means. Most career advisors recommend that young business professionals spend at least two or three years in the working world before seeking a graduate degree — and that's good advice! Delaying the decision lessens the chances that you'll decide midway through the degree program that you weren't really interested in that career, after all. On a more practical level, if you wait a few years, you may be working for an employer that will pay for some part of the degree.

✔ **Are you up to the grind?** Don't be too quick to answer this question. You may have fond memories of your college years, sitting around a table in the college coffee shop arguing about politics and philosophy. Remember though, you weren't working full-time. So even if you take what seems to be a light course load — one class per semester, for example — you need to factor in your homework and out-of-class commitments, which typically include group projects that can run throughout most of the semester. Some experts recommend tripling the number of credit hours to better estimate your total time in and out of class each week.

✔ **Which school should you choose?** Depending on where you live and how flexible your work schedule is, you may not have too many options. But if you have a choice of schools, try to get a firsthand look at as many of them as you can. Read the catalogs carefully so you know exactly what the degree requirements are and what courses you'll be taking. Talk to the professors who will be teaching you — and, if possible, the department heads. And see if you can sit in on a class or two. That way you'll get a chance to talk to the people best qualified to tell you whether it's worth your time and money to attend: the students.

Table 4-2   The Pros and Cons of Earning an Advanced Degree

Pros	Cons
Enhances your marketability and earning power in many professions and could well be an essential requirement in others.	Expense. It may take you as long as ten years to recoup in salary raises what you spend on the degree.
Gives you a leg up on other candidates competing for the same job, everything else being equal.	A major time commitment, even if you're taking a reduced course load.
Broadens your network.	Lack of interest. You're often obliged to take some courses that you may not necessarily like.
Opens your mind to career opportunities that you may not have considered.	

Distance learning

On the surface, the powerful new trend in education known as distance learning appears to be the ideal solution for business professionals whose career goals require additional education but whose schedules make it difficult to attend conventionally scheduled classes. The term itself encompasses any course that doesn't oblige the student to be physically present at a class (this includes the old-fashioned correspondence courses). But more often than not, when people say *distance learning,* they're talking about courses that are delivered via the Internet.

It's easy to get excited over the basic concept of online distance learning. You can sign up for a course on almost any subject you can imagine, without having to worry about where it's held or at what hour. You can "attend class" from your office, your kitchen, a hotel room, your villa on the Riviera — anywhere you can find a phone jack for your modem. What's more, it is possible to pursue a bachelor's degree or an advanced degree electronically with a number of reputable schools, including University of Wyoming, Florida State, and Syracuse University.

Things you want to find out before you sign on the dotted line

Before you sign up for any online course, here's a list of questions to ask the organization that wants your tuition money:

- ✔ What exactly is covered in the course, and how detailed are the lessons? (Try to request a review of a typical lesson.)

- ✔ Who's teaching the course, and is that person a recognized expert in the field?

- ✔ What sort of accreditation does the organization have — and from whom?

- ✔ How long has the organization and instructor been offering the course online?

- ✔ What materials (textbooks, for example) are you expected to buy, and what additional learning materials (videotape lectures, perhaps) are included as part of the course?

- ✔ Approximately how many hours per week do you need to devote to classwork in order to keep pace?

- ✔ How will your grade be determined?

- ✔ How many other people are going to be in the same class? (This is a key issue, especially if the course is advertising interactive sessions with the instructor.)

- ✔ How extensive — and easily accessible — is the school's online library, and do you, as an online student, share the same rights as a student on campus?

- ✔ What is the school's refund policy in the event that you decide after the first session or two that you don't want to take the course?

- ✔ How much direct feedback can you expect from the professor?

If you can't find someone in the organization who can answer these questions, you may need to find another program.

There must be a catch somewhere, right? Well, there is — several catches, as a matter of fact. But the problem is that so much is happening so quickly in distance learning, especially in the area of technology, that whatever is written here could well be out of date by the time you've finished reading this sentence. So here is a look at some of the underlying issues that need to be considered regardless of what happens with technology:

✔ **Learning styles:** No matter how sophisticated online delivery processes may become, the very nature of distance learning makes it a dubious choice for certain types of learners. You may be one such person. To fare well in a distance learning environment, you have to be self-motivated and you need to be able to function well in a nonstructured environment. Many courses offer chat room opportunities and lots of e-mail messages back and forth between professor and student, but no matter how much interaction you're promised, it's not the same kind of attention and discussion you can find in a classroom.

✔ **Accreditation blues:** You see the word "accredited" over and over when you read descriptions of organizations offering online courses, but the questions you need to ask are: Accredited by whom and for what? Accreditation standards vary significantly from profession to profession and from region to region within the same profession. The only way you can be sure that the online credits or degrees you earn will help you in your career is to speak directly with the people responsible for issuing the credentials you need.

✔ **No day at the beach:** If you think you're not going to have to work as hard in an online course as you would in a traditional course, think again. The online programs offered by reputable organizations are no less rigorous than their classroom counterparts — and they may even be tougher, considering that you can't stay around after class to get some assistance from an understanding professor.

Tooling Up for the Future

Are you ready to start chipping away at those career goals and action items? Congratulations! But as you focus on your specific objectives, keep in mind some general guidelines:

✔ **Set realistic goals.** How successful you are in achieving the ultimate goal of your action plan — a job that you can get truly excited about — greatly depends on how disciplined you are. Focus and follow-through are the keys to reaching your final destination. So think small — at least at first. Break a large goal, such as "Become a better public speaker," into smaller, more concrete objectives, such as "Get the names of local organizations that offer public speaking courses," or "Research course information online." Create a timetable for all of your objectives. Begin each week with a half-dozen or so goals, and review your progress at the end of the week to stay on track.

✔ **Start to network now.** Even though you may not be actively involved in the field you hope to pursue, start networking in that industry as soon as possible. Ask friends, relatives, and business associates for names of people who are working in the kinds of jobs you want. Get in touch with professional organizations to find out about events that give you an opportunity to speak with professionals in the field. Set up an organized system for keeping track of names, including e-mail addresses. When the time comes to make your move and look for a job, you'll be that much further ahead of the game.

✔ **Continue to hone your basic skills.** Apart from anything else you may be doing to enhance your marketability, don't overlook the basics. Take advantage of the following opportunities and solidify your proficiency in the skills that are the cornerstone of every job you'll ever get.

- **Reading:** Career success in most fields depends on how quickly you can learn, which means, in turn, that you need to be a fairly fast and efficient reader. If you're not, look for ways to improve your reading speed and efficiency. Read how-to books or take courses in speed-reading. And make a conscious attempt to increase your reading speed without sacrificing comprehension.

- **Writing:** The fact that so much communication takes place these days via e-mail means that you can't get away with inadequate language skills. Plenty of help is available — through books, tapes, online courses, and continuing-education classes.

- **Math skills:** Even if you're in a nonsales or nontechnical position, the ability to work with numbers and figures can be a key asset. For example, you may need to critically analyze simple statistics while conducting research on an important issue or quickly compare vendor bids on products and services. To exercise your math skills, try to rely less on your calculator and more on your mind.

- **Computer skills:** Technology continues to be integrated with everything you do at your place of business, from electronic scheduling to PC-based video-conferencing. While you may not use every high-tech tool on the market right now, the more familiar and at-ease you are with technology in general, the more you'll be able to make the most of them in the future. Explore opportunities to find out more about technological developments.

Part II

Succeeding in the Corporate Culture

The 5th Wave   By Rich Tennant

PSYCHIC HOTLINE
NOW HIRING

"We don't care where you see yourself in five years, as long as you can see where our clients will be."

In this part . . .

You know where you want to go in your career, but you need to know the rules of the road. From finding the ideal job to practicing workplace diplomacy to bouncing back from adversity, this part spells out the do's and don'ts of on-the-job success. You also get insight into the traits of peak performers and find out about new ways to work.

Chapter 5

Getting the Job You Really Want

● ●

In This Chapter

▶ Looking for a job in today's market

▶ Writing winning resumes and cover letters

▶ Taking your job hunt online

▶ Making the most of interviewing

▶ Evaluating the offer

● ●

*R*egardless of where your career ambitions may lie and what sort of a timetable you've set, you share at least one career-related challenge with almost everyone else on the planet who has to actually work for a living. Periodically throughout your life, you're going to hear about a job opportunity that you would very much like to have, and you're going to do your best to get hired for that position. But here's the rub: Whether you get hired will depend not only on how qualified you are, but also on how skillfully you manage the job-hunting process itself.

This chapter gives you a crash course in the art of successful job hunting, but with an added wrinkle. The underlying assumption here is that you've already created the foundation for a successful job hunt: You have a reasonably clear idea of the kinds of jobs you would like — or need — to get to reach your overall career goal. Your objective is more than getting a good job. It's finding a job that either achieves or brings you closer to the ultimate goal of your strategic career plan.

In light of this objective, research plays a big role, and your mission is to be as thorough and as focused as possible in the front end of the job hunting process, identifying those companies that are likely to have the kinds of openings you're looking for. After you identify those firms, you need to do more than wait for news of an opening — you need to be proactive and strategic. This chapter shows you how to do it.

Narrowing Your Focus

No matter what type of job you're seeking, you must set general criteria before you begin your search. Otherwise, the number of options open to you will overwhelm you. And this narrowing of your focus is especially important when the job you're looking for has implications for your career plan. What someone else may consider a good or even great job may not work for you, because it doesn't meet the criteria of your plan. In other words, it doesn't move you any further along the career path you've set for yourself or strengthen your marketability in the field you want to pursue.

Uncovering the job leads you want

You could spend several hours scouring the classifieds for jobs. There's nothing wrong with this approach, but even if you come across an ad that captures your interest, you've now become one of zillions of people competing for the same position.

Is there a better way? Yes, but it will take some work. And most of that work consists of selecting companies where you'd like to be employed based on a set of criteria you've set (see Chapter 2). It's possible that you may have to either expand or narrow your criteria in order to develop a base list — 30 or 40 companies. Consider creating your own database that you can update as you research each company. You can create as many fields in the database as you like, but be sure to reserve some space for a list of networking contacts. As time goes on, add names of people who either work at the company, know something about the company, or know someone who works there.

If the job you're seeking is industry-specific — if, for example, you know you want to work in the finance field — you've already narrowed down your list of possibilities. If it's not industry-specific — perhaps you want a job in marketing, but you would be happy in any number of different fields — you need to select a handful of industries that appeal to you most. You may also consider company size and regional location to help narrow your list of target companies.

Your overall objective in this process is to develop a customized profile of each company. This information helps you determine how to approach the firm and what to say when you do. This way, you'll be ten steps ahead of the competition.

Working your way inside

After you identify a number of companies that represent realistic job opportunities (either now or in the future), your next challenge is to find out the inside scoop on hiring. Sending an unsolicited letter, along with your resume, isn't a bad strategy, by any means, but the better strategy is to use your network. If you don't know anyone who works for the company, call your contacts and ask them if they know someone at the firm. After you're able to speak with an insider, you'll get a better sense of your job opportunities there.

Taking a Crash Course in the Basics of Job Hunting

Certain time-honored principles apply to job hunting in general, regardless of what kind of a job you're looking for or how high-tech you are in your approach. While this advice may sound familiar, you may be surprised at how many job seekers sabotage their efforts by not being more aware of the principles at the heart of this advice.

Committing yourself to the process

You've probably heard this many times before, but it bears repeating: Job hunting is a job unto itself. As with any job, you can't do it well unless you're committed to it. Are you prepared to set aside a certain amount of time each week to do nothing else but focus on some aspect of your job search? If not, you may not be ready to launch your search. Exactly how much time you need to set aside each week depends on your sense of urgency and your other commitments. If you're working full-time, you may not be able devote more than a handful of hours each week to your job search activities. That's fine. It isn't so much the number of hours you spend working on your job search that's important; it's the regularity of it. You can't be passive. For a well-organized job search, you have plenty to do.

Creating a game plan

Job searching, at its root, is a logical process that's highly sequential. Before you can go before a hiring manager and expound on your exemplary professional qualities, you first need to find out about the job opening and then secure an interview.

With this logic in mind, you'll be far more productive in your job search if you break the process down into three distinct but overlapping steps:

1. **Uncover new leads.**
2. **Pursue opportunities you've uncovered.**
3. **Prepare to knock the socks off the person who will interview you.**

If you do this, you'll always have clearly defined tasks to work on and you'll be able to set interim goals on a weekly basis. One week, try to identify at least three companies that could conceivably offer you the kind of job you're looking for. During the following week, zero in on researching one of those companies. Or maybe you can focus on tracking down two or three people who can introduce you to someone at that firm. The point is to create objectives that are reachable and sequential — that is, they get you one step closer to where you want to be.

Being systematic

One of the occupational hazards of job hunting today is the abundance of information. Unfortunately, you may feel the need to wade through it all before you can get around to taking action on that research. The only way to protect yourself from this common pitfall is to set up a system for organizing the information you gather. It doesn't matter whether you do this the old-fashioned way (file folders in a box) or set up a database for the various kinds of information you're collecting, such as company data, industry information, interesting articles, and names of people. What matters is that you aren't simply dumping vast amounts of information into a bottomless pit. Research is useful only to the extent that you can use it as the basis for purposeful action and access it when you need it.

Nailing down your story

Long before you make your first call or write your first letter, you need to take time to formulate what may best be described as a 15- to 20-second *self-pitch*. In two or three sentences, you want to introduce yourself, describe your current occupation or background, and identify just what it is you want from the person you're calling. For example:

> "My name is Alexander the Great, and I'm the King of Macedonia. For the past several years, I've been conquering the world, most recently Asia Minor, and I've had a good opportunity to learn a variety of foreign languages. What I'm hoping to do now is to become an interpreter at the U.N., and I'm wondering if you could give me some names of people I might contact."

This is more or less the kind of summary you use over and over whenever you're networking, so take some time to nail it down before you begin calling. You may also want to develop an expanded version, which you will need when someone who is interviewing you poses the inevitable question: "What can you tell me about yourself?"

Networking

An irrefutable truth of job hunting is that it's impossible to know too many people. The more people you know — or, to be more precise, the more people you've enlisted as allies in your job search campaign — the more job leads you're able to turn up. In addition, you can be more prepared when following up on those leads, thus increasing your chances of setting up interviews. Keep in mind, however, that if you're trying to conceal the fact that you're looking for a job, you want to network more selectively and less candidly.

There's no great secret to successful networking. It's mainly a numbers game. And the most important skill you need for networking isn't really a skill; it's simply the courage to ask people for help. If you're hesitant about requesting information from people you don't know, first call the people you do know: family, close friends, and former classmates. True, your Uncle Luke — the one who falls asleep at family dinners — may not seem like a fruitful source of career-related information, but he may know someone who knows someone who . . . well, you get the idea. You may be surprised at how many people are willing to help you when you're willing to ask for it.

Casting a wide net

Job leads can materialize from any number of different sources, some more fruitful than others. And one of the easiest ways to kindle an argument among career experts is to ask them to choose the *best* source. The fact is, there isn't one best source of job leads — certainly no source that works best for every person looking for a job. Internet postings, referrals from friends, classified ads, job fairs — any one of these sources can produce a lead that will eventually help you get the job you want. The best policy is to utilize all sources.

Getting the most out of recruiters

Recruiters — sometimes referred to as *employment agencies, staffing firms,* and *executive search firms* — are playing an important role in the job market, and they can be particularly valuable to you if you're looking for a job in a specific industry. Recruiters are in the business of matching a candidate's skills and abilities with a company's needs and opportunities.

Here's how to get the most of this resource:

- ✔ Work with recruiters who specialize in the field or industry in which you're searching.
- ✔ Pay a personal visit to the office of any recruiter you're considering and work only with those you trust.

✔ Take advantage of the recruiter's expertise and request feedback on enhancing your marketability.

✔ Be honest. If you misrepresent yourself, it will invariably come back to haunt you.

✔ Never work with a recruiter who charges a fee or pressures you to sign up for career counseling that his or her firm happens to offer.

Job Searching, Millennium-Style

Despite the profound changes that have occurred in workplaces across America during the last few years, the fundamentals of effective job hunting are essentially the same as they've always been. You need to be able to do the following:

✔ Uncover job leads

✔ Determine which opportunities are worth pursuing and how best to convert those leads into interviews

✔ Convince those doing the hiring that you're their next employee of the day, month, and year

What has changed in a big way, however, is how you carry out the mechanics of these fundamental steps. Consider, for example, the role that the Internet plays in the job search process versus just a few years ago. In 1995 (the Stone Ages, in Internet terms), online job hunting was considered an esoteric art, practiced mainly by a relative handful of technical professionals. By the turn of the millennium, however, the number of Web sites offering job-posting services had reached into the tens of thousands. If you decide to do nothing else but explore at least 25 sites every day, including weekends (and this doesn't say much about the quality of your life!), it will take you more than three years to work your way through the list, by which time there will probably be an additional 50,000 sites. The Internet has become such a bountiful source of information and resources for job hunters, in fact, that carrying out a job search without taking advantage of the Internet would be the job-hunting equivalent of entering the Indianapolis 500 with a horse and buggy. You'd be eating a lot of dust.

But the Internet isn't the only factor that's changing the nature of job searching these days. The advent of e-mail has brought an unprecedented degree of efficiency to the process. You can now dispatch your resume to hundreds of would-be employers in a matter of seconds (although this isn't necessarily a recommended tactic), and without having to stuff envelopes and lick stamps. Big changes, too, can be seen in the methods interviewers are now using to evaluate candidates. In the past, your chances of being hired for most jobs hinged primarily on how closely your previous work experience and hard skills matched the job description. Your track record and technical abilities still count for a lot in most hiring situations, but more and more interviewers these days want to know who you are as a person. They want to know, in particular, how closely your competencies — both hard and soft skills — match those needed to perform specific tasks in a certain environment.

Wire to wire: What you can find on the Web

If you're a seasoned surfer, you already have a basic idea of what you can expect when you log into the typical job site. But if you're new to the constantly changing world of online job hunting, here's a brief summary of the typical mix of offerings.

- ✔ **Recruiters and job boards:** The job openings advertised on most of these Web sites originate from two sources:

  - • Direct from companies (they may also list their available positions on their own sites).

  - • The classified sections of newspapers from around the nation (some job boards gather the listings from newspapers and publish them online).

  Each site has its own way of organizing the data. Usually, though, you can quickly narrow the list of possible jobs on the basis of profession and region. Some sites ask questions about your education background, current salary, and so on, in an effort to target the list of possibilities. In most instances, you reply directly to the company posting the ad.

- ✔ **Resume posting:** Many sites offer you the opportunity to post your resume in a resume bank, which is then accessible to companies in search of candidates. Most sites have worked out reasonably efficient protocols for transferring your data to an online form, and some sites even have online tools that actually help you build the resume. What differs from site to site is the degree of protection they offer, how long they keep the resume online, and what policies they have with respect to trading lists with other sites.

- ✔ **Company listings:** The company listings on many sites consist mainly of links to company Web sites, but some sites have begun to develop their own company profiles. You choose a profession and a city and are given a partial listing of the companies that may have openings that match your criteria.

- **Career planning advice:** Many sites that advertise job openings or offer resume posting services include departments that focus various aspects of career planning. Some of this information is homegrown. Others are simply links to other information sites. The quality varies.

- **Chat rooms:** Chat rooms give you an opportunity to network with other job seekers and take online seminars and presentations from career experts.

The only way to find out which career and job sites are best is to spend some time exploring these resources. It shouldn't take more than a half hour or so for you to get the feel of a Web site: how easy it is to navigate, how the job offerings are organized, the quality and relevance of the information in the career resource sections, and so on. If you're going to make regular use of the Internet, find three or four sites that you can rely on, and then, just to make sure you're not missing out, spend at least one night a month window-shopping new sites.

Working the Web

Here's a quick look at a few of the many job and career Web sites that are worth taking a look at.

- **CareerCity:** www.careercity.com

  Main offerings: Job listings, resume postings, company and industry research, salary surveys, career resources

  Most useful features: Extensive links to other sites; clean user-friendly format

- **CareerMosaic:** www.careermosaic.com

  Main offerings: Job postings, free resume postings (with the option to edit or delete), *Fortune* Magazine career articles, company directories

  Most useful feature: Special department (called Communities) that focuses on jobs and career advice in six areas: technology, accounting and finance, health care, human resources, public sector, sales and marketing

- **CareerPath.com:** www.careerpath.com

  Main offerings: Job search, resume postings, career resources, company research, industry research

  Most useful feature: Huge number of classified ads from nearly 80 major newspapers

✔ **Job Hunt.org:** www.job-hunt.org

  Main offerings: A clearinghouse for Internet career services and job-posting sites

  Most useful features: Clean, easy-to-use site with lots of valuable links

✔ **Monster.com:** www.monster.com

  Main offerings: Job search, resume posting, company research, career resources, salary information

  Most useful features: Side-by-side city comparison reports, Q&A segment that features interviews with people in a wide range of professions

✔ **The Riley Guide:** www.riley.guide.com

  Main offerings: Job search, salary surveys, companies, industries and careers, career planning resources

  Most useful features: Salary data, ease of use, listings that are unusually comprehensive

✔ **Headhunter.net:** www.headhunter.net

  Main offerings: Job search, resume posting, ability to restrict resume exposure, company research

  Most useful feature: Can search for jobs that are 30 days old or less

It's 10 p.m. Do you know where your resume is?

On the face of it, placing your resume on one of the posting services offered by many job sites sounds like a terrific idea. It doesn't cost much (many Web sites offer the service at no charge) and if your skills are in high demand, you're likely to have more than a few companies beating a path to your door. But be careful. After you post your resume on a site, you have no control over where it goes, who reads it, and what people do with it. It's been widely reported, for example, that telemarketers rummage through resume banks for names, addresses, and phone numbers. (Consider deleting your address and telephone number and leaving a post office box or your e-mail address.)

Perhaps more worrisome, though, is the possibility that your resume could wind up on the last place you want it: your boss's hands. More and more sites allow you to block certain companies (your current employer, for example) from accessing your resume. But these precautions can only protect you so far. Companies that are determined to find out which of their employees are shopping their resumes can always log in with a different name, thereby circumventing the block.

Remember that your resume will be on display for all to see. Choose wisely.

Resumes: Yes, They Still Matter

Here's a quick question for you: Is there anything that anyone can say about resumes that hasn't already been said or written tens of thousands of times in tens of thousands of places: books, articles, newspapers, audio tapes, Web sites, and software packages? Probably not. And yet putting together a solid resume continues to be a challenge for many job hunters.

If you think you need major help with your resume, check out my book *Job Hunting For Dummies,* 2nd Edition (IDG Books Worldwide, Inc.), which devotes no fewer than five chapters to this subject. Or go to any of the job sites on the Web and type **resumes** in the search box. You'll find an abundance of resources. But assuming you've mastered the basics of Resume 101, the following sections give some advice that's designed to make a good resume even better.

Making it look good

The trick to making your resume look good is to give it some air. Take a look at the resume in Figure 5-1. Notice how the dates in the left-hand column create white space. Notice, too, the use of bullets and the spacing between items. But if you plan to send your resume electronically as ASCII text, don't include any formatting. Asterisks, capitals, spacing, and hard line breaks can be substituted in the areas where bullets and special fonts would otherwise be used. (See the "Making it computer friendly" section, later in this chapter.) Paying attention to these little elements may not seem very important, but because your resume is an extension of you, it should communicate the best possible impression.

Using a chronological versus functional arrangement

A *chronological resume* lists your work experience in a reverse-chronological sequence — the most recent first. The principal advantage of this format is that it gives employers exactly what they're looking for: an easy-to-follow snapshot of your work experience. The alternative is the *functional resume,* which is organized according to your skills and attributes, as opposed to your work experience. With this format, you run the risk that interviewers will assume you were trying to hide some dark secret about your background by not listing your job experience in chronological order. In fact, in a survey commissioned by Robert Half International of executives with the nation's largest companies, 78 percent of those polled said that they prefer to receive a chronological resume rather than a functional one. Many career experts are now recommending that job seekers create a primarily chronological resume, but include a section in which skills and attributes are listed. The technical term for such a resume is a *hybrid resume.*

BEVERLY A. HILLS

123 Park Place, Seattle, WA 98115
(111) 222-3333
bhills@sellerslane.com

Summary:

Ten years of progressive experience in sales and management. Proven ability to deliver increased productivity through sales training development and client-relations management skills.

> Each statement conveys the idea of accomplishment and success.

Employment History:

10/99 – present, Account Manager at Futuristica, Seattle, WA
- Initiated and developed new accounts that now generate 20 percent of team's revenue goals.
- Implemented comprehensive marketing strategy to the field.
- Created sales presentations for field representatives.
- Trained sales representatives through team-based activities and group discussions.

6/96 – 10/99, Sales Manager at Piffany and Co., Seattle, WA
- Supervised national/international accounts.
- Researched new business acquisitions.
- Created customer needs-assessment questionnaire to improve satisfaction.

8/93 – 6/96, Sales Representative at Blue, Inc., Portland, OR
- Coordinated, promoted at all product-related trade shows.
- Restructured marketing strategy for western region.
- Acquired new clientele, 25 percent more than annual quota.

> Note use of bullets and spaces between items.

7/91 – 8/93, Inside Sales Assistant at LPD, Inc., Portland, OR
- Monitored client relations.
- Managed client files.
- Updated and reorganized client data into database to improve targeted reporting.
- Researched demographics for future sales campaigns.

Education:

> Note the use of white space.

Portland University, Portland, OR, June 1991
B.A. in Communications

Additional Skills:

- PC and Mac proficient
- Word, Excel, PowerPoint, Lotus 1-2-3, PhotoShop

Figure 5-1:
Use white space and bulleted text in your resume for a professional look.

Making it computer friendly

If you're submitting your resume to a large company, chances are, the first person who reads your resume may not be a person at all. It could be a computer equipped with OCR (optical character recognition) software. This software is programmed to screen resumes on the basis of certain words — words that describe job titles, departments, organizations, and computer programs that the employer feels are essential qualifications. If those words don't get spotted, your resume doesn't get past first base. (This doesn't mean you shouldn't be truthful, however. You won't get far if you incorporate words or phrases that don't accurately reflect your experience.)

So after you write your resume, consider the following suggestions to help make it scanner-friendly:

- ✓ Look closely at the key words used in a classified ad or Internet job board posting. If applicable, use these words in your resume.

- ✓ Contact your network of people helping you in your job search to see if you can get documentation for specifications or a job description from them.

- ✓ Use ASCII or plain-text formats (see Figure 5-2), which are options within Save As functions in most word-processing packages. These formats can be read by nearly every computer, including a PC and a Macintosh.

- ✓ Remove all columns, bullets, and bit-mapped graphics from your resume. (See Figure 5-2.)

- ✓ Use a fixed-width font (such as Courier, 10-point) and set the page width to 4.75 inches. (Take a look at Figure 5-2 for an example.) Save the file as "text with line breaks" so that each line will be separated by a hard return.

- ✓ Set your line length to no more than 80 characters so that your text will not wrap prematurely when viewed by the other person.

- ✓ If you indent information, be sure to use the same number of spaces from the margin each time. Just because it appears vertically aligned on your system at home doesn't mean it will appear that way after it reaches the hiring manager.

Using accomplishment-oriented words

Without stretching the truth, use the summaries of your work history to do more than list your duties. Showcase your accomplishments with results-oriented statements. Instead of listing "created database for customer service department," write "created database that reduced response time by 35 percent." To see this principle in action, refer to the resume in Figure 5-1. Notice how each statement in the Work Summary section conveys the idea of accomplishment and success.

BEVERLY A. HILLS
123 Park Place, Seattle, WA   98115
(111) 222-3333
bhills@sellerslane.com

Summary:
Ten years of progressive experience in sales
and management. Proven ability to deliver increased
productivity through sales training development and
client-relations management skills.

Employment History:
**10/99-present, Account Manager at Futuristica,
Seattle, WA**
--Initiated and developed new accounts that now
  generate 20 percent of team's revenue goals.
--Implemented comprehensive marketing strategy to
  the field.
--Created sales presentations for field
  representatives.
--Trained sales representatives through team-based
  activities and group discussions.

**6/96-10/99, Sales Manager at Piffany and Co.,
Seattle, WA**
--Supervised national/international accounts.
--Researched new business acquisitions.
--Created customer needs-assessment questionnaire
  to improve satisfaction.

**8/93-6/96, Sales Representative at Blue, Inc.,
Portland, OR**
--Coordinated, promoted at all product-related
  trade shows.
--Restructured marketing strategy for western
  region.
--Acquired new clientele, 25 percent more than annual
  quota.

**7/91-8/93, Inside Sales Assistant at LPD, Inc.,
Portland, OR**
--Monitored client relations.
--Managed client files.
--Updated and reorganized client data into database
  to improve targeted reporting.
--Researched demographics for future sales
  campaigns.

Education:
Portland University, Portland, OR, June 1991
B.A. in Communications

Additional Skills:
--PC and Mac proficient
--Word, Excel, PowerPoint, Lotus 1-2-3, PhotoShop

> Set margin at
> 4.75 inches.

> Replace bullets
> with plain text.

> Use a fixed-
> width font, such
> as 10-point
> Courier.

Figure 5-2:
Make your
resume
scanner-
friendly.

Read your own resume to see if it passes this test. If not, don't automatically
assume that you don't have a success story to tell. Focus on the results of
your actions and you may surprise yourself.

Split personalities: Creating multiple resumes

Creating a series of resumes, each tailored to a specific job, sounds duplicitous, and indeed would be dishonest if you were fabricating the content. But tailoring a resume to different jobs means highlighting the relevant experience. If one of the principal requirements of a job appears to be the ability to handle a multitude of responsibilities, make sure this skill gets the appropriate emphasis on that particular resume. The only downside to multiple versions is that you have to go into your computer and make any necessary changes to each version, which opens up the possibility for typos. Be extra careful of that when you're making revisions.

Writing Cover Letters

A cover letter is a letter that accompanies your resume. It introduces yourself and points out the highlights of your work experience. This letter is more than just wrapping paper for your resume; it's an opportunity to strengthen your chances for getting an interview. In fact, a nationwide survey commissioned by Robert Half International found that 60 percent of executives believe the cover letter is either as important as or more critical than the resume.

The following are key considerations when writing your cover letter, whether a traditional or e-mail version:

- ✔ **Keep it brief.** Cover letters should never be more than three paragraphs in length.

- ✔ **Link it to the resume.** Use the cover letter to direct the reader to those aspects of your resume that have the most relevance to the job. However, don't rehash your resume; merely restate the information in prose.

- ✔ **Play it straight.** Don't waste your time trying to come up with a peppy or lively opening. Keep it professional. Think about what you would say if you were opening up a phone conversation. Let that message govern the beginning of your letter.

- ✔ **Be "you" oriented.** Short though the letter may be, make sure it emphasizes what you can offer. And don't be afraid to show enthusiasm for the position or company. Take this opportunity to demonstrate your knowledge about the firm's success and let them know how you can contribute to future endeavors.

Hitting Pay Dirt: Ten Keys to Making the Best Interview Impression

Testing, multiple-person interviews, and trial periods are all part of the hiring strategies of many companies. It's true that it takes more than a great interview performance to get hired for most good jobs today. It's also true, however, that a mediocre interview performance can knock you out of the running. So even in these changing times, you want to make sure that your face-to-face meeting with a hiring manager makes the best possible impression.

You can find a staggering amount of advice on interviewing strategies in books, articles, newspapers, and on the Internet. (In my book, *Job Hunting For Dummies,* 2nd Edition, published by IDG Books Worldwide, Inc., I discuss interviewing tools in-depth.) Help is available, too, from not-for-profit agencies and continuing education centers in the form of seminars and coaching sessions. Truth be told, though, the best way to improve your interviewing skills — after you nail down a few of the basics — is to learn from each experience. The advice in the following sections should help get you started.

Putting yourself in the interviewer's shoes

It's only natural in an interview to be preoccupied with yourself: who you are, what you want, and what makes you special. But you'll be doing yourself an immense favor if, instead of focusing on your needs, you put yourself in the shoes of the interviewer. Going through this mental exercise is not as difficult as you may think. After all, you already know what's going on in the mind of that person.

One way or the other, he or she wants the interview to yield answers to the following questions:

- Do you have the skills and temperament to do the job?
- How long is it going to take you to get up to speed in the job? (In other words, can you hit the ground running?)
- Will you fit into the company's culture?
- How much of an asset are you going to be to the company?
- How motivated are you?
- How do you compare with other candidates in these areas?

Whatever you do in the way of preparation, keep these questions foremost in your mind. And when you're rehearsing the answers to typical interview questions, let these considerations guide your answers.

Doing your homework — and then some

Some of what happens during a job interview is beyond your control. You can't control the number of distractions the interviewer has to deal with — including the phone call from his five-year-old who just swallowed a nickel. But the one thing you can — and should — control is your level of preparation. Being prepared means, above all, that you know as much as you can about your would-be employer. This knowledge not only enhances your ability to carry on productive dialogue during the interview itself, it also sends a message to the interviewer that you're resourceful and know how to gather information.

What follows is a list of questions that you should be able to answer before you walk into any interview. You may need to adapt these questions when preparing for interviews with not-for-profit or educational organizations.

- ✔ How does the company earn money? (What are its products and services?)

- ✔ What industry (or industries) is the company in?

- ✔ Who are its main customers?

- ✔ How long has it been in business?

- ✔ How big is it (number of employees)?

- ✔ How profitable is it (revenues, earnings, and so on)?

- ✔ How large of a share (roughly speaking) of the market does it have in the area you may be working?

- ✔ What are its main competitors?

- ✔ Who is the president and CEO, and how long has that person been there?

- ✔ What major events (if any) have taken place in the company over the past year (new product launches, acquisitions, major personnel changes, and so on)?

Any information that you can gather that goes beyond these basics can only work to your advantage. It may be useful to know, for example, whether the company is in the midst of any sort of cultural makeover, whether it's losing or gaining market share in its industry, or whether it's had a recent turnover in senior personnel. Much of this information can be gleaned from articles, annual reports, or marketing materials that you can access on the Internet or from your local library, but you may have to rely on your network of people helping you with your job search to give you the latest info.

Interview checklist

The following are some suggestions for setting the stage for your interview:

✔ Get a good night's rest.

✔ Rehearse your 20-second self-pitch (see the "Nailing down your story" section, earlier in this chapter).

✔ Arrive early.

✔ Bring copies of your resume and/or work samples.

✔ Bring paper and pen to take notes in the meeting.

✔ Greet every person you meet with a smile.

✔ Review the three or four key points you'd like to make in the interview.

Dressing appropriately

Even though formal dress codes in most companies have gone the way of carbon paper and the typewriter, job interview etiquette still dictates that you always dress up for an interview. A dark-colored business suit with a white or light shirt (or blouse) is the preferred, professional look. Everything else connected with your appearance should follow the same principle: nothing flashy or provocative; nothing that would catch anyone by surprise. Make sure your shoes are shined (and check the soles to make sure there are no holes). Avoid strong-smelling perfumes or colognes. And go easy on the jewelry.

Minding your manners

Without being aware of it, you can shoot yourself in the foot before you even shake hands with your interviewer. How? By acting in a quirky or unintentionally rude way. Realize that your interview begins the minute you walk inside the company's front door. Treat the security guard (if there is one) as if he or she is the CEO of the company. Refrain from any distracting behavior — such as making a call from your cell phone — while you're waiting for an interview. More often than you may imagine, an interviewer asks other people who've observed you for their impressions of you — according to a survey by Robert Half International, 91 percent of executives consider their assistants' opinions an important factor in the employee selection process, up from 60 percent five years ago.

Getting off to a good start

The first few moments of an interview are always the most awkward — for both you and the hiring manager. In time, as you become more and more accustomed to the interview process, the uneasiness will fade. But here's some advice to heed in the meantime:

✔ **The handshake:** If the interviewer doesn't extend his or her hand, take the initiative. Use a firm (but not crushing) handshake, and thank the person for taking the time to meet with you.

✔ **Preliminary small talk:** Most interviewers will begin the interview by making small talk. Join in, but don't launch into any lengthy soliloquies about issues that have no bearing on the job.

✔ **Name game:** Pay attention to the name that the interviewer uses during your introduction, and refer to him or her by that same name. (If she calls herself "Susan," don't call her "Sue." If he calls himself "Robert," don't call him "Bob.")

Showing enthusiasm

A job interview isn't a poker game. And there's little to gain and much to lose by going out of your way to conceal the fact that, hey, this is a job you might sell your soul to get. Most employers today are looking specifically for high-energy, enthusiastic people. True, you don't want to force things. If you're laid-back by nature, fine. Just make sure your laid-back attitude doesn't come across as apathy.

Giving focused answers

Savvy interviewers are often less interested in the content of your answers (they figure you've anticipated most questions, anyway) than they are in how you communicate the answer: how precise and succinct you are and how logically you string your thoughts together. Before you answer any question, do two things:

✔ Make sure you understand exactly what you're being asked (if you're not sure, ask).

✔ Give yourself a few seconds to think through your answer.

Using specific examples to back up your responses

Whenever you're asked predictable questions, such as "What are your strengths?" be prepared to back up your statements with some solid evidence. If you say, "Well, I'm very good at project management," follow that assertion with a specific example that proves the point, as in, "In my last job, I managed 20 separate projects in six months with overlapping deadlines for event planning, day-of-event logistics, and post-event follow up." If you want to drive home the point that you work well under pressure — an important quality in today's job market — be prepared to offer an example or two that demonstrates it.

Interesting interview situations

Robert Half International asked its managers to describe the most unusual occurrences in interviews they had ever heard of from clients and colleagues. The following examples certainly left an impression, but not necessarily the kind that the candidates may have intended.

✔ "When asked about formal education, the candidate replied, 'I don't need any. I'm certified by the school of real life.'"

✔ "The applicant's reference sheet listed a person with the title 'Dad.' When the interviewer asked if this was his dad, he said, 'No, but he is a dad.'"

✔ "When asked about her proficiency with software programs, the candidate pulled out a photo of herself standing next to a computer and said, 'This shows my familiarity with today's office equipment.'"

✔ "A beeping noise was coming from the candidate's briefcase. He opened it, switched off an egg timer, and said he could answer one more question without being late to his next interview."

✔ "Responding to a question about his ideal job, a candidate said, 'To lie in bed all day, eat chocolate, and get paid.'"

✔ "The candidate walked into the hiring manager's office with a brown bag and proceeded to eat lunch during the interview, saying she was 'multitasking' during a long day of interviews."

✔ "When discussing why the candidate had been fired from several jobs, he said his previous employers had conspired to place a curse on him, and he was conducting his own secret investigation."

✔ "When the hiring manager walked into the lobby to greet the candidate, she was 'feeding' her virtual pets and asked him to wait just a minute."

Debriefing yourself after each interview

Regardless of how well or badly you think you've handled yourself in an interview, try to set aside at least 15 minutes as soon as possible after the meeting to reflect upon your interview performance. Take notes. Jot down the questions that may have given you trouble and think about how you might answer them if given another chance. Don't beat yourself up, but keep in mind that you can always improve. Some specific points you may want to focus on include the following:

✔ **Appearance:** Were you dressed appropriately?

✔ **Preparation:** Did you know as much as you should have?

✔ **Your mental state:** Were you as relaxed as you wanted to be? If not, why?

✔ **Listening:** Were you focused enough? If you had trouble concentrating, why?

Being strategic when you ask questions

Most hiring managers, particularly those who've been coached in the art of interviewing, give you an opportunity toward the end of the interview to ask questions. If you've paid attention and listened carefully, your questions will come naturally, and they should also demonstrate that you've done at least some homework (research on the company).

But if you're at a loss for words — and assuming these issues haven't been covered during the interview — you may want to ask one of the following questions:

✔ What are the two or three qualities that are the most important for success in this job?

✔ If I were hired to do this job, what would be my number-one priority?

✔ How would you best describe the future of this company?

What's especially good about these questions is that they get the interviewer to envision you in the job. They also can provide some insight into your chances of being hired.

Following up

Be sure to send a thank-you note to each person with whom you interviewed as soon as possible. Your letter should express your gratitude, reinforce your interest in the job, and recap the two or three strongest points working in your favor. Keep in mind, too, that according to a survey commissioned by Robert Half International, 76 percent of hiring managers with the nation's largest companies said that it is helpful for a promising job candidate to send a thank-you note following an interview.

If you haven't heard from the hiring manager after a few weeks, it's acceptable to call him or her. Remind the person of your name and simply ask for the status of the particular job for which you interviewed. If you discover that an offer hasn't yet been extended, ask when it may be — a few days, another week? If an offer has been made to someone else, thank him or her again.

Evaluating the Offer

If you've effectively targeted your job hunting and have researched the company with which you interviewed, being offered the job will be a reason to celebrate — not a source of conflict. Having laid the groundwork, you already have every reason to believe that this is the right job with the right company at the right time.

Sometimes, however, regardless of how diligent you've been, issues arise during the interview that may cause you to have some second thoughts about taking the job, if indeed you're offered it. Those issues may relate to salary, to the nature of the job, to the company, or to any number of things.

In these situations, you owe it to yourself (not to mention to the company) to give careful thought to the offer. Don't allow the fact that you've invested a lot of time and effort into the process to sway your thinking. No one wins if you accept a job that isn't right for you, but you're the only one capable of making that decision. Table 5-1 helps you evaluate the situation and, more important, identify which aspects deserve more thought. Rate, on a scale of zero to five (five the highest), how much you agree with each statement. Answer each question on the basis of your current perception.

Table 5-1	Is the Job Suitable to You?
_____	Being a success at this job will bring me closer to my ultimate career goal.
_____	I can afford to live on the salary and benefits that I'm being offered.
_____	I'm likely to enjoy the day-to-day responsibilities of the position.
_____	The job is well suited to my strengths.
_____	The commute isn't going to create any great inconvenience for me.

(continued)

Table 5-1 (continued)

_____	The hours I need to put in, along with the travel commitments, are doable and acceptable.
_____	As far as I can tell, the people who work for this firm look like people with whom I'd enjoy working.
_____	The overall culture of the company is a match with my values and personality.
_____	The company is in solid financial shape. I don't have to worry about getting a paycheck.

If your score totaled between 35 and 45, the job is probably a good fit for you. If you got a score between 25 and 34, you may want to closely examine those items that received a mid to low rating and decide how important they are to you for overall job satisfaction. But if you received anything less than 24, you probably want to keep your eyes open for other opportunities.

Culture clash: Measuring the things that count

It isn't always easy to get an accurate read of a company's culture on the basis of the research you've done or what you've experienced during the interviewing process. Sometimes you have to trust your instincts. The following list spells out some of the key elements that differentiate one corporate culture from the next.

You can use the list — and the suggestions that accompany it — to determine whether there's a good match between you and the culture of the company you're thinking of joining.

- ✔ **Management style:** Is it top-down and bureaucratic or collaborative and participatory? Are most decisions made by one or a handful of people or do senior managers delegate? Possible indicators include the following:

  - How are offices arranged (for example, do senior execs have their own floor)?

  - How often does senior management seek input from employees before making major decisions?

  - How prevalent (if at all) are self-managed teams?

✔ **Work/family balance:** How committed is the company to helping employees balance work pressures with family responsibilities? The best indicators include:

- Flexible-schedule policies

- Telecommuting options for appropriate positions

- Broad benefit offerings

- The presence of on-site employee services, such as dry cleaning, banking, and take-home meals for people who work late

✔ **Work ethic:** Are 60- and 70-hour work weeks for key people the exception or the rule? How often do people spend their weekends at the office?

✔ **Quality of day-to-day work life:** To what degree is day-to-day life in the company dictated by rules that relate to individual behavior (apart from work responsibilities). Some indicators include:

- The general atmosphere in the office

- Whether people are relaxed or formal with one another

- How personal the individual work spaces are

✔ **Community focus:** Is it important for the company to be a good corporate citizen? Best indicators include:

- The company's involvement in charitable causes

- The extent to which employees are encouraged to take part in community projects

- Corporate policies regarding issues like recycling

✔ **Office politics:** Do the various departments work collaboratively or are they constantly at war with one another? Are policies and practices specifically designed to foster teamwork, or is teamwork simply a slogan? Possible indicators include:

- A team approach to decision making

- Purposes for meetings made clear

Negotiating for more money

If it turns out that the only negative aspect of the job you're being offered is the salary, it's quite possible that you can close the gap between what the company is offering and what you want.

Is there a dot-com in your future?

Some job offers hold open the possibility (okay, the dream) that if everything goes well, you'll be making more money than you ever imagined. With stock options and the opportunity to get in on the ground floor of an IPO (initial public offering), the offer may seem too good to be true.

You wouldn't be human, of course, if you weren't tempted by this prospect. Some companies that have yet to show a profit have nonetheless made millionaires (on paper, at least) out of employees who were part of the original crew. But for every overnight success story, there are a dozen more tales of tough luck. So before you hitch your wagon to a start-up and pass up an offer with an established company, make sure you know what you're getting yourself into. Here are some suggestions to keep in mind:

✔ **Recognize the tradeoff.** If you're considering joining a start-up, be prepared to put in long, hard hours. Getting a business up and running takes a lot of time and energy from every employee. (So if you were looking to cash-in your first paycheck for a three-week cruise to the Bahamas, you may want to reevaluate your options.)

✔ **Analyze the business.** If a company has been in business for only a short time, research its goals and prospects for development before you accept an offer of employment. Simply because a company announces its intention of going public is no guarantee of success.

Make sure the firm has a viable product or service and a well-thought-out plan to capture market share. Find out if the company has sufficient funding to achieve its goals — even if there isn't a public stock offering — and pay particularly close attention to the background of senior managers. Do they have the knowledge and experience needed to not only get the company off the ground but also to sustain momentum?

✔ **Consider the culture.** Do you prefer to work in a company with somewhat established practices and guidelines or do you want to be part of the group that invents these things along the way? Are you interested in a traditional business environment or do you like new or alternative ways to work? Many start-ups are exploring new management techniques and innovative corporate cultures. Not everyone thrives in the same surroundings, so be sure you know what works best for you.

✔ **Look for clicks and bricks.** Are you lured by the flash of the dot-com industry but prefer the business practices of a *Fortune* 500 firm? You may want to consider seeking employment with a progressive company that's incorporating Internet strategies and services into its traditional business practices. You may find the best of both worlds.

Consider the following suggestions when it's time to negotiate.

✔ Never negotiate salary or benefits before you're actually offered a position.

✔ Make sure you have an accurate reading of the market value of the position you're being offered, based on what your counterparts with comparable background and experience are getting. (You can usually get salary data from staffing firms, professional organizations, or Internet career sites.)

✔ Be sensitive to how much — or how little — power the person with whom you're negotiating has to give you what you want.

✔ Be aware of your leverage — how badly the company wants you and how prepared you are to walk away if you don't get what you want.

✔ Look at the total package being offered as opposed to the salary in and of itself. Consider the value of benefits, vacation time, and cost of living. The gap that separates you and the company may not be as wide as you think.

✔ If accepting an offer obliges you to uproot yourself and your family, you're going to incur substantial relocation expenses. When you negotiate who's going to pay for what, make sure you have estimates in hand and are able to document each estimate with paperwork.

✔ Keep the atmosphere friendly. Your goal is not to win but to arrive at a conclusion with which both you and your new employer are comfortable.

✔ Who should make the first move? Negotiating specialists tend to be split about the question of who should make the first move when discussing salary. Forget the game playing. You should have a figure in mind. For example, you could say, "Well I'm making $60,000 right now, and I was hoping to increase that or, at the very least, come close." Or, "I need at least $60,000 a year to support myself, but I'm looking for $65,000." Don't be embarrassed to talk about money.

✔ Be ready to compromise on issues that aren't that important to you. ("Okay, so I won't bring my horse to work with me — except maybe on casual day.")

✔ After you agree on terms, ask for a letter of agreement that details the specifics of the offer, such as the position's key responsibilities and tasks, the salary, and any special arrangements that were negotiated.

Chapter 6

Making Your Mark Early in the Game

*H*ow often have you heard an athlete, coach, or a CEO make the following statement: "We had a great plan, but we didn't execute"? Well, if you're not careful, this familiar observation can also apply to career management. You can have a great overall career plan: one that, on paper, is strategically sound and logically thought out. But if you don't successfully execute the components of that plan — that is, perform well in each of the jobs you hold — your chances of realizing your career goals are remote.

This chapter focuses on one of the most important and yet most frequently overlooked aspects of job performance: how you handle yourself during the first days and weeks on the job. You get some general advice on how to make the best possible impression when you're first starting out. You also find out how to get an early read on the company culture and, if necessary, how to adapt to that environment. Finally, you get some insight into what your strategy ought to be, should it become clear early on that you've made a terrible mistake by accepting this job.

Welcome Mat: Who's Orienting Whom?

What happens to you during your first few days on your job depends mainly on whether the company you're joining has a formal, well-thought-out orientation program or whether you're left to your own devices to get the lay of the land. Chances are, your orientation to your new company will fall somewhere in between these two extremes.

Philosophies about orientation programs vary widely across the corporate landscape. Some companies — Disney, for example — takes orientation very seriously and puts newcomers (entry-level employees, in particular) through rather lengthy, highly structured programs. These orientations typically include presentations, tours, welcome-to-the-company lunches, speeches from senior executives, get-acquainted activities — the whole nine yards. In other companies — including, surprisingly, many *Fortune* 1000 companies — orientation tends to be more impromptu, with most of the focus on explaining the benefits package. In still other companies, those in which there is no HR department, orientation may be nothing more than a walk through the office with your boss and introductions to other employees, after which you're expected to roll up your sleeves and get to work.

Whatever form it takes and however active a role the company plays in your orientation, you need to make sure you're being oriented properly, obtaining the kind of information you need to acclimate yourself, get up to speed in your new job as quickly as possible, and make a contribution early on.

Getting into an opening-day mindset

First, the good news. Unless the company you're joining is run by direct descendants of Genghis Kahn, you can expect something of a honeymoon during your first few days and even first weeks on the job. No one is going to call for your resignation if you inadvertently park in the CEO's spot, trigger the alarm system, e-mail your HR forms to the entire company, or fail to recognize that the voice on the other end of the line is your boss's spouse.

Even so, people are people. This means that even though your employer may not be evaluating your job performance too strictly when you first start out, they are nonetheless forming impressions that will either confirm or call into question their decision to hire you. These impressions are based on any number of factors, including the following:

✔ Appearance (your grooming, in particular)

✔ Work habits

✔ Personality

✔ Intellectual curiosity (or lack thereof)

✔ Ability to blend into the flow of the workplace

Ultimately, of course, you are also judged by how effectively you do your job. But the early observations of you go a long way to affect those judgments, as well. The better the overall impression, the more patient employers are likely to be as you ramp up in your responsibilities. Bad impressions, on the other hand, create doubt and set into place a negative dynamic that is often difficult to overcome.

Avoiding opening-day jitters

You can expect to be more than a tad apprehensive on your first day of work. (If you're not, it could mean that succeeding in the job isn't as important as it should be.) The following bits of advice cover some basic points that help you ease, if not entirely eliminate, the jitters that nearly everybody experiences in this situation. Remember that little things count the most during your first few days on the job.

- ✓ **Be an early bird.** Give yourself plenty of extra time the morning of your first work day just to make sure you arrive relaxed, with plenty of time to spare. You don't want to experience the agony of watching time race by as you sit in a traffic jam that seems as long as the Mississippi River. Plan to arrive at least 30 minutes earlier than required, even if it means you have to sit in the reception area for 30 minutes until your new boss arrives. The fact that you're already there when your boss shows up isn't going to hurt. Arriving late for work, on the other hand, is never a good way to make a positive impression, even if you're just transferring to another department within the company. This is an all but unforgivable sin on your first day.

- ✓ **Dress up.** Regardless of how casual the company's dress code, pay extra attention to what you're wearing and be equally diligent about your grooming. Even if you know for certain that the dress code is casual, make sure you're dressed on the higher end of the scale. And if you have any doubts, wear interview attire. You're going to meet a lot of new people for the first time, and you only get one chance to make a good first impression. Make it count. You can adjust your dress code accordingly after you settle into the job.

- ✓ **Adopt a flexible mindset.** Even if you're working for a company that has arranged to cater to your every whim, be prepared to overcome any obstacle that may materialize. Who knows what could happen? Maybe the security guard will not have been informed of your arrival. Maybe your workspace won't be ready, or your computer can't be configured. Or maybe the manager you were looking forward so much to working with won the lottery two days earlier and has high-tailed it to Tahiti. Without driving yourself crazy, be prepared for whatever may come your way and be ready to adapt or respond. That way, if things go great, you'll be pleasantly surprised, but if you run into problems, you'll have an excellent opportunity to demonstrate to your new employer that you're flexible and adaptable — two of the most important qualities in today's workplace.

Brushing up on the basics

Even if you have to give up your lunch hour, or arrive an hour earlier in the morning, or stay after work, try to familiarize yourself as quickly as possible with the company's basic procedures and policies. And follow the same practice with respect to the various practical and logistical matters that relate to your job and your immediate work area. If no one has been assigned the task of bringing you up-to-speed in these matters, ask your manager to recommend someone in the company who, in one or two sessions, can give you an overall introduction to the facilities. If the company has a procedures manual or handbook, take it home with you and read it cover to cover, making notes of any questions you may have.

If there's no manual, create a list of questions of your own that covers the basic policies and procedures and arrange a meeting with your manager or someone else in the company to discuss the information. The following list of topics can serve as a guide:

- **Basic company procedures:** Ask about protocols regarding everyday events, such as using security precautions.

- **Normal working hours:** Beyond the official company hours, be sure to find out what the firm's corporate culture involves regarding overtime, taking work home, or coming in on weekends.

- **Time off:** Find out the policy on holidays, vacation, personal days, sick time, and so on.

- **Benefits coverage:** Get details on health and life insurance, 401(k) plans, stock-option programs, flexible spending accounts, tuition reimbursement, and so on.

- **Location of key office areas:** Find out where the restrooms, break room or lounge areas, supply room, mail room, and other areas are located.

- **Supply-request procedures:** Ask where and how you obtain paper, staplers, pens, and other basic materials you need to do your job.

- **Computer procedures:** Inquire about passwords, useful macros, tech support, and company policies on e-mail and Internet surfing.

- **Who's who:** Request the names of all key personnel in the company, the names of the company's main customers, and names of key vendors.

After you gather this information, get it organized on your computer, print the information out, and keep the list at arm's reach for the first couple of weeks. You'll probably be amazed at how often you refer to it — and how much time you can save by having the information so close at hand.

Going back to school at work

A big part of most orientation programs consists of filling you in on the background of the company: its history, mission, and values. This information can be extremely important if you're hoping to make your mark in the organization. (Of course, if you did your homework while preparing for the interview — see Chapter 5 — you're already ahead of the game.) Make a point to be super-attentive and alert during your first few weeks on the job, learning as much as you can about every aspect of the business.

If you're looking for some inspiration on this point, look no further than Michael R. Quinlan, former chairman and chief executive officer of McDonald's Corp. Quinlan, who started out in McDonald's as a mailroom clerk at the age of 18, reports that by keeping his ears open, he was able to deepen his knowledge of hamburgers, operations, real estate development, and purchasing.

Understanding your job responsibilities

Regardless of how many discussions you may have had during the hiring process about your job responsibilities and tasks, it's still critical that you sit down with your boss in the first few days to revisit those issues. Your goal is to make sure that you share a common vision of the job, implementation, and expectations for achievement. The basis of this discussion should be a written job description, and each of you should have a copy of it so that you can go over it point by point. If for some reason a job description isn't available, draft one yourself based on your knowledge of the basic responsibilities. (Make sure, though, that when you discuss it with your manager, you emphasize that it represents your initial understanding of the position — a work in progress.)

If your new boss is skilled in the art of management, she will probably take the initiative and communicate to you her expectations. But you can't always count on this. Your manager could be inexperienced or so consumed by pressures that she hasn't thought about what she really expects. If this is the case, assume the initiative and responsibility by being the one to ask questions.

Whatever else, you want to make sure that by the time the first meeting is over, you have clear answers to the following questions:

- ✔ **What are my responsibilities?** Try to get a specific list of the duties you'll be expected to perform.

- ✔ **What are the priorities?** Ask what percentage of your time during a typical workday should be spent on each responsibility.

- ✔ **Who are my colleagues?** Find out with whom you'll be interacting most often. If you're collaborating with others on projects, where do the lines of responsibility lie?

✔ **How frequently should I give updates?** Some managers want detailed daily or weekly status reports in writing. Others prefer very concise e-mails that only touch on the highlights. Still others prefer informal, unscheduled updates at the coffee machine. Find out your supervisor's preference.

✔ **How will my performance be evaluated?** Find out who will do the evaluation and what the criteria are. It's also helpful to know how frequently performance reviews take place.

During the course of that initial conversation, you may uncover some disparities between the job description you were originally presented and the description as you now understand it. As long as the disparities aren't too great and you can live with them, there's probably no need to dwell on the issues. But if you see significant differences, ask your boss if you may rewrite the job description.

Don't be reticent about asking these or any other basic questions about your responsibilities and what's expected of you. And don't hesitate to probe if the answers you get are vague and general. As long as you're cordial and respectful, don't worry about coming on too strong. Most managers will appreciate the fact that you're concerned about the job and about doing your best. You're making his or her job easier.

All this lengthy talk about your job and the responsibilities may strike you as overkill, but keep this in mind: The number-one reason, by far, that most job experiences go south is a communication breakdown between manager and employee.

Understanding your boss

Early meetings with your boss serve another useful purpose: They give insight into how your manager likes to work and communicate. You get an initial sense of whether he's a hands-on manager or a delegator. You also get a feeling for how he likes to process and deliver information — whether he's a cut-to-the-chase person or someone who takes a more measured and reflective view of things. That information will hold you in good stead after you settle into your job.

Adopting a team mentality

It's only natural when you begin a new job to want to prove yourself quickly. But in many corporate cultures, your ability to work as part of a team is more important than your individual achievements. In such environments, your goal should be to establish yourself as a team player. You can accomplish this by demonstrating a sincere desire to become a productive member of the team.

Here are some of the ways to establish yourself as a team player in the first few days on the job:

- ✔ **Take the initiative.** Rather than waiting for other people to introduce themselves to you or to be introduced to them, take the initiative to introduce yourself.

- ✔ **Get to know your coworkers.** Arrange to spend some time (no more than 15 minutes — and keep it informal) with anyone in the company you'll interact with, to get a sense of what he or she does and how you can help.

- ✔ **Try to see the big picture.** Find out how your job, team, and department fit into the overall strategic priorities of the business.

Don't rock the boat — not right away, anyway

If you're good at what you do and you've worked for highly successful companies, it's a safe bet that during your first few days on the job, you're going to notice policies and practices that, to your way of thinking, could be improved. You may be sorely tempted in these situations to point out the error of these ways. Resist the temptation — at least at first.

Your first priority when you're joining an organization is to establish trust and build chemistry with the folks you're going to be working with side-by-side in the trenches. You have plenty of time, after you earn that trust and develop that chemistry, to offer suggestions for improvement. You may find, too, that after you establish trust and are more familiar with the company, you're able to present a more persuasive argument for change.

Be especially careful of how you handle yourself during the first few meetings. Here are some key guidelines:

- ✔ **Be measured and diplomatic.** Offer opinions only when asked to do so. Even then, keep your comments brief.

- ✔ **Don't compare past and present.** Avoid beginning any comment with the phrase, "Well, when I was with . . . ." Comparing your present and previous employers will almost always get you into hot water.

- ✔ **When in doubt, be silent.** Avoid saying anything that may be interpreted as critical or judgmental. Better to hold your peace than create unnecessary upheaval.

- ✔ **Observe the reactions of others.** Pay attention to how people respond to your comments. If you sense — without being oversensitive — that someone is less than receptive to what you have to say, take the person aside in private and find out if you did something inadvertently to upset him or her.

Ten sure-fire ways to make a bad impression

Remember, I'm only kidding!

✔ Interrupt your manager as often as possible to dispute every comment he or she makes.

✔ On your first day of work, ask if you can have the afternoon off so that you can watch an important episode of your favorite soap opera.

✔ Arrive with a huge box of personal mementos and spend most of your first morning decorating your workspace. Ask your manager if she thinks you should hang the 18" mural of your dog above your computer or off to the side.

✔ Arrange to have all your friends call you on the first day to find out how you're doing — or, better still, invite them to drop by the office for a tour.

✔ Call the CEO "Pops" or "Big Mama."

✔ Offer unsolicited criticism to your colleagues, especially about their wardrobe choices.

✔ Rearrange all the office furniture for "improved energy flow."

✔ Solicit your coworkers for donations to your personal legal defense fund.

✔ Bring a hotplate to work and prepare your own lunch in your office (the more aromatic, the better).

✔ Call the information technology department to complain about the fact that you can't play any of your favorite computer games on your PC.

Asking for help

One of the biggest mistakes you can make when starting a new job is also one of the easiest to avoid: putting too much pressure on yourself by not asking for help when you need it.

The main reason people are reluctant to ask for help is that they don't want to appear foolish or uninformed. But the fact that you're new to a job gives you the right to ask questions and request assistance. People expect you to ask for help, so take advantage of this expectation. Without making too much of a pest of yourself, seek help when you need it, and don't make the mistake of trying to play the Lone Ranger when you're asked to do something you don't know how to do.

Here's a simple example. It's your third or fourth day of work and your boss, who assumes you're familiar with presentation software, has asked you to put together a presentation. Suppose, for the sake of argument, that you're familiar with the basic features of the software, but you're not quite up to speed on the more sophisticated capabilities, such as animation.

So what do you do? The best thing to do in a situation like this is to admit right up front that you can handle the basics but you're not too sure about the animation. Ask if there is someone with whom you could consult on this particular aspect. Your boss may decide that he doesn't really need the animation, or he may enlist someone else to help you with the presentation. Either way, you're much better off than you would have been if you had decided to wing it, putting extra pressure on yourself and running the risk of failure.

By the same token, don't hesitate to accept or to volunteer for assignments that are a stretch for you — they'll help you grow and develop. The key is to be candid about your abilities and not to bite off more than you can chew.

Getting initial feedback

In most companies, you're unlikely to go through any sort of formal appraisal process until you've been with the company for at least three months and sometimes as long as six months. But it's in your best interest to request some reasonably formal feedback much earlier — as soon as three or four weeks after you've started.

It doesn't have to be a big deal. Simply suggest to your manager that the two of you sit down for half an hour to review your job performance. Before the meeting, draw up a brief agenda — the points that you want to cover. And when you're discussing each of these items, seek specific feedback as opposed to general comments about whether you're doing a good job. Ask about particular aspects of a project as in, "Was there enough documentation in that last report?" or "Was the tone right? I was a little concerned that I was coming on too strong." Remember, the first step to strengthening a weakness is to become aware of it. Remember, too, that by strengthening your weaknesses, you're assuming more direct control over your career future.

Getting a Fix on the Company Environment

At the same time that you're acclimating yourself to the nuts and bolts of your job, be sure to pay some attention to the company culture or environment. Corporate culture has been a hot topic in recent years, but the fact is that with only a handful of exceptions (Disney, Marriott, GE, and Southwest Airlines, to name four), few companies today are known for being culture-driven from top to bottom. What you find in most companies is an organizational style — a certain way of doing things. The extent to which the prevailing company style governs the day-to-day atmosphere of the office varies not only from one company to another but also from one department to another. In smaller, entrepreneurial companies, the personality of the workplace is usually a reflection of the owner or president and perhaps a handful of senior people.

If you've done your research during your job search and if you've been observant throughout the hiring process, you should have a fairly accurate sense — even before you begin work — of the general tone of the office. But it's not until you've had a chance to work in that environment and become directly involved in the processes that you can confirm those initial observations. The following sections detail some of the areas to keep in mind.

Noting the work ethic

It is a given in business that success requires hard work. But not every organization has the same definition of hard work, especially when considering the number of hours that constitute a typical work week. You'll find out soon enough — and mostly through observation — what the guidelines are in your company. Take note of how early most people arrive, how late they leave, and how laden they are with paperwork when they walk out the door. Yet another indication is how often you find people at the office on weekends.

The purpose here isn't to judge what's right or wrong but to understand the prevailing style in the company. Even if you are unusually efficient and can get your work done without working a 60- or 70-hour work week, the fact that you're arriving a little later and leaving earlier than most people could be construed as a sign that you're not as committed as everyone else. You have to decide if you're willing to adapt to the culture or risk possible career stagnation.

Determining who makes decisions

If you hope to make any sort of mark in your new company, try to discover as soon as possible who makes the key strategic and operational decisions. In traditionally structured companies, key decisions and strategic initiatives are generally made by a handful of people, with little or no input from others in the company. Hence the term, *top-down management*. That style of decision-making still prevails in some companies, but many progressive organizations today favor a much more empowered approach to decision making.

It shouldn't take long to figure out where the seat of power really lies in the company. One fairly reliable sign is how much authority — budgetary control, in particular — is exercised by managers in the middle levels of the company. If your manager answers most of your questions with, "Well, I'll have to check that out with . . .," you're probably working for a top-down company.

If that's the case, be sure to work within the chain of command: Consult your manager on key initiatives and decisions and provide information and updates as necessary. Your responsibility is to help your supervisor make a decision or take action. However, if you're in a company that empowers its employees to make many of the important decisions that relate to their jobs, you need to exercise the responsibility that goes along with the authority. In other words, you need to be the one who gathers important facts and information so that you can make an informed decision. You may choose to speak with your manager for her insight, but you may also want to seek input from peers, other managers, and external sources.

Of course, even in an empowered culture you still need to update your manager. And in a top-down management structure, you still need to gather facts and information. The difference between the two corporate cultures lies in how much responsibility you have for acting on information.

Documenting your decisions

Making a decision about anything more complex than what color pen to use can be a little unnerving when you're just getting to know your company, let alone the scope of your own job responsibilities. But if you keep notes throughout any decision-making process, you can ease your concerns as well as those of your manager. For example, if you need to evaluate and select a hotel for an upcoming meeting, take notes on your discussions with each hotel representative, your boss's instructions or insights, and your conclusions throughout the process. While this may seem tedious at first, you'll be better able to discover any holes in your research as you go along. And after you've made your decision, you also have documentation to support your actions should anyone need an explanation.

Heeding communication style

A company's communication style is best measured by the way information flows from one person to another or from one department to the next — whether it's by memo, e-mail, phone, or face-to-face conversation. Typically, the communication style is a reflection of how the manager or owner likes to communicate. Other times, however, there's a pronounced company style. Within the first few days, get a sense of how the people you work with prefer to communicate. If you want to succeed in this organization, it may be necessary for you to adapt to their style.

The adjustment that many people find the most challenging is the move from an oral, face-to-face style of communicating to the written format (e-mail, in particular) that has become increasingly prevalent now in today's global economy. If writing doesn't come easily to you, the best approach is to build more time into your daily schedule for writing tasks.

Observing interactions

It's unlikely that you're going to find yourself in an environment in which people blatantly mistreat one another. And in the unlikely event you find yourself in such a company, it's not in your best interest to hang around. In most cases, though, you simply want to take note of how formal or casual the atmosphere, and how open people are with one another. Here are some examples:

✔ Some companies are known for encouraging frank, open discussion, and if you're working for such a company, don't be too quick to assume that you're being picked on.

✔ Pay attention to how people treat senior managers — are they referred to as Mr., Mrs., or Ms., or as Frank, Marilyn, or Betty?

✔ Be alert to the unwritten rules of staff meetings. Is it the general practice to simply speak your mind or to wait until opinions and feedback are requested?

Be careful not to participate in any inappropriate conversations, jokes, or behavior in an effort to fit in. Your goal is to adapt to any acceptable, not unacceptable, means of conduct.

Undoing the Wrong Move

Regardless of how perfect your new job may have seemed when you were competing and interviewing for it, you may discover in the first few days that you have made a terrible mistake. Why that happened is less important than doing your best to avoid the two most common pitfalls:

✔ Jumping ship prematurely (and, in many cases, for all the wrong reasons)

✔ Hanging in there too long, even though you have ample evidence to suggest that you're not going to be able to salvage the situation

Certain situations give warning signs so loud and clear that you can't afford to avoid them. Here are some of them:

✔ **Breach of agreement:** The company that hired you has reneged (and can't give you a justifiable explanation) on critical points in your agreement, such as salary, signing bonus, fundamental responsibilities, or the amount of support you could count on.

✔ **Legal problems:** You discover that the company is engaged in illegal or unethical activities (and, worse, that you're expected to be a party to these actions).

✔ **Unhealthy or unsafe conditions:** You find yourself working in an abusive, angry environment or for an abusive boss.

Situations like these are the exception, not the rule. In most instances, any misgivings you may have about your job will likely be less conspicuous. It may be that certain responsibilities — the ones you like the least — are taking up most of your time. It may be that you underestimated the inconvenience of a very long commute or the demands of travel. Or you may not be receiving the support staff that you want or need.

Meeting with your manager

Whatever the reason, you owe it to yourself and to the company to refrain from any hasty decisions. At the very least, request a brief meeting with your manager to discuss your concerns, many of which may be easy to correct.

Here are some suggestions on how to get ready for that meeting:

1. **Write down any important aspects of the job that you find unpleasant or distasteful.**

   But be reasonable: There's no need to cite the color of your trash bin as a critical issue that needs to be addressed.

2. **Categorize each item.**

   After you set the list to paper (and I hope the list isn't too long), try to organize it according to the following outline:

   - **Job:** The specific responsibilities of the position

   - **Environment:** The corporate culture

   - **People:** Coworkers or management

   - **Other:** Problems with equipment, the condition of your workspace, lack of support, and so on

Try to determine ahead of time what changes need to occur in each of these areas to eliminate the problems you're having.

If you go through this exercise, you will probably find some overlap between categories. It may be hard for you, for example, to separate the specific tasks you have to perform from the atmosphere of the company or the people you're working with. But the more time you spend thinking through each of these issues, the more productive your meeting with your boss is likely to be. You'll be much better able to determine whether the problems you're having are solvable. And, most important, you'll be more prepared to recommend solutions.

Deciding to leave

If the conversations you've had with your boss convince you that it's better to leave than to stay, try to make your departure from the job as civilized and pleasant as possible. Forget about who's to blame: There's nothing to be gained by dwelling on history. If you've been working on a specific project, you may want to offer to complete it. Otherwise, the sooner you leave, the better. (The company, in fact, may want you to leave that very day.) If, during the recruiting and interviewing stage, some people in the company went to bat for you, call them or drop them a line. Fill them in on what has happened and thank them again for their help.

One last thing: After you have a few days to gain some perspective, you may want to recreate in your mind the steps that led you to make a bad choice. Don't beat yourself up. Instead, try to figure out if there were signs early on that you were either unaware of or chose to ignore. Use that insight to help prevent you from making the same mistake the next time around.

Chapter 7

Workplace Diplomacy: The New Rules for Getting Ahead

*T*he phenomenon generally known as *office politics* exists to some degree in almost every organization — and it's no wonder. Regardless of how much people may like and respect each other and how strong their commitment may be to a common goal, disagreements invariably arise. Coworkers may not agree on how things should be done, who should do them, who should get the credit for things that go well, or who should take the heat when things go wrong.

Fortunately, most organizations are able to keep the negative aspects of office politics under reasonable control. Clearly, though, some companies are more political than others. Even in today's performance-driven workplace, you still run into people who owe whatever career success they've achieved not to their skills, talent, or work ethic, but to how shrewdly they play the game of politics. In fact, such an individual may have assumed a position of power in your organization, your department, or — heaven forbid — the cubicle next door.

You need to be sensitive to the political undercurrents in your organization. But you don't need to engage in manipulative games to do your job and succeed. That would be a mistake. What you need to do, quite apart from mastering the skills that are crucial to your job, is deal effectively with those aspects of your position that may best be described as your *unwritten job description*. In other words, you need to be able to work cooperatively with others at the same time that you're focusing on your job. You need to be able to communicate openly without offending or alienating others, knowing when to speak up, when to keep quiet, and how to get the credit you deserve without undermining the efforts and accomplishments of others. You need to practice workplace diplomacy.

This chapter offers insights into coping effectively with the less-than-comfortable political situations that may arise in your organization. It also includes an introduction to an important but often neglected subject today: office etiquette. You get advice on how to be politically savvy without becoming so consumed by office politics that your work suffers and you lose enthusiasm.

Understanding Your Environment

Giving advice on workplace diplomacy is a lot like advising people on how to get along with their families. Generalizations are risky. What works for you in a given environment or situation may not work for someone else. And the same advice that applies in one environment could get you into trouble somewhere else.

The guidelines in the following sections are general — and deliberately so. This information isn't designed to make you a better political player but to enhance your ability to operate effectively in your company's environment.

Getting to know coworkers

One of the most effective — and simplest — ways to avoid problems with your coworkers (and to get their support when you need it) is to find out as much as you can about the pressures that they themselves are up against in their jobs. Lacking this awareness, you run the risk of underestimating the difficulty of what you may consider a routine request for help.

The best way to gain this knowledge is through direct observation. If you're going to be interacting frequently with people in the accounting department, for example, take note of how they work. Get a feel for which of their job functions are routine and which are complicated. The better you understand what others do, the more effectively you can assess the difficulty of any request you make and take steps to ease the burden.

Working through the chain of command

Even though many companies are no longer as structured and bureaucratic as they once were, a chain of command (informal though it may be) still exists, and you want to make sure that you're observing it. Whenever you run into problems, the first person you should consult is your manager.

In some cases, however, the source of your problem may, in fact, be your immediate supervisor. But even then, do your best to work it out with him or her before you decide to break the chain of command. (However, in cases of sexual harassment or unlawful discriminatory treatment, your company may have a policy in place that directs you to the human resources department.)

Observing protocol

In diplomatic circles, protocol refers to the practices that govern behavior at official functions. Protocol dictates how you greet Queen Elizabeth and what sort of a gift you bring when you've been invited to the home of a tribal leader in Borneo. In most business situations, protocol can be best thought of as the internal rules of the road. Given the chain of command in your organization, for example, the only person you may officially need to seek feedback from on a new initiative is your immediate boss. However, protocol may dictate that you also seek the blessing of a certain individual who is, for example, recognized as the resident expert in that field.

Protocols aren't necessarily documented in your procedure manual; they tend to evolve out of tradition and precedent. Here are some other protocol-related issues to consider:

- ✔ **Practice teamwork.** If you notice that a coworker is swamped with a project, volunteer to help out. Of course, you need to be sure that your helping hand will not limit your ability to fulfill your own responsibilities. But in general, be a team player.

- ✔ **Don't criticize publicly.** If you disagree with a position your boss has taken during a staff meeting, request a private meeting to ask for clarification and, if appropriate, voice your concerns.

Minor as any given issue may seem, you can create difficulties for yourself by not being aware of the unwritten rules.

If you've just joined a company, don't make the mistake of assuming that the protocol you followed in your former company is the same in your new organization. Spend some time with veterans and get a sense for how things are done.

Commenting with discretion

Even when you're urged to do so, and you've been given assurances that your answer will be kept confidential, never say anything about anyone in your company that you wouldn't say to his or her face. And even then, be discreet. Be especially careful about what you write when you're sending an e-mail. The written word is binding, and you never know whether your message will be forwarded to others.

Never send a memo or e-mail when you're upset or angry. (You can write it, but don't distribute it until you've had a chance to look at it at least 24 hours later, when you can be more objective.)

Maintaining appearances

Even the faintest hint of scandal or impropriety can trigger rumors. So regardless of how noble or innocent your motives may be, think twice before doing anything that may send an erroneous message to your staff members, coworkers, or manager.

Here's an example. You're browsing in your local bookstore and come across a book that you think one of your staff members would enjoy and benefit from. (Perhaps *Managing Your Career For Dummies*?) If it's customary for you to give books or other small gifts to your employees, go ahead; you can buy the book without agonizing about the reaction of others. But if you've never made such a gesture before, your thoughtfulness could be interpreted as favoritism and create problems not only for you but also for the person who receives the gift.

Building support for new initiatives

New initiatives have a way of stirring up ownership issues — disputes over which individual or department should have the final say in certain types of decisions. Assume, for example, that one of your responsibilities is organizing market research, and you're looking to improve the software currently used to crunch survey numbers. You have a new package in mind, but the change you're advocating requires additional training for the IT people who have traditionally been responsible for the analysis. This means that although you're making life easier for yourself, you may be complicating their responsibilities. They may balk at the suggestion and remind you that choosing software is an IT function and not your area of expertise. The result: stalemate.

The main thing to keep in mind about ownership issues is that even when you get your way, you may not enjoy the fruits of victory for very long. The ill feelings spawned by most of those disagreements can poison future dealings with the person or persons who lost. The better way is to anticipate whose territory you may be invading whenever you come up with an idea or a new initiative and then approach that person early on to enlist his or her support. A good mentor can help you navigate the situation. (See Chapter 15 for more information on choosing a mentor.)

Any initiative you want to advance needs to be favorably perceived by those in the company whose day-to-day activities and responsibilities will be impacted by the initiative.

Protecting your credibility

Next to your job performance, nothing has more bearing on the stature you attain or the influence you ultimately wield in your company than your reputation for integrity and honesty. Difficult though it may be at times, resist taking any action that may jeopardize your reputation as a straight shooter.

Here are some suggestions:

- **Be honest.** If you don't know the answer to a question that you're asked, admit it — even though you're supposed to know the answer.

- **Keep your word.** Never make any promises you're not sure you can keep.

- **Honor deadlines.** And if you're not going to be able to meet a deadline, let your supervisor or coworkers know well in advance.

- **Admit when you're wrong.** When you mess up, admit it, and let people know that you're going to rectify the situation. Even when it's not your fault, don't blame others.

Watching your back

Regardless of how far you've been able to distance yourself from the politics of your company, it's still possible that someone in the organization — someone you may have long considered an ally — may see you as a threat (or just may not like the way you comb your hair). This individual may start acting in ways designed to undermine your reputation and effectiveness.

You have to be careful, of course, not to jump to conclusions. But don't be naïve, either. If you have any reason to suspect that someone is sabotaging your efforts, don't be passive. Make it your business to discuss the situation with that person. Be careful, though. Skilled players are good at covering their tracks. Be prepared to provide concrete evidence for any suspicions you may have.

In the meantime, keep your guard up whenever you're dealing with anyone who does the following:

- **Speaks negatively:** Watch out for poison tongues — especially when they encourage you to talk negatively about others in the company or about the company in general.

- **Steals ideas:** Beware of coworkers who frequently come to you to pick your brain but never give you credit when presenting your ideas to senior management.

- **Reneges on promises:** Steer clear of people who make commitments but don't tell you until the last minute that they're not going to be able to meet them, thereby making you look bad in the eyes of others.

Sharing credit

An almost sure-fire way to make enemies in your company is to assume all (or most) of the credit for accomplishments to which others have contributed. Forgetting for the moment the unsavory ethics of this practice, taking credit for the accomplishments of others always costs you in the long run. Apart from the antagonism you trigger, you will usually find it difficult to get information or help from people you've relied on in the past. Little things matter. If you're reporting the results of a project in which you were one of several people involved, always use "we" instead of "I" in both your written and oral presentations. And if you're the team leader, always mention the specific contributions made by various members of the team.

There's a flip side to the advice: Don't shed all responsibility for failures.

Resolving conflicts

If, in spite of your best efforts, you still find yourself locking horns with a coworker (and don't worry for now about who's to blame), do your best to try to resolve the problem informally, without involving your boss or the other person's boss. While you may not be comfortable with the idea of working things out one-on-one with someone with whom you're not getting along, resolving workplace conflicts has become a critical skill and it's not as daunting a challenge as you may think. It's simply a willingness to talk things out — difficult issues can be resolved amicably with a little preparation and thought.

Chances are, if you were to go to your supervisor for help, the first thing he or she would ask is whether you've tried to work out the problem on your own.

Here is some additional advice on how to settle conflicts with coworkers:

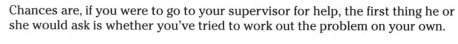

- ✔ **Make the first move.** There's a good chance the other person is even less comfortable than you are in these kinds of situations and will welcome your gesture of peace.

- ✔ **Choose the right time.** Try to have your sit-down conversation at a calmer time — perhaps at the end of the day.

- ✔ **Adopt a conciliatory stance.** Keep in mind that the purpose of this meeting is to resolve the conflict, not to vent your feelings.

- ✔ **Own your part of the problem.** Recognize that you may be acting in ways that are exacerbating the conflict.

If confronting the individual doesn't ease the problem, suggest to him or her that the two of you sit down together with a third party. You need to reach this decision mutually and agree on who should mediate.

Setting boundaries

Volunteering for assignments that lie outside your normal responsibilities is usually a good career move, especially when those assignments enable you to develop new skills or make new contacts. But don't allow yourself to become a dumping ground for assignments that no one else wants to take on. Sure, it's important to be nice and willing to pitch in when the need arises, as long as your sense of altruism doesn't prevent you from meeting your own responsibilities. And if you sense that your department's ability to get the job done is in jeopardy, diplomatically express your concerns, making sure, of course, that you do it in the appropriate setting.

If you have one of those bosses (heaven help you) who frequently assigns you low-level tasks that aren't part of your job description (and, worse, interferes with your ability to do the job for which you've been hired), set up a meeting in which the two of you can come to an agreement on priorities. The same is true if you're the only member of a team who winds up doing most of the grunt work: Don't be afraid to discuss the issue with your team leader or supervisor.

Developing a thick skin

At times, colleagues or coworkers who bear you no malice — and who, in fact, like and admire you — do and say things in the heat of the moment that seem incredibly insensitive and hurtful. You're entitled to your feelings, of course, and there's no reason for you to put up with behavior that is blatantly abusive. But keep in mind that many of the things that people say and do during periods of stress aren't really directed toward you but toward the situation. Carrying a grudge isn't in anyone's best interest.

Office Etiquette: When in Rome . . .

Many of the behavioral guidelines that are part of your unwritten job description boil down to common sense and courtesy. Unfortunately the busier and more pressured the workplace gets, the more likely these guidelines will fall by the wayside. What follows is a list of guidelines for office etiquette. Chances are, you're already heeding much of this advice. Just in case, though, circle any principle that you may not be consciously adhering to and see if you can improve in that area the next time you show up at the office.

✔ Treat everyone — from the company president to the clerk in the mailroom — with respect and dignity. Never engage in any actions that may make people feel embarrassed or uncomfortable.

✔ Never assume that anyone from whom you seek information or a favor is less busy or less stressed than you. Keep in mind that nearly everyone in the organization has more to do than can be comfortably handled.

✔ When coworkers come to you for information, give them your undivided attention. And if you're talking to someone over the phone, don't work on your computer while you're carrying on a conversation. (It's not polite and they can hear the clicking of keys on the other side of the line.)

✔ Be punctual for all meetings. If you arrive late, apologize and skip the "dog ate my homework" excuses — they aren't relevant.

✔ Celebrate with others. Busy as you are, always do your best to make an appearance (even if it's very brief) at all informal get-togethers — such as a lunchtime birthday or five-year anniversary celebration for a coworker.

✔ If you're good with computers and you work with people who aren't, don't be a *cybersnob*. Share your expertise without making others feel inadequate.

✔ Be sensitive to other people's need for privacy. Example: If you're in someone's cubicle and he or she receives a personal call, offer to excuse yourself before you're asked to leave.

✔ Don't let the fact that you're on a break and have this really funny joke to tell induce you to interrupt your coworkers while they're in the middle of an important project.

✔ Do your best to return every call or respond to e-mail within 24 hours. If you have to violate this principle, be prepared to offer an apology.

✔ Whenever you're leaving a voice-mail message, always leave your telephone number, the time you called, and the reason for the call.

✔ Keep your voice-mail messages clear and concise.

✔ Don't make cell phone calls in public places, such as the break room.

✔ If a fax isn't addressed to you, don't read it. By the same token, if you're sending a fax, be alert to the possibility that other people may read it, even though it is not addressed to them.

✔ Try to limit any fax to no more than three or four pages. (Otherwise it ties up the recipient's machine.) If the message is going to be longer, call the person ahead of time to let him or her know it's coming.

✔ Be careful with humor. Never tell an offensive joke and keep your sarcasm under wraps. It can easily be misinterpreted.

✔ Never make changes to anyone's computer unless you've been specifically instructed to do so — even if you're just trying to help.

✔ Dress in accordance with your company dress code. Even on so-called dress-down days, never wear anything that may be considered unprofessional. Also, remember to go easy on the perfume or after-shave. Some people are allergic or are highly sensitive to cologne and other scents.

✔ When you're making conversation, steer clear of any subject — ethnicity, sex, religion, politics — that could spark antagonism and create misunderstandings. Stick to the basics: sports, movies, restaurants, gardening, the kids, or the precipitous slide of the Euro (just kidding).

✔ Call people by their names, as opposed to "Hon," "Love," or "Sweetheart."

✔ If you have to attend to personal matters or personal calls, do so on your break time.

✔ Don't bring your personal problems to work with you. A dark mood can be contagious.

✔ Don't show up for work if you have a bad cold or any other medical condition that may be spread to others. If you need to be in the office, let others know that they may want to keep their distance.

✔ Don't complain about little things. If your company no longer stocks your favorite pens or the year-end party is not within walking distance from home, keep your disappointments to yourself. Pick your battles and realize you can't always get everything you want.

✔ Be a good neighbor. If you eat lunch at your desk, avoid foods that emit a strong smell. And if you borrow something, such as a directory, a stapler, or computer disk, return it as soon as you're finished.

✔ When in doubt about the appropriateness of any behavior, ask yourself the following question: What would it be like to work here if everyone acted this way?

Making the Best of Three Tricky Situations

No matter how adept you are at handling interpersonal issues in general, you may very well find yourself in situations for which there are no clear-cut right or wrong answers. The following sections detail three such situations, along with some general advice on how to respond. Keep in mind, however, that you have to deal with each situation on its own terms — and with an appreciation of all the factors. (For a discussion of more situations like these, see Chapter 20.)

Stop the talk: When a colleague is spreading rumors

The situation: A coworker in another department appears professional whenever senior-level managers are around, but after they've left the area, gossips about colleagues and starts rumors. In fact, he's so good at it that some people have begun to believe his lies, and a coworker's professional reputation may be damaged.

Response strategy: Your instinct may be simply to ignore him and hope that others will do the same. But if the behavior continues, employee morale and motivation may suffer, if they haven't already. You need to bring the matter to your boss's attention, and you need to do it in an objective, professional manner. Present your manager with the facts of the situation as they occurred, but try not to get caught up in condemning the person. You're merely passing along information, not recommending disciplinary action. If your supervisor chooses not to address the problem, don't push for a resolution or go over her head to your boss's boss. Just begin documenting the gossiping coworker's behavior, in case your manager decides to take action at a later time. Your notes may be helpful.

Teacher's pet: When you think coworkers are getting preferential treatment

The situation: Not long after your request to telecommute two days a week is turned down by your manager, one of your coworkers is given the thumbs-up for a similar request.

Response strategy: Even though you may have good reason to believe that you're getting the short end of the stick, withhold final judgment until you've explored the situation. Special circumstances in your coworker's case — a crisis at home, perhaps — may explain what you perceive as a double standard. There's nothing wrong with asking your manager for clarification on the decision, just as long as you do it in a reasonable, nonconfrontational manner and it doesn't jeopardize the arrangement your coworker has secured. If, after hearing the reason, you're still convinced that you're being treated unfairly, ask for specific guidelines to follow so that your request may be considered in the future.

Candid camera: When the truth may hurt

The situation: Your boss's boss calls you aside one day and begins to ask you questions that, if answered truthfully, may cast the person you work for in a less-than-favorable light.

How to respond. The conflict here is clear. If you fudge the truth, you're not being honest. Saying everything you're tempted to say, on the other hand, could be viewed by many as a gesture of disloyalty. A lot depends on the nature of the behavior in question. If you know for certain that your boss has been behaving unethically or in ways that are clearly not in the best interests of your company, and you're asked directly about these issues, tell the truth. You may want to let whoever is asking these questions know, however, that you don't feel comfortable talking about your boss. In addition, you should never represent as a fact anything you're not able to back up with proof.

If the questions are meant to solicit your views on your supervisor's competence or judgment, weigh your answers extremely carefully. If you admire and respect your boss, by all means express that view. But if you have mixed feelings, keep your responses brief.

Keep in mind that nothing — nothing! — will do more to poison the relationship between you and your boss than having him or her learn, through a third party, that you've been saying negative things.

Chapter 8

Different Strokes: Taking Advantage of Flexible Work Arrangements

*W*orking arrangements in most corporations today are far more flexible than they used to be. People are working every bit as hard and are committed to their careers, but when and where the work gets done is no longer the issue it once was. Scheduling arrangements that were rare and, in some cases, unheard of 10 or 15 years ago have become more prevalent. And going to work these days is no longer synonymous with catching the 6:35 train or driving from your home to your office.

In this chapter, you find out about the various work arrangements that may be available to you, but the emphasis isn't so much on the arrangements themselves as on their career implications. You get a look at the pros and cons of the four main alternate work options today:

✔ Part-time work

✔ Job sharing

✔ Flextime

✔ Telecommuting

For each of these arrangements, I give you insight into how each can affect your job performance and career progress. I also share solid advice on how to gain management approval for the arrangement you seek. Finally, I include some guidelines for how to make a smooth transition from the old arrangement to the new.

What's Going on Here, Anyway?

The dramatic change in the way companies view working arrangements that deviate from the 9-to-5, 40-hour week norm didn't just happen overnight. The change has occurred gradually, driven by several concurrent trends:

- The changing demographics of the workplace and, in particular, the growing number of dual-income households

- A growing desire among employees to balance their job responsibilities with their family priorities

- Technological advances that allow for 24-hour-a-day, 7-day-per-week remote access to information and people

Whatever the factors, this much is clear: Companies throughout the world now recognize that to attract and hold on to good people, scheduling policies need to be in sync with the lifestyle needs and desires of their employees. A survey conducted by Robert Half International found that balancing work and family demands is a bigger concern to working men and women today than salary and job security. Other survey results in recent years have found that flexible scheduling policies, coupled with various family-friendly initiatives (child care subsidies, for example), can help reduce absenteeism, improve morale, lessen turnover, and in certain instances, decrease overhead costs. Many organizations have also discovered that by broadening their definition of normal working hours, they can provide better service to customers.

Flexible work arrangements aren't a passing fad. Even the most bottom-line oriented executives of all — chief financial officers — report a significant change in focus. According to another recent survey by Robert Half International, 90 percent of CFOs say that their companies are much more concerned about work/family issues today than they were five years ago.

Looking at the Options

Alternate work arrangements is a catch-all phrase that describes any working schedule that deviates from the 9-to-5, 40-hour week pattern. For the purposes of this book, it doesn't include independent working options such as consulting or project-based work, which we cover in more detail in Chapter 16. What we discuss in the following sections are four arrangements that may be available to you as a firm's paid employee.

Part-time, regular employment

As a *part-time employee,* you work fewer hours per pay period than do full-time employees but are still considered part of the company's workforce and, therefore, are entitled to most benefits. (Note that sometimes, benefits are reduced or paid on a prorated basis.) Part-time employment can be structured in any number of ways, such as three 8-hour days per week, five mornings (or afternoons) per week, or whatever arrangement happens to work for both you and your employer.

While part-time work is hardly a new development, what's different today is that the arrangement is being sought by an increasing number of professionals and managers. A reduced work week is an especially attractive option for workers who are pursuing advanced degrees or changing careers. It's a popular option, too, among senior-level managers who want to transition to retirement. One drawback to part-time work, of course, is the financial implication. With fewer hours, you earn fewer dollars. Another possible drawback is that as a part-time employee, you may not be available for high-profile projects that could be important to your career growth. You may be out of the office when key decisions, crises, or meetings occur, and your manager may need someone who can participate on a full-time basis. While you can't necessarily avoid this, you can work with your team members or coworkers to help stay in the loop with e-mail and voice-mail updates. And you need to give 100 percent of your energy and focus to the job when you are in the office to avoid any possible perception that you're less committed to your work than others are.

Job sharing

In *job sharing,* two part-time employees share the duties and responsibilities of a full-time job. The tasks and responsibilities are typically divided 50-50, but the division of labor can also be based on the preference or proficiencies of each partner. Job sharing is best suited for positions in which the tasks are clearly defined, and the pressures of the job are reasonably contained and predictable. The downside to job sharing is that finding the right job-sharing partner can be as tough as finding the perfect job. Possessing the skills and attributes that the position requires is not enough. The two of you also have to be able to communicate well, respect one another's judgment, share the same work ethic, and be willing to give one another the support you'll each need. (Fortunately, you don't have to like the same football team, but it helps!) Another possible challenge with job sharing is that you're no longer in full control of your own career accomplishments. Your ultimate success depends as much on your partner as it does on you.

Job sharing gone wrong!

The following are five sure signs that the people you're considering as potential job-sharing partners are Mr. (or Ms.) Wrong.

✔ He can only work on the fifth Friday of every month and can't work during any month that has an "r" in it.

✔ He's interested in the arrangement but he'd like you to be interviewed first by his cat.

✔ He has one simple request: Split the first few paychecks 90 percent for him and 10 percent for you, so that he can catch up on his gambling debts.

✔ He asks you (for reasons you're not sure of) if you're afraid of snakes.

✔ When you ask what software he's familiar with, he responds, "Software?"

Flextime

Flextime is one of the most widespread alternate work options. This arrangement is geared more to employees who normally work a fixed number of hours each day, as opposed to managers or salespeople whose schedules fluctuate according to the daily demands of their job. In a typical flextime situation, you work the same number of hours as in a standard work day, but your start and finish times may be earlier or later than those of other employees, depending on how you structure the arrangement.

Most companies set parameters on how early you can arrive and leave, and usually require that you're in the office during the core hours. You may also be asked to keep the same schedule as your teammates to facilitate communication. Flextime is popular with working parents because it reduces the need for after-school childcare. The practice is also widely encouraged by municipalities in areas that are plagued by heavy rush-hour traffic. The downside? None, really, other than the fact that you may not always be available for meetings or events that take place when you're not there.

A common variation of flextime is the so-called *compressed work week*. Instead of five eight-hour days, for example, you work four ten-hour days, resulting in one less day in the office per week.

Telecommuting

Telecommuting (short for telecommunication commuting) is used to describe any scheduling arrangement in which you spend some portion of the week working from a nonoffice environment, such as your home. Your schedule remains the same, but what you eliminate is travel time. Telecommuting wouldn't be a viable option for most people today if it weren't for advances in technology that enable you to access information and communicate with others from virtually anywhere. The option has obvious appeal to employees — working parents, in particular — who have lengthy commutes. Of course, some types of jobs lend themselves more readily to telecommuting than others. Sure, you can still participate in meetings and discussions through conference calls, but you'll likely miss the subtleties of group interaction. And it's important to remember, too, that telecommuting requires the ability to work well independently and remain focused in a nonoffice environment. Sometimes the distractions of working at home or in an alternative workspace can be as troublesome as the commute you're trying to avoid.

Thinking Through Your Decision

Making a fundamental change in your work arrangement requires serious thought, regardless of what your career ambitions may be. You need to make sure, above all, that any decision regarding where and when you work is in sync with your strategic career plan. And whatever else you do, make sure that you will be able to accept the negatives as well as the positives of any arrangement you choose. To help you work your way through this self-examination process, the following sections pose four questions to ask yourself before pursuing any changes.

How will it affect my work performance?

Any change to your basic working patterns is likely to affect your job performance — especially at first. So the key question isn't whether your job performance will be influenced by the change you're considering, but how. And after you answer that question, you need to figure out how to prepare for and prevent any challenges that may arise.

All too often, people become so enamored with the idea of changing their work arrangements that they fail to consider the practical implications until after the change, when they find themselves knee-deep in problems.

The following exercise can help you prepare.

1. **Get a sheet of paper and divide it into three columns.**

2. **On the left-hand side list all the various functions and tasks you now perform in your job.**

3. **Use the second column to describe how you currently handle each task.**

   Think about your access to certain equipment — a high-speed copier, for example — that you may use for certain projects.

4. **Use the third column to describe how you would handle things under the new arrangement.**

   If you're going to telecommute two or three days, for example, ask yourself if the work flow would suffer because you're no longer able to have frequent face-to-face interaction with your coworkers.

Take your time with this exercise, and if you're going to err, do so on the side of caution.

How will it affect the people I work with and manage?

The degree to which your new working arrangement affects the job performance of other people you work with depends on two factors:

- ✔ The number of people with whom you interact
- ✔ How dependent these people are on your physical presence in the office

The more solitary and self-contained your job is, of course, the less these issues should concern you. But if your job is people-oriented and closely linked with the activities of your coworkers and staff members, you can't afford to gloss over the question of how others will need to adapt when you're not there.

Ironically, the more indispensable you are in your current arrangement, the bigger the adjustment you'll have to make. If, for example, you're a manager who spends a great deal of time mentoring and coaching your staff members on an informal basis and you intend to telecommute or cut back on your hours, you'll probably want to schedule blocks of office time that are expressly set aside for this kind of interaction.

Most of the people problems that may result from the change you're contemplating are solvable — as long as you're willing to recognize and address them.

How will it affect my career prospects in my company?

All things being equal, the degree to which your advancement opportunities in your current company may suffer as a result of your new work arrangement will depend on two factors:

✔ The nature of your occupation

✔ The culture of your company — or, to be more specific, the work habits of the senior executives in the company

In certain corporate cultures and in some fields (law, accounting, and management consulting, in particular), it's tough (though not impossible) to stay on the fast track unless you're willing to work unusually long hours and spend a lot of time on the road. You may struggle to meet these requirements under the new working arrangement.

Even in companies that actively encourage and support alternate working arrangements, your chances for advancement may still be hampered if the new arrangement has a negative impact on any of the following:

✔ **Your availability:** If you're unavailable time and again for key, high-profile assignments, a flexible work arrangement may reduce the likelihood that you'll be considered for a promotion.

✔ **Communication:** Make sure the quality — and frequency — of the communication you have with senior management doesn't diminish with the change in work schedule.

✔ **Goals and deadlines:** Your new arrangement shouldn't impair the ability of coworkers or your entire department to meet goals and deadlines.

How will it affect my home life and family?

Most people choose alternate work arrangements because they desire more control over their personal lives, so the answer to this question may seem obvious. Even so, make sure that you're aware of — and can accept — whatever adjustments may be necessary in your personal life when you start following a new routine. If the flextime arrangement you're seeking will oblige you to arrive at work an hour earlier in the morning, for example, you may need to make some adjustments in your nightlife — leaving the club at 2 a.m. instead of 3 a.m.!

If you're reducing your total number of hours, you may need to rebudget, to ensure that you'll have enough money to pay your bills. And if you're going to telecommute, don't underestimate the difficulty of "leaving the office behind" at the end of the day.

The purpose of Table 8-1 is to give you an overall picture of the career-related pros and cons of the various types of alternate work arrangements that your company may offer. Keep in mind that each alternate work arrangement is different. The pros and cons can vary considerably depending on your job, your company, and of course, you.

Table 8-1	Alternate Work Arrangements at a Glance	
	Pros	*Cons*
Part-time	Reduced total working hours. Access to most benefits and perks (sometimes on a pro-rated basis) that full-time workers enjoy.	Reduced total salary. Possible prorated benefits. Limited ability to take an active role in high-profile assignments.
Job sharing	Reduced total working hours.	Reduced total salary. Possible prorated benefits. Requires an unusually compatible relationship between you and the person with whom you're sharing the job. Overall job performance depends on skills and abilities of other person.
Flextime	Scheduling flexibility without reduced responsibilities or salary.	May prevent you from getting involved in important projects or meetings. Need to manage your time wisely.
Telecommuting	Eliminates commuting time. Flexibility with full-time status.	Doesn't lend itself to certain types of jobs, especially those requiring frequent, non-scheduled interactions with customers and with coworkers. Requires a home office or alternative workspace setup, which may entail expenditures on either your part or your company's part.

Making Your Case

Deciding to modify your working arrangement represents only one half of the alternate working arrangement equation. The second — and in some ways, more difficult — half is securing your company's or manager's approval. As you may expect, any number of factors can influence the final decision. Certain arrangements (flextime, for example) are easier to arrange than others (such as telecommuting), simply because the arrangement has less direct impact on how the work gets done.

Looking at things through their eyes

The mere fact that you're asking for a change in your working arrangement presupposes that the change is going to work for you. So rather than focusing your presentation on all the reasons the new arrangement is important to you ("My dog really needs me. He gets very upset when I'm not home."), focus instead on the business implications.

Look for the business benefits of the new arrangement. Perhaps the working hours you're seeking as part of the flextime arrangement enhance your company's ability to serve its customers. It's possible, too, that by telecommuting several days a week, you can free up additional office space.

Be careful, though. More often than not, your benefits from any alternate working arrangement outweigh the company's advantage. Be sure you can convince your manager that the change in working arrangements isn't going to impede the company's ability to achieve its strategic goals.

Waiting for the right time

If possible, wait until you've established yourself as a productive and valuable employee before you request any basic change in your working schedule. There's one notable exception to this principle. If you've already established an impressive record at one company and you're actively recruited by another, you can often negotiate the arrangement you want as part of your acceptance agreement (see Chapter 5). Otherwise, take the time to learn the job, build trust, and establish yourself as a valuable asset.

The more valued you are, the more leverage you have when negotiating your arrangement.

Getting your ducks in a row

Laying the groundwork before you present your ideas to your manager increases your chance of getting what you want. If you're interested in job sharing, first consider the job market. If good partners are hard to find, your arrangement may never happen. If you want to telecommute or scale down from full-time work to part-time, chart how projects you've completed under the old arrangement can be handled under the new arrangement. That way, when you eventually pitch the idea to your manager, you'll be better prepared to address any concerns.

Putting the proposal in writing

Your chances of getting approval for any alternate work arrangement are almost always better if you put the request in writing rather than winging it. Here's why writing the proposal is a good idea:

- ✔ **It's thorough.** When you take the time to write the proposal, you have to think your case through and explain it completely.

- ✔ **It's serious.** By putting the request in writing, it acquires more gravity.

- ✔ **It's documented.** Your supervisor receives tangible information that can be shared with the next level of management, if necessary.

If you lack confidence in your ability to write an effective proposal, seek help from a friend or colleague who's a skilled writer. And give yourself plenty of time to put together a proposal that is written clearly, concisely, and persuasively.

Estimating your leverage

The leverage you bring to any discussions about alternate working arrangements almost always depends on the value your company places on your work and contributions. If you're recognized as a top performer and your talent is in short supply in the local labor market, you're probably in a strong bargaining position.

As with any negotiation, though, you don't want to force the issue. And because you're still going to be working with your manager, whether the arrangement is approved or denied, you never want to take an adversarial stance. Nobody wins when a negotiation ends on a bitter note.

Allowing review time

However eager you may be to start your new arrangement, allow your supervisor time to mull it over and to discuss it with his or her manager. It's a good idea to have a target date in mind, but stay flexible: The decision-making process may involve several factors, and pushing for a quick answer may jeopardize your chances.

Offering something in return

Your chances of reaching an amicable agreement with your manager about your new schedule will always be better if you enter the discussion with the mindset of a negotiator. And, like any negotiator, be prepared to give up something in exchange for something you want.

In the beginning of any arrangement, offer to spend some extra time (without necessarily being paid for it) to make sure the transition goes smoothly. For example, as you begin your new flextime schedule, arrive early and stick around for an hour or so at the end of the day, just to make sure that all responsibilities are handled.

Telecommuting: A special situation

Telecommuting is one of the most sought-after alternate work arrangements, but it can also be the most difficult to establish. That's because telecommuting raises numerous issues that your company may have yet to completely resolve. Here's a look at some of those issues and what you should know about them:

✔ **Deciding who pays:** Telecommuting is such a recent practice that established norms regarding financial arrangements have yet to be established. Depending on the situation, you may be able to work out an arrangement in which your company agrees to either provide you with equipment or share some of the expense. But don't count on this support. To play it safe, be prepared to bear the brunt of whatever costs are involved in setting up your home office.

✔ **Making the transition:** Face-to-face communication is an important aspect of almost all jobs. In most telecommuting arrangements, you and your manager determine ahead of time how many days (and which days) you need to come in to the office. That number may range from a few times a month to two or three times a week. Whatever the number, the transition should be gradual so that everyone — you, your manager, and coworkers — has ample time to adapt.

✔ **Understanding insurance:** Most company insurance policies that relate to property are limited to equipment located on company premises. However, some companies have policies that also cover computers and other equipment located in the homes or apartments of employees. To ensure that you get the coverage you need, consider purchasing your own policy and negotiating partial reimbursement from your employer.

✔ **Workers' compensation:** Technically, you're covered by this insurance program when you become ill or are injured on the job. The problem with working out of your home or apartment is that your daily activities are often a mix of work and personal activities. For example, if you sprain your ankle while you're walking from your home office to your kitchen, are you covered? No easy answer exists. The best advice is to consult with your lawyer, insurance carrier, and state officials so that you can familiarize yourself with the rules before you begin your new work arrangement.

✔ **Protecting your work:** Telecommuting raises some security issues that are all the more critical if intellectual property is involved. If you want to work from your home, develop a plan to establish reasonable security precautions. (Your dog that sleeps by your computer isn't exactly what the risk-management folks in your company have in mind.) You may be asked to sign a written agreement that spells out your company's confidentiality policies and guidelines.

Adapting to Your New Routine

Assuming your request for an alternate work arrangement is approved, the next challenge you face is making a smooth transition from your old routine to the new. Take the initiative to make sure the arrangement works. There are no surefire formulas for guaranteeing success, but the guidelines covered in the following sections get you off to a good start.

Adopting a transition strategy

Give yourself (and the people you work with) at least two or three weeks to adjust to your new work arrangement. Change things gradually. If you're going to be job sharing, for example, be prepared to spend several days during the first few weeks of the arrangement working side by side with your new partner. If you're going to telecommute, be prepared during the first few weeks of the arrangement to go into the office — for a few hours, at least — on what would normally be a home day. If you're making a transition to flex-time, work some extra hours at first. Think of all these as insurance for the success of the arrangement.

Preventing problems

Without driving yourself nuts, be sensitive during the first few weeks to any glitch, problem, or unexpected challenge that may surface. Remember that any problem, no matter how minute, can mushroom into a crisis if you don't address it. Pay attention, too, to your own productivity as well as that of your staff members. If you see a significant drop in the quality of work, try to get to the root of the problem as soon as possible. Be aware of any changes in interactions with your manager. Request feedback on the transition and be sure to communicate frequently. Be proactive. Showing a willingness to make adjustments at the start will greatly reduce the possibility of much more significant changes later.

Staying in the loop

Be careful not to lose touch with what's going on in your company. Right from the beginning, give yourself time — when you're at the office — to talk with your coworkers or staff about recent developments. Be sure to schedule a little extra time when you're offsite to write lengthier e-mail messages or make additional phone calls that keep the lines of communication open.

Homework: Ten keys to working efficiently at home

Establishing a productive home office is critical to the success of a telecommuting arrangement. Here are ten guidelines that can help:

✔ Set up your office up in a separate room, if practical. Choose a quiet part of your house or apartment so that you can insulate yourself from day-to-day distractions.

✔ Establish protocols for answering your business phone. Make it a capital crime for anyone other than you to pick up your business line. If you can't take a call, let your answering machine or voice mail pick it up.

✔ Schedule repair or maintenance appointments at off-peak times. Arrange for your telephone to be dismantled during periods when you're least likely to get phone calls from the office or customers.

✔ Consider putting a lock on the door of your work area. At minimum, keep anything that's important — letters, files, computer disks, and so on — well out of the reach of young children.

✔ Set up a routine for backing up electronic files. The simplest option is a Zip disk that allows you to store hundreds of megabytes on one disk.

✔ Designate your computer for business use only. If others in your family need to use a computer, buy a separate one. You can't risk the possibility that your business files will be inadvertently deleted or revised.

✔ Create a work schedule and stick to it. Try your best not to blur the boundaries between your personal life and your work activities.

✔ Buy basic office supplies. Rather than taking them from the office, stock your own supply of printer paper, notepads, pens, paper clips, and so on. Keep a record of such expenses for reimbursement, if this is what you arrange in advance.

✔ Coordinate tech support. Get the name — before the need arises — of someone who can come to your rescue when you run into a computer crisis.

✔ Plan your telephone system very, very carefully. Depending on how much time you spend on the phone, how often you send or receive faxes, and how much you use the Internet, you may want to get a DSL line that allows you to share voice and data.

Chapter 9

Becoming a Peak Performer

*I*n business, as in most endeavors, your ability to excel depends on more than just your talent, skills, and knowledge. It also depends on whether your day-to-day work habits are helping you maximize those attributes.

This chapter gives you a chance to focus on the basics of day-to-day job performance. You get a look at the attributes — apart from talent, knowledge, and skills — that separate peak performers from everyone else in their respective occupations. You also get some insightful advice on how to adopt a peak performer mindset and how to do something that everyone needs to know how to do well: manage time. Finally, you get some advice on yet another critical skill — decision making.

The Road to Mastery: What You Can Discover from Peak Performers

Every field, from business to music to sports, has its own elite cadre of *peak performers* — people who are able to maintain consistently high levels of performance over extended periods. And they are capable of doing so without wreaking havoc on themselves or the people with whom they live and work. Among the individuals whose names spring to mind when the term "peak performer" is mentioned are high-profile entertainment and sports celebrities such as Michael Jordan, Bill Cosby, and Barbara Walters. But the vast majority of peak performers aren't athletes, entertainers, or household names. They're businesspeople, lawyers, teachers, physicians, scientists, designers, editors, sales professionals, and politicians who, quite apart from their differences, all share one quality. They're able to accomplish more — and in less time — than the typical practitioner in their respective fields.

What sets these individuals apart from their counterparts is a question that has been of interest to behavioral scientists for nearly 20 years. A psychologist named Charles Garfield got the ball rolling in the 1980s with a book called *Peak Performers,* but numerous books and studies have been released since then. And the effort to gain more insight into what makes peak performers soar has led to the HR practice generally known as *competency modeling.* This is a practice of establishing hiring criteria based on the skills and attributes of the most successful performers in any given job specialty.

Unfortunately, the results of this research have yet to produce a true science of peak performance. Not every investigator has reached the same conclusions or has used the same terminology to describe specific attributes. Still, certain patterns are clearly emerging from this research. What follows is a brief description of six different attributes that are shared, to varying degrees, by all peak performers.

As you read through the descriptions, ask yourself whether you possess these attributes and to what extent. Keep in mind that what underlies peak performance is not so much excellence in one or more of these categories but outstanding performance in all of them.

- **They focus on the goal.** All peak performers possess what Charles Garfield first described in the 1980s as "an image of a desired state of affairs that inspires action." In other words, they're goal-oriented. They have a clearly defined, well-thought-out vision of where they want to go in their lives, and their day-to-day actions are rooted in a set of clearly defined values. This clarity of vision is the chief reason peak performers tend to manage their time so efficiently. Constantly tuned in to their priorities and values, they have little trouble differentiating essential and nonessential tasks. So while peak performers don't necessarily work as hard or as long as others on the same tasks, they invariably focus on the right tasks and they get the most out of their efforts.

- **They're committed to personal mastery.** Whether they earn their living shooting a basketball, composing music, writing code, or teaching math, peak performers have an unadulterated commitment to excellence, a desire to excel that originates from within. Although they may enjoy public recognition and other external rewards of success, peak performers typically judge the quality of their work by their own standards of excellence — standards that are invariably higher than the norm.

✔ **They're positive thinkers.** Peak performers tend to be optimists. The glass is always half-full, never half-empty. Whether this optimism is driven by the success they've attained — or vice-versa — is one of those chicken-and-egg conundrums. This much, however, is clear. Peak performers aren't simply wishful thinkers. They neither ignore nor oversimplify problems. They don't let problems intimidate them. Problems are there to be solved, not fretted over. Setbacks are an opportunity to learn and do a better job next time. No sulking allowed. Their optimism goes a long way to explain why peak performers tend to bounce back so quickly from adversity. It was often said of basketball legend Michael Jordan that he was always the most dangerous in a game that followed one in which he hadn't played well.

✔ **Each knows how to keep his or her eye on the ball.** Peak performers have an uncanny ability to focus their attention on the task at hand, regardless of how much chaos may be raging around them. Some people refer to this attribute as the ability to *compartmentalize*. Whatever it's called, it's not an attribute that comes naturally or easily to most. One of the keys to concentrating fully on the task at hand is, of course, motivation: You need to know why you're doing something and why it's important. But other factors — some of them surprisingly routine — can have an impact as well. Your physical condition, for example — simply being in good shape — can go a long way to keep you mentally alert. Your diet, sleeping habits, and general lifestyle are also important.

✔ **They seek — and receive — the support of others.** Contrary to myth, peak performers aren't generally Supermen or Lone Rangers who neither need nor seek the help and support of others. On the contrary, they are able to practice what Stephen R. Covey has described as *creative cooperation*. Peak performers are usually well aware not only of their strengths but also their limitations. They know how to ask for — and receive — the support needed from coworkers, teammates, family, and friends. They also understand that cooperation is a two-way street: If you rely on others for support, you need to reciprocate.

✔ **They're emotionally well balanced.** Behavioral scientists who study peak performers describe this quality in different ways. Some refer to it as *centered*. More recently, it's been described as *emotional intelligence*. However you describe it, the implications are the same. Peak performers do a good job of managing their emotions. They're centered. They can be passionate without being out of control, alert without being obsessive, and vigilant without being fearful. Whether this ability to put emotional energy to productive and positive use is innate or an attribute that peak performers have developed over time is a matter of debate. But it's generally agreed that this particular attribute — emotional balance — is the linchpin of peak performance qualities.

The qualities described above are interrelated. The more clearly defined your goals are, for example, the more likely it is that you'll invest the time and effort it takes to develop personal mastery. The more emotionally balanced you are, the easier it is for you to get the most out of your ability to concentrate and bring a positive outlook to your day-to-day life.

Developing a Peak Performance Mindset

Business books and publications are a fertile source of advice on emulating the practices of peak performers. But your ability to put this information to effective use in your life depends on two things: your values and your mindset. Self-improvement begins with self-knowledge — a clear understanding of what you want and why you want it. With this observation in mind, the following sections cover four principles to think about before you try to incorporate any time-management techniques into your day-to-day activities.

Clarifying your priorities

To some people, becoming more productive is essentially a technical challenge. It's all about setting goals, creating daily to-do lists, rolling up your sleeves, and making sure that each item on the list is checked off before the end of the day.

There is undoubtedly something to be said for this way of thinking. And you may indeed be justified in feeling a sense of accomplishment if, at day's end, you can look at your to-do list and see the comforting presence of little check marks after every item.

But as most time-management gurus will tell you, a set of goals and daily to-do lists (as well as other time-management systems) are simply tools designed to help you keep track of and accomplish daily tasks — no more, no less. The fact that you've completed all the tasks doesn't necessarily mean that you've operated effectively that day in your job. And it doesn't mean that you've accomplished anything that produces long-term satisfaction or brings you closer to strategic career goals. Implicit in this observation is the need to prioritize — and equally important, to prioritize on the basis of criteria that are keyed to your long-term life goals. Every time-management product or system has its own recommendations on how to manage priorities. The most common method consists of giving each task on your to-do list a numerical value (1, 2, or 3) that reflects its relative importance. A to-do list that has 12 items, for example, may include three 1s, (high priority), four 2s (normal priority), and five 3s (low priority).

But the value you ultimately derive from this approach can nonetheless be limited. The critical issue in prioritizing isn't so much differentiating tasks on the basis of their importance. It's establishing the criteria that define the tasks as high priority. In other words, what's important are the values that underlie your decisions. A common failure among less productive workers is not necessarily a lack of planning, prioritizing, or hard work. It's simply that their method for prioritizing focuses too much on immediate tasks and deadlines — with little attention paid to long-term strategic goals and personal values. Consequently, many people spend the bulk of their days putting out brush fires that keep flaring up time and again, and they rarely get around to doing something to prevent the fires from occurring in the first place.

Unfortunately, there is no quick fix for this common syndrome. It requires a willingness to invest the time and effort in self-examination as you clarify where you want to go in your life and your daily objectives. You may need to revisit your strategic career plan and review your objectives (see Chapter 1). Are they still relevant? You may want to request a meeting with your manager to discuss your job priorities and responsibilities. Do you have a clear picture of what's expected? As you continue to refine both your long-term and short-term goals, your priorities will become more clear.

Using systems thinking

Systems thinking as outlined by Peter Senge in *The Fifth Discipline* is the process of seeing the big picture instead of merely individual parts. (See Chapter 22 for more on *The Fifth Discipline*.) Viewed in the context of peak job performance and career management, systems thinking helps you view your job as more than a series of disparate tasks and responsibilities (some of which you may be good at and enjoy but others with which you struggle and don't enjoy). You see things as an integrated whole. For example, instead of seeing a typical work day as a series of job parts — a string of tasks, meetings, and interactions, each with its own challenges — you see everything as an integrated entity. When you run into problems, you don't focus solely on that part that's giving you trouble. You look instead at the system and try to figure out what has happened structurally in that system to create the problem.

Consider the following example. Assume that you head a department that provides graphic design for executive presentations. Over the past few weeks the managers giving these presentations have complained about glitches (ouch!). Logic may lead you to find out who is responsible for the mistakes, but if you're a systems thinker, you don't stop there. In addition to talking to employees who've been working on the presentations, you step back and consider the overall process by which the graphics are generated: the software that's used, the software's compatibility with hardware that managers use, and the communication between your staff and the managers who deliver the presentations. You then use this insight to implement solutions that affect the system, not just one symptom of it.

The value of systems thinking is that it helps you develop and maintain a big-picture perspective. Because you're focusing on how all the various parts of your day relate to one another, you can begin to think more synergistically — that is, manage your time so that each task you perform enhances your ability to perform all tasks.

Becoming more sensitive to process

Whether you realize it or not, you already go through a process in every aspect of your job. The question is whether you're consciously aware of it and whether the process is the most efficient and productive way to get the job done.

A critical first step in improving your productivity is carefully analyzing every aspect of your job to isolate those areas that need improvement. After all, before you can change habits and develop new skills, you need to identify where you need improvement. To perform this analysis, set aside several hours of quiet time to consider the following:

- **Method:** Is there a particular reason for handling this task the way you're now handling it? Is this the only or most efficient way to do things?

- **Side effects:** Which aspects of the process (if any) are creating problems and interfering with your efficiency and productivity (and perhaps the efficiency and productivity of others you work with)?

- **Process improvements:** What changes can you make to either solve or minimize the impact of these problems?

- **Outcome:** How will you measure the results of those changes to be sure you're achieving the desired effect?

To get the most from this exercise, be willing to examine every aspect of your job, no matter how rote or mundane it may seem to you. It's obvious, too, you need to set aside — temporarily, at least — any preconceptions you may have about the best way to handle a particular task. To expand your frame of reference, consider how others tackle a similar responsibility or assignment. Approach this exercise with an open mind, and you may be surprised by your ability to develop creative new ways to handle old challenges.

Becoming Better at Managing Your Time

Any initiative to enhance job effectiveness ultimately obliges you to focus on how efficiently you manage your time. Simply put, you have to make sure that you're not only working hard but also working smart — getting maximum results from the time and energy you spend on specific tasks.

The ultimate goal in time management isn't simply to accomplish more in less time. The ultimate goal is balance, harmony, and overall job satisfaction. You want to be as productive as you can possibly be, but you don't want to become so focused on getting things done that you lose sight of long-term goals. And you don't want to push so relentlessly that you neglect the personal priorities in your life and run the risk of falling victim to burnout.

The best way to gain more control over your time is to conduct your own time-management audit. (Relax, this task sounds a lot more intimidating than it actually is.) A *time-management audit* is nothing more than a detailed log of how you spend time on a moment-by-moment basis over the course of a week.

You don't need to go to extremes in this process and, for example, hire an assistant who follows you around and keeps a record of every time you blink. All you have to do is keep a notepad (or an electronic organizer, if you have one) handy in your office. Every hour or so, take a few minutes to note how you spent the previous hour. The more detailed you can be, the better, but don't drive yourself crazy trying to account for every second. Just be sure to indicate how much time you spend doing routine things like talking on the phone or filing paperwork.

After keeping a log for at least five days (and, for best results, these should be typical work days), analyze your time-usage patterns. To make things easier, divide the various activities you've written down into discrete categories, such as "conversations with customers," "personal errands," business meetings," "writing memos," and so on. Don't worry at first about having too many categories; you can always consolidate later. The key question is this: Is there a logical connection between the importance of an activity and the amount of time spent on that activity?

This exercise helps you gain insight into how much time you squander on tasks that don't produce the results you want. Here are some other questions to ponder as you go through this exercise:

- ✔ **What are the results?** Generally speaking, are you able to achieve the goals you set for any given day? And if not, what changes can you make that may help you do so?

- ✔ **How can you change?** Is there any way to spend less time on less important tasks without decreasing your overall productivity?

- ✔ **Are there time constraints?** How often — if at all — are you under extreme pressure to meet deadlines?

- ✔ **Who's in control?** Are you, for the most part, in control of you time, or is your schedule controlling you?

- ✔ **What are your priorities?** Are you able to allocate sufficient time — quality time — to the tasks that are the most important to you, your job, and your career?

Resist the temptation to take action before completing the exercise. The time will come for action, but first you need some time to thoroughly review and evaluate the situation. And don't worry for now about making judgments on how well you're managing your time. Focus instead on which tasks and priorities are taking up the bulk of your time. Make sure those tasks are moving you in the right direction. If this isn't the case, readjust your priorities or rethink your strategic career plan (see Chapter 2).

Success Secrets for Time Management

Time management is one of the most frequently discussed skills in business today, and so you may have had your fill of advice on how to handle the purely technical aspects of this challenge. But the fundamentals that underlie the information in the following sections are always worth a review. For more information on the subject, take a look at *Time Management For Dummies* by Jeffrey J. Mayer (IDG Books Worldwide, Inc.).

Creating a time-management system

No one — particularly anyone who leads a very busy life — can expect to manage time without the help of some external tool or system (as opposed to keeping everything in your head). There are countless gizmos, software packages, and calendar-based diaries on the market today that are designed to help you manage your time more efficiently. Prices can range anywhere from $10 or less for an at-a-glance diary to several hundred dollars for a Palm Pilot that can link to your PC. But as most time-management experts can tell you, your success has less to do with which method or system you use and much more to do with your commitment to using that method or system.

Don't be afraid to experiment. Chances are, the software you're currently using already has a calendar program of sorts. Start using it. And if you're reluctant to invest money in a system that you may not find to your liking, start off with nothing more than a legal pad. Make lists and rough out a daily schedule. In short, start developing the discipline and the habits that underlie successful time management before you start investing heavily in the technology of the process.

Drawing up a daily plan

Time-management experts have different views about the more subtle aspects of their advice. But they share a universal belief in the importance of spending at least 10 or 15 minutes at the start of every day mapping out priorities. Use this time not only to develop a general snapshot of what you hope to accomplish that day, but also to sketch out a rough schedule. Don't fall victim to the misconception that setting up a structured schedule somehow limits your options. On the contrary, the structure and control you create by mapping out a daily plan usually enhances your ability to take advantage of alternatives and options.

Should you find yourself on a particular day with two or three hours of open time, you may want to refer to your master list and find a task that has strategic importance, but that you haven't been able to attend to. You can also use that open time to focus on tasks — reorganizing the files on your hard drive, for example — that increase efficiency.

Consolidating similar tasks

People are often more productive when working for an extended period in the same mental mode, as opposed to changing mental gears frequently. Do your best to cluster tasks that require similar efforts or resources into the same time frame. For example, if you're working on three or four projects, each of which requires Internet research, try to gather the information for all the projects during the same block of time. If several of the projects require e-mail or other correspondence, handle those writing tasks at the same time.

Controlling distractions

Distractions and interruptions are unavoidable in most workplaces, but with discipline, you can minimize their impact. Here are some ideas on how to accomplish this often elusive objective:

- **Find the right space.** Whenever you're working on a task that requires concentration — writing a report, for example — find a place where you can you work in relative peace and quiet, such as a conference room. (Note: Asking to go the beach so that you can concentrate may not be well received.)

- **Curtail interruptions.** Discourage family members and close friends from calling you (except for emergencies, of course) during those periods of the day when you're likely to be the busiest. (And don't even think about encouraging them to drop by the office when they're in the neighborhood.)

- **Screen calls.** Unless you have a job in which every phone call you get has critical significance (or protocol forbids this), let any calls that come during busy periods roll to your voice mail. Set aside certain blocks of time during the day when you check your messages and return calls.

✔ **Defer requests.** When people come to you with important requests while you're trying to maintain your concentration, ask politely if you can address the issue at another time. (Key exception: When the request is to verify your name and address for forwarding your state lottery check, you may want to respond promptly.)

Setting up disciplined protocols for routine tasks

Imagine for a moment what it would be like if every time you got into your car, you had to stop and think to yourself, "Okay, let me see. I guess the first thing I should do is put in the key. Okay, what's next? Oh, yeah. I should turn the key. But which pedal should I press? The one on the left or the right?" None of this happens, of course, with experienced drivers. That's because after you master how to drive, tasks that once required conscious thought become automatic. You no longer have to think about the steps and yet you're still able to start the car.

Now consider how you handle routine aspects of your job. How much time do you spend — or waste! — making decisions about such routine tasks as storing certain files in your computer or organizing hard-copy correspondence? How much time do you waste looking for the phone numbers of people you call two or three times a week? Take some time to note the tasks you perform repeatedly during a typical day. Little by little, set up protocols to handle these tasks as efficiently and as effortlessly as starting your car. The following are some areas you may want to focus on:

✔ **Location of key supplies:** Do you know exactly where to go when you're looking for routine office supplies, such as envelopes, paper clips, pens, or stationery?

✔ **Streamlining computer tasks:** Have you experimented with methods — macros, for example — that can reduce the number of key strokes for certain functions, words, or phrases that you use over and over? (If you think you need assistance, refer to the *...For Dummies* book for your particular word-processing program, or ask for the help of a computer whiz.)

✔ **File organization:** Do you have a logical filing system, whether it's on computer or in a filing cabinet? (Here's a clue: If you can't get your hands on a filed document in less than 30 seconds, you need to rethink your system.)

✔ **Speed dialing:** Have you taken the time to program your phone (assuming it has that capability) to speed-dial numbers you call frequently? If not, do you have a list or computer file that allows instant access to the numbers of people you call regularly?

Allowing time to recharge

Like the fuel in the car you drive, the mental energy that keeps you alert and gives you the power to concentrate needs replenishing. If you're not doing so already, regularly schedule some time to mentally recharge. Five- or ten-minute breaks, strategically scheduled throughout the work day, can mean the difference between consistent productivity and fatigue that sneaks up on you (yawn!) during a staff meeting. And if you've been through several months in which you were constantly under the gun, give yourself time to unwind. Even if you can't spare the time to take a lot of time off, ease up on your schedule a little — request the opportunity to come in an hour or so later or leave earlier for a day or two.

Finding a way to say "no"

Sometimes, especially when you're on task overload, you may need to politely decline some less critical requests. At issue are tasks and requests that aren't crucial to your job or the strategic goals of the organization.

If the person asking you to do one more thing is your supervisor, be careful. Sit down with your boss, explain your scope of responsibilities, and get some direction on which priorities you should focus. Similarly, you want to be a team player, which means that if other members of your department or team need help, don't whine about how much stress you yourself are under. Simply explain that you're currently a bit overloaded but would be happy to help on the next project.

Customizing your schedule

As much as possible — and as long as it doesn't inconvenience the people with whom and for whom you work — try to structure your day in a way that's well suited to your style of working. Because many people are more productive during the morning hours, time-management gurus usually recommend that the most mentally challenging tasks of the day be scheduled for this time. That's good advice if you're like most people, but if your biological clock doesn't work like everyone else's, you may want to schedule your best work during the late afternoon. Don't be afraid to experiment. Find your own peak times and organize your schedule around those hours.

Growing from experience

When mapping out a schedule for a new type of project or event, make a reasonable guess as to how long it will take and then add some extra time. If you're finished ahead of time, adjust your estimate the next time around. But if the task turns out to be much more time-consuming and difficult than you originally thought, you'll appreciate the padding. Adding extra time to your schedule is a good idea, especially if special circumstances existed the last time that don't apply to your current project.

If you find yourself constantly running late on projects, you probably suffer from a common time-management malady: underestimating the time needed to complete a task or project. Program in more time than you think you're going to need just to be on the safe side.

Accepting mistakes

Don't be too quick to condemn yourself when, despite your best efforts, you find yourself hopelessly behind or bogged down occasionally. Remember, tomorrow is another day — a fresh start.

Kicking the Procrastination Habit

Putting things off until the last possible moment or neglecting tasks that are unpleasant, boring, or uncomfortable is easy to do. As long as you keep yourself in check, occasional procrastination is nothing to lose sleep over. But if it becomes a habit, the consequences can be severe — not only for you, but for the people who depend on you.

Fortunately, procrastination isn't a disease; it's a pattern of behavior. Yes, there may be some deep-rooted psychological reasons behind the habit — fear of failure, fear of success, fear of finding out what you're afraid of — but it's something you can control and if you work at it, overcome. The following advice represents the best wisdom on how to get your procrastination tendencies under control.

- ✔ **Figure out what it's costing you.** Calculate how much time you waste when you have to bail yourself out of a problem that wouldn't have arisen had you addressed a situation more promptly.

- ✔ **Think small.** Whenever you're faced with a big, complicated project that you avoid tackling, break it down into smaller tasks, and commit yourself to work on it step-by-step until you're finished.

✔ **Audit your procrastination habits.** Think back to all the things you intended to do over the past three months but never got around to and consider the following:

- **The missing link:** How many important events did you have to either miss entirely or cut short because you had to attend to tasks that had been put off?

- **Interpersonal strain:** How often have work relationships been strained because you failed to follow through on your obligations?

- **Inner stress:** How much unnecessary pressure did you put upon yourself by not taking care of things earlier?

Striving for Perfection

One of the occupational hazards of aspiring to peak performance is a behavioral pattern generally known as *perfectionism.* A good way to define perfectionism is to think of it as taking a good thing too far. The "good thing" is high standards, which, of course, you need to set for yourself in order to be successful. But when the standards you set are unrealistically high or virtually impossible to achieve in light of the realities of any given situation, that positive tendency can become an obstacle to your success and a source of frustration for both you and the people you work with. Some of the problems that perfectionism can cause include the following:

✔ **Missed deadlines:** You spend too much time on details or considerations that aren't critical to the ultimate objective.

✔ **Strained work relationships:** Staff or coworkers resent spending extra time or effort on truly unimportant details, thus neglecting critical aspects. In addition, you don't trust others, making it difficult to share responsibility or delegate.

✔ **Lack of direction:** Defining goals and expectations for others is extremely difficult.

✔ **High anxiety:** You develop a general (and usually unwarranted) sense of anxiety about being good enough. This can even lead to physical ailments such as ulcers, migraine headaches, and clinical depression.

Numerous theories have been advanced to explain what compels certain people to take their perfectionist tendencies to excessive and usually self-defeating extremes. But most psychologists who've studied this behavioral phenomenon agree on at least two points. The first is that most perfectionists developed these habits at an early age. The second is that even those perfectionists who recognize the folly of their ways have a difficult time making any meaningful change in their behavior. For many, a major crisis — a heart attack, for example, or the loss of a job — is the only catalyst for change.

Fortunately, most people who have a strong desire to excel and set high standards are able to maintain the perspective that separates peak performers from perfectionists. But if you find yourself developing a perfectionist's mindset, here are four suggestions to keep in mind.

- ✔ **Select a realistic goal.** Whenever you're setting standards for a task, consider first your ideal goal, but adjust it to meet expectations that you and everyone else can reasonably accept. You can aspire to the ideal standard, but if you don't establish realistic goals, you'll never truly succeed.

- ✔ **Ask for help:** Find coworkers whom you trust and respect and ask for their assistance in monitoring your efforts. In other words, give them the right to tell you that enough is enough.

- ✔ **Reduce stress.** Take note of any added stress you may put on yourself or others because of your tendencies. Revise your goal to limit unnecessary stress and disruption.

- ✔ **Find ways to relax.** Choose leisure activities in which there is no benefit to achieving or excelling. Prove to yourself that you can enjoy something without necessarily being the best at it.

Making Better Decisions

Making decisions is such a fundamental component of most people's day-to-day business routine that there's a tendency to underestimate the skills and attributes needed. Your ability to make effective decisions inevitably affects your job performance, so understanding the process is critical. The following sections outline several general principles to keep in mind.

Gathering information carefully

To make an informed decision, you need good information. And thanks to the Internet, gathering information is much easier than it used to be. This improved access to information has proven to be a mixed blessing because it easily leads to information overload. The challenge, then, is to be disciplined in gathering information. Decide ahead of time what you need to find. If you want to research and select a vendor to process your company's mail, first determine the criteria you're going to use to make the decision. Which factors are important: price, speed, reputation, familiarity with your business? After you establish the criteria, rank them according to importance. You're then in a position to effectively evaluate and sort the information you gather.

Becoming aware of your biases

A bias is a preexisting attitude or judgment that diminishes your ability to objectively evaluate information. Here's an example: Assume that ten years ago you had a horrific experience with a computer manufactured by a certain company, and decided that, sure, you'd be willing to buy a product from that company again — but the sun would have to freeze over first. Now assume that the company has addressed the problems it once had and now makes, hands down, the best product on the market. If your bias against that company overrides this information, you're not going to make the best decision.

Everyone has biases. The trick is to be sufficiently aware of them when making decisions.

Talking it out with others

As long as you don't allow discussions to drag on for too long, seeking out people you can use as a sounding board for important decisions makes sense. Consider this approach to be like thinking out loud. The people you select should not only be knowledgeable enough to provide objective feedback, but should also be candid. You don't need advisors who tell you what they think you want to hear. As you network professionally, you'll develop a large bank of collective wisdom from which you can draw — and to which you can contribute.

Trusting your instincts — sometimes

Sometimes, when making decisions, logic tells you one thing but your intuition tells you something else. Intuition is any thought or opinion that simply feels right to you. It has been formed without the use of any conscious cognitive process. Many successful CEOs rely as much on their intuition as they do on the facts. (Keep in mind, however, that intuition is usually the product of many years of decision-making experience.)

The best advice: Don't hesitate to consider your intuition during the decision-making process — but don't allow it to blind you to the facts.

Evaluating the process versus the result

Don't fall victim to the common practice of judging the effectiveness of a decision on the basis of its result. Here's an example. Assume that two weeks ago you were shopping for a printer and had narrowed down your choice to two models: the Megaprint and the Gloriprint. Assume, too, that the Megaprint had a couple of additional features but cost $200 more. You thought about it, decided that the extra features weren't worth the $200 (who needs a printer that plays polka music) and decided to buy the Gloriprint. You're happy with your decision until you read in the paper two weeks later that the manufacturer of Megaprint has lowered the price of its printer by $250.

In other words, you think that you made a bad decision. Wrong! However natural it may be to assume that you made a mistake when things don't turn out the way you hoped they would, don't second-guess yourself. Based on the information you had at the time and the criteria you were using, you made the right decision to buy the Gloriprint.

The soundness of a decision is based on how diligently you handled the decision-making process and not necessarily on the outcome. No one can predict the future. What you can do, however, is to make the best possible decision based on the information you have at the time.

Improving on your mistakes

One good way to improve your decision-making skills is to look back on decisions you've made and analyze the process. Here are some questions to ask yourself:

- **Was the information sufficient?** Did I gather enough data to make an informed decision? If not, where did I go wrong?

- **Was the information reliable?** Did I base my decision on false information?

- **Were assumptions accurate?** Were some of my assumptions reflexive or automatic? Did I make incorrect assumptions about the quality of the information? Or did I overlook certain information and make inaccurate assumptions as a result?

- **Did my biases and prejudgments interfere?** What effect did they have on my final decision? If I had the decision to make over again, what would I evaluate differently?

Chapter 10

Bouncing Back from Adversity

- -

In This Chapter

▶ Anticipating the bumps ahead

▶ Avoiding burnout

▶ Getting back on your feet

- -

*I*f you read the biographies of highly successful people — business people, in particular — you can't help but notice how often you come across the word "failure."

✔ In 1966, for example, an explosion occurred in a General Electric pilot plastics plant, and the person who "failed" in this example was a plant manager, Jack Welch, who went on to become one of the most successful and best-known CEOs of the 20th century.

✔ In 1978, a retailing executive named Bernie Marcus was fired by his boss at a company called Handy Dan's. Not long afterward, Marcus and his partner secured some outside financing and opened up the first in what would eventually become a multibillion-dollar chain of hardware stores known as Home Depot.

These are just two of the numerous examples illustrating a paradox that nearly all highly successful people experience: Success includes failure. True, when you're the person whose project blows up (figuratively speaking), or you're fired or passed over for a promotion, this paradox can be hard to accept. The point, however, is that highly successful people don't necessarily fail less frequently or suffer fewer setbacks than others. On the contrary, they typically take more smart risks than others, and, therefore, experience a fair share of failures. But they have an uncanny ability to rebound from setbacks and, more importantly, convert failures into success.

This chapter looks at an aspect of career management that's unpleasant to think about but important to consider: career setbacks — everything from major blows, such as getting fired, to minor bumps in the road, such as receiving a less-than-stellar performance review. In this chapter, I also include insights into recognizing — without overreacting to — danger signs that may indicate job-related problems down the road. This chapter also shares information about an increasingly common workplace phenomenon known as job burnout, and you discover how to prevent it and how to deal with it when it strikes. And you receive some solid, real-world advice on how to get back on the right track quickly and decisively when your plans and aspirations have been temporarily derailed.

How to Head Trouble Off at the Pass

The best thing you can do to cope effectively with career setbacks is to be proactive — that is, to prepare as well as possible for whatever lies ahead, professionally speaking. To do this, of course, you need to be able to recognize — before you break an axle — that the road ahead may have unexpected bumps. And that's not always easy to do. You may have no way of knowing, for example — until you hear about it on the 11 o'clock news — that somebody else has already applied for and received a patent for the invention you've been working on for the past seven years. And you may have no way of knowing that one of your most trusted lieutenants (who is now asking for a prolonged leave of absence) is really looking for other employment and has no intention of returning to his current position.

More often than not, however, setbacks don't suddenly materialize. The circumstances that lead up to the ultimate event are often warning signs that point in that direction. In retrospect, you sometimes wonder how you could have been so blind. The challenge, of course, is to be able to recognize these signs early enough so that you can either prevent the situation entirely or, at the very least, minimize its impact.

With this observation in mind, here are some of the common situations in business that can be notoriously fertile breeding grounds for future setbacks. As you read through the sections that follow, keep in mind that these situations don't inevitably indicate trouble. You simply need to be on guard.

Riding out a drop-off in business

Nobody can afford to rest easy when a company's sales and profits are on the decline. If your organization is experiencing rough times, you should be doing two things:

> ✔ **Make every effort to help your company weather the storm.** This may mean working extra hours at the office, looking for ways to cut expenses without sacrificing productivity, or volunteering for extra assignments that may bring in new business.

> ✔ **Draw up a contingency plan.** Make sure you're prepared to launch a job search. Update your resume and make a list of contacts who can help you uncover leads (see Chapter 5). If you even suspect a remote chance that you may be laid off, you need to get your finances in order. (Now may not be the best time, for example, to lay out $2000 on a home entertainment system.)

What you don't want to do in this situation, of course, is push the panic button too soon. Your company may ride out the storm, and your contributions during that difficult period may be recognized and rewarded. But if business progressively declines and you're prepared, you're in a much better position to take the hit with minimum damage to your career, psyche, and life in general.

Weathering a changing of the guard

You wouldn't be normal if you weren't at least a little uneasy about any change in management that affects your job performance and its evaluation. And if the change results in a new supervisor, a business-as-usual attitude is not in your best interest.

The issue here isn't competence — yours or your new boss's. It has more to do with working styles. Your new manager, for example, may not believe in delegating as much as your old boss. Or he or she may allow you a good deal more — or less — autonomy than you previously had. You'll have to adjust. You also have no way of knowing — until you've had a chance to work together — whether the two of you share a common vision of your role and the priorities that govern your day-to-day actions.

You don't want to overreact. Keep in mind, however, that if you don't have a good relationship with your new manager, your performance reviews may reflect this and raises may be hard to come by. It will also be extremely difficult for you to enjoy your job or progress in your career.

Take the opportunity early on to create a positive, harmonious relationship. Here are some simple guidelines to help you get off to a good start:

> ✔ **Keep an open mind.** Regardless of how many horror stories you may have heard about your new supervisor ("Attila the Hun was a pussycat compared to this guy!"), reserve judgment until you've had a chance to meet with and work for this person.
>
> ✔ **Go out of your way to be supportive.** Avoid the temptation to compare your old boss and your new boss (especially in his or her presence). If asked to do so, offer suggestions on how things could be done, but if you and your supervisor disagree, be flexible. Give your new manager time to adapt, evaluate, and establish the practices he or she deems appropriate. You'll have other opportunities in the future to suggest changes and offer your opinions.

✔ **Link your job with strategic goals.** If you have reason to believe that your new supervisor is under pressure to cut staff, make sure you can articulate the strategic implications of your job — how your responsibilities are keyed to the company's strategic goals.

Surviving the project from hell

Being involved in (or, worse, being responsible for) one of those projects that has been plagued from the start with nightmarish problems is never a happy experience — and not usually a good thing for your next performance review or career move. The best case scenario, of course, is to rescue the project and emerge as the hero. Some projects, however, are simply not salvageable.

If you're convinced that this is the case in your situation — and be sure not to overreact — here's what you may consider doing:

✔ **Recognize the demise.** If you're the key decision maker on a project that has spiraled out of control and has little chance of achieving its objectives, summon the courage to end the project and redirect your efforts, thereby cutting your losses. You'll have to take some heat — that's a given — but better now than two or three months later when the damage is far more extensive. However, if you're not the key decision-maker, make sure that at the very least you're fulfilling your responsibilities to the best of your ability. As long as you're pulling your weight and planning ahead, it's unlikely that you'll be blamed for the failure.

✔ **Own up.** When the time comes to accept responsibility for things that may have gone wrong in a failed project, be willing to shoulder your share of the blame (even if, in your view, the other guys caused it). If there were miscalculations from the start, let others know what those miscalculations were — and what you've learned from them. Don't dig yourself into a deeper hole by trying to pin the blame on other departments or on senior management.

✔ **Put it behind you.** Everyone in business makes mistakes. The one mistake you don't want to make is allowing the aftereffects of a failed project to erode your confidence and sabotage your efforts in future projects. After you analyze what went wrong in the previous project and take responsibility, put the experience behind you — and leave it there.

Losing the edge

The one factor that can significantly affect the number — and severity — of career setbacks you absorb is also the one aspect over which you have the most control: your ability to maintain sufficient enthusiasm and passion for your work. After your enthusiasm starts to ebb, you'll have a tougher time focusing on each task and maintaining a high standard of performance. What happens, instead, are careless mistakes. You're not as diligent as you once were in meeting deadlines. And projects that used to go smoothly are now running into constant problems — not because you lack the skills required to do the job, but because you're simply not paying attention to what you're doing.

If you find yourself in this type of pattern, it's usually due to one of two reasons:

- **You're overworked and beginning to burn out.** If the problem is burnout, the next section offers some helpful advice.

- **You're bored.** If boredom is the culprit, take the initiative. Look for ways to adjust your job to recapture the enthusiasm you've lost. Here are some suggestions on how to do this:

  - Ask yourself when was the last time you learned something new in your job. If you can't come up with an answer, look for opportunities within your position to expand your knowledge and awareness — especially in areas that will enhance your long-term career prospects.

  - Talk to your manager about acquiring some additional responsibilities, making sure, of course, that you have the skills, time, and resources required to handle those responsibilities.

  - Analyze your job on a task-by-task basis to see if you can minimize the time you spend on tedious and uninteresting aspects of the position. Try to concentrate on those areas of responsibility that you enjoy.

Don't allow short-term disappointments to sabotage the quality of your work. If you decide that you want a change, careless or shoddy work won't persuade anyone to assign you new responsibilities.

Coping with Burnout

Burnout is best defined as psychological exhaustion brought on by prolonged periods of job-related stress. There may or may not be anything wrong with you physically when you're burned out, but you've nonetheless reached the point at which even the most routine job tasks — dealing with a customer complaint, writing a memo, filling out an expense sheet — seem to be challenges of Everest-like proportions. Among the most common symptoms of job burnout are the following:

- **Physical problems:** These may include loss of appetite, increased susceptibility to colds and other minor ailments, or a generalized and prolonged feeling of fatigue and overexertion.

- **Mental agitation:** This is usually manifested through sleep difficulties (insomnia, bad dreams), short-term forgetfulness (your left hand doesn't know what you're right hand is doing half the time), an inability to focus, or difficulty concentrating.

✔ **Emotional upset:** This can express itself as increased irritability and impatience (a short fuse) or as a pervasive feeling of being overwhelmed all the time. You may experience excessive reactions to trivial problems.

The primary cause of burnout is something organizational psychologists like to call *task overload*. That's another way of saying that you don't have enough hours in the day to meet the basic responsibilities of your job. As it happens, most people in the workforce — high achievers, in particular — are dealing with task overload in one form or another, but not everyone is equally susceptible to burnout.

Burnout tends to rear its ugly head when you combine task overload with one or more of the following conditions:

✔ **Lack of control** over your work load, schedule, or deadlines.

✔ **Imbalance** between work and personal commitments.

✔ **Absence of feedback,** which creates an inability to see appreciable results for efforts.

✔ **Conflict** with a boss or with coworkers.

✔ **Anxiety** about job security or possible reprisals if you fail.

If you experience symptoms of burnout, first determine whether the situation is temporary or long-term. If you're convinced that the pressure will ease soon, the best strategy is to ride out the storm without making any major alterations to your work practices or lifestyle. And if you haven't done so already, enlist more support from coworkers, family, or friends. If, on the other hand, you're convinced that there is no light at the end of the tunnel, you need to take some decisive action — and soon.

There are no simple cookie-cutter solutions to dealing with job burnout. If your situation is severe, you may have no choice but to take some time off to rest, renew yourself physically and mentally, and if need be, rethink your career objectives. Otherwise, the following sections give you concrete steps to help you deal more effectively with burnout and minimize its long-term consequences.

Conducting a stress audit

The one thing that's clear when you're suffering burnout symptoms is that you're experiencing job stress. That's a given. But the specific factors in your job that produce the stress may be less obvious. To get a better understanding of why you're so stressed out, analyze a typical work day and determine which conditions or responsibilities create the most stress for you. Possibilities include the following:

- ✔ **Pressure:** The need to meet deadlines is unremitting.

- ✔ **Overload:** Despite your best efforts at multitasking and organizing yourself, you simply have too many things to attend to at one time.

- ✔ **Tension:** Because everyone is under pressure and overwhelmed by the demands of their jobs, the potential for constant conflicts with coworkers is very high.

- ✔ **Disagreement:** There's no consensus about what's important and strategic.

After drawing up your list, develop some coping strategies. Here are some suggestions to get you started:

- ✔ **Prune responsibilities.** If the problem you're facing is simply an overload of responsibilities, review your daily tasks and identify those that could be eliminated, cut back, or delegated to others.

- ✔ **Focus on what you can control.** Make a distinction between factors in your work life that you can control and those you can't. Direct your efforts accordingly.

- ✔ **Resolve conflict proactively.** If you're having people problems, arrange to meet with the individual(s) with whom you're in constant conflict. Try to work out your differences. Perhaps you are a major source of the stress that the other person experiences!

- ✔ **Keep priorities in mind.** Be sure that whatever you work on in a given moment is, in fact, strategically linked to short- or long-term objectives.

- ✔ **Avoid the nonessential.** Evaluate assignments or requests based on how essential they are to achieving goals.

- ✔ **Evaluate your position.** Consider the possibility that your job description, as it is now structured, may be unrealistic. If, for example, your company has grown significantly and rapidly, your scope of responsibility may have gradually expanded beyond what one person can truly manage. Consult your manager and look for ways to restructure the position, perhaps by delegating certain tasks or requesting additional help from others.

- ✔ **Set measurable goals.** A common cause of burnout is a failure to recognize a connection between your efforts and their results. Even if your goals are modest, they should be quantifiable.

- ✔ **Seek guidance.** If all of the previous efforts don't seem to improve your situation, you may want to speak with a professional counselor. Sometimes, an objective opinion and fresh perspective are what you need to pull yourself out of a pattern of stress.

Pacing yourself

Up to a certain point (which varies from one person to the next), the number of hours spent on the job is not necessarily related to stress. The key is pacing yourself. Whenever you intend to work really long hours at your desk — more than eight hours a day — take a microbreak every hour. (If necessary, set an alarm to help you do this.) Stand up, stretch, breathe deeply — even take a short walk. Instead of eating lunch at your desk, go somewhere else — and for a few minutes, get away from what you've been concentrating on all morning. Don't delude yourself into thinking you can't afford the time. By taking these breaks, you're conserving energy, recharging, and allowing yourself to work longer without losing your mental edge.

Leaving it all behind

When you're finished with the workday, try to relax and get your mind off work. If you can possibly avoid it, don't bring work home with you. And if you have to bring work home on a weekend, set aside one day (or at least a portion of the day) to focus on anything but your job or career. But if you can't seem to separate yourself from the concerns of the office, consider seeking professional guidance or assistance.

Asking for help

A common symptom of burnout is a feeling of isolation — the feeling that it's you against the world. Of course, that's usually not the case. In high-pressure situations, help is typically available. But you have to know what type of help you need and ask for it. If you're part of a team (and even if you're the leader of a team), let others know about the difficulties you're facing — without bemoaning the situation — and request their support and assistance. You won't be perceived as a complainer as long as you objectively outline the challenges you're experiencing and ask for assistance in resolving the situation. You may be surprised at how much cooperation you'll get when you're willing to open up to others.

Paying attention to your health

One of the best ways to prevent burnout is to focus on your physical health. You know the drill: Eat a balanced diet, get plenty of rest, and exercise regularly. Do your best to schedule at least 30 minutes of activity each day — a brisk walk is great.

Eight steps to prevent staff members from burning out

When attempting to avoid burnout, the old saying — "An ounce of prevention is worth a pound of cure" — certainly holds true. Here are eight ways to reduce stress, diffuse tension, and keep burnout from claiming your talented staff:

✔ **Be flexible.** Help your staff balance work and family commitments. Give people some latitude (without compromising a project) to attend to personal matters.

✔ **Be proactive.** Intervene quickly when pressure-related disputes arise. Sort out the difficulties promptly and fairly.

✔ **Bring in support.** Hire additional staff on a project basis to help during peak workloads.

✔ **Forget about egos.** Let your actions demonstrate that each person is there to help everyone else.

✔ **Provide a little extra.** For example, order pizza for people who are working long hours.

✔ **Praise your staff often.** Never stop telling the people who are working hard how much you appreciate their commitment.

✔ **Offer educational opportunities.** Provide formal and informal instruction in skills required by the new workplace, including stress management, communication, and conflict resolution.

✔ **Celebrate.** Set aside time — at least once a quarter — for a departmental celebration. Encourage everyone to get together and simply relax (the sillier you can make the celebration, the better).

✔ **Allow time to recharge.** After a major project is complete, encourage staff to take some time off or leave a little earlier for a few days.

Minimizing other stressors

The physical consequences of stress and burnout are cumulative. So if you're experiencing difficulties at home as well as at work, you're accelerating the burnout process. Family support is critical. Work out some arrangement to help you balance work and personal obligations. For example, if you're in the middle of a huge project that requires late nights at the office, ask your family to join you for a quick picnic one night at a spot nearby so that you can be close to the office without sacrificing all of your personal time. With cooperation and creativity, you can usually find a way to be there for your family and at the same time deal with pressures at the office.

If you know you're going to be in a high-pressure situation, start your day on a slow, relaxing note. Set the alarm a half-hour earlier than usual. And do everything you normally do in the morning a little bit more slowly. That way, you arrive at work in a reasonably relaxed state of mind.

Don't underestimate how stressful it can be to change mental gears too quickly. Even a few minutes to ease into a routine can make an enormous difference in handling stress.

Rebounding from a Career Setback

Certain people are better at coping with adversity than others, but only within the past 25 years have scientists investigated the attribute at the core of this ability — resilience. Because this field is relatively new, the number of published studies is small, and most of them to date have focused on young people who've become successful, productive adults in spite of traumatic childhoods.

Even so, the findings from these studies can apply to anyone who has dealt with adversity. Research has shown, for example, that no single skill or attribute distinguishes resilient people from others. Rather, they share a number of characteristics, to varying degrees. These include the following:

- **Low levels of defensiveness and aggressiveness:** Resilient people demonstrate a high propensity toward cooperation and participation.

- **Positive sense of self:** Their attitude reflects a steady confidence in their own abilities.

- **Sense of control:** Their behavior suggests a sense of personal power rather than powerlessness (a belief that they are capable of exercising a degree of control over their environment).

- **Strong sense of faith:** Whether it be in the future, in a higher power, or in themselves, resilient people exhibit steadfast beliefs.

- **Positive outlook:** The ability to see bad times as temporary and surmountable.

Most of the behavioral scientists who've studied resilience insist that it's not an innate characteristic. They also agree that there is no surefire formula for bouncing back from adversity. Your ability to cope is affected by your personality, support system, and, of course, the severity of the setback. The sections that follow are a series of how-to-bounce-back suggestions.

Taking stock

After allowing yourself to recover emotionally from any career setback (a couple of days or so), set aside some time to take a long, hard look at the situation. Be as objective as you can, which isn't easy. Fight the tendency to blame other people or outside events for what happened. At the same time, don't assume all the blame yourself. As you reflect, keep a notepad and pen in hand so that you can make notes. The following are some good questions to ask yourself as part of this exercise. Notice that each of these questions encourages you to come up with positive, productive answers — the purpose is to learn from the situation so you can prevent a recurrence.

- ✔ **Was the purpose clear?** Did you have a thorough understanding of the mission or objective of the project? If not, what did you miss at first, and what steps could you have taken to better understand?

- ✔ **Were the resources there?** Did you determine — before beginning the project — the resources necessary for success? Did you avail yourself of those resources?

- ✔ **Did external factors impact the outcome?** What circumstances would have been necessary to achieve your objective?

- ✔ **Were you in the driver's seat?** How much control did you have over the factors central to success?

- ✔ **What can you change?** Which skills do you need to develop to avoid making the same mistake in the future?

- ✔ **Can you imagine a different outcome?** In retrospect, would you have done anything differently?

Don't be in a hurry to answer these questions. And don't worry, either, if you're not really sure of the answers. What you're looking for is insight.

Avoiding the victim syndrome

While it's easier said than done, try your best to avoid what many people refer to as the *victim syndrome*. People caught up in this way of thinking refuse to accept any responsibility for what happened and instead choose to pin the blame on circumstances or other people. Whatever short-term ego boost may be gained by this practice is far outweighed by a dangerous mind-set of helplessness.

Studies show that one of the most important characteristics of resilient people is an objective view of their role when faced with adversity. They don't view themselves as helpless victims; they recognize and accept the power to control their reaction to whatever happens around them. This confidence enables them to take steps that people who feel helpless would be unlikely to take.

Writing down your frustration

If you're having trouble letting go of your anger and you feel you were truly wronged by your boss or anyone else, you need to release that frustration without getting yourself into more hot water. Do this by writing a mock-letter to the person, expressing your feelings. Relax, you're never going to mail this letter. But the mere fact that you've released your feelings can be highly therapeutic. Some psychologists recommend repeating this exercise several times until you've released most of the anger.

Art Berg

Art Berg is an entrepreneur, author, and public speaker who addresses more than 150,000 people each year. He's also a powerful example of what you can accomplish in your career if you're flexible enough to make major changes when opportunities present themselves.

A quadriplegic since an automobile accident in 1983, Berg nonetheless achieved success in several different career tracks, first as a salesman for Bell Atlantic CompuShop, where he won national sales awards three years running and then as a book store entrepreneur. Then, in 1989, he published a book entitled *Some Miracles Take Time*. He became in such demand as a public speaker that, three years later, he was persuaded by a friend to pursue it as a full-time career. Since then, he has formed his own firm, Invictus Communications, to market his speaking engagements and related educational materials. He's also the president of eSpeakers.com, Inc., a company that creates and markets a Web-based calendar and event-management tool for professional speakers, agents, and bureaus.

What's his formula for success? Here's a glimpse of how he views many of the key issues of career management.

✔ **On taking responsibility for your own future:** "Even before my accident, I was determined to be responsible for my own career rather than leaving it in the hands of other people. That's what attracted me to sales: I wanted to be responsible for my own success or failure."

✔ **On pursuing dreams:** "Leaving a somewhat secure career in the book business for a riskier goal as a public speaker took a leap of faith and a lot of hard work. However, by doing what I love, I've found that work is more of a joy than a burden."

✔ **On succeeding as an entrepreneur:** "It starts with a good business plan. But you also need to be flexible and willing to adapt. And remember that even the best-laid plans require time and patience."

✔ **On knowing what you want:** "Determine your long-term reputation — what you'd like to be known for — several years down the road and create your own future through your habits, behavior, and accomplishments."

✔ **On career advancement:** "My advice is to develop an entrepreneurial spirit. Become cross-funcional in both your skills and understanding. Learn to see more of the big picture outside your sphere of responsibility. Never stop educating yourself. Read constantly. Ask questions — always."

Separating yourself from the failure

Failure is always situational. In other words, you don't simply fail; you fail in your attempts to achieve something. This distinction is essential when reflecting on your setbacks. Limit your thoughts to those aspects of your performance (and only those aspects) that significantly influenced the outcome of the project. Chances are, you're already adhering to this discipline in many of the routine activities in your life. If you make a bad menu choice, for example, it's unlikely that you view your failure as a reflection of your overall decision-making ability.

Follow the same principle when analyzing your business setbacks. Focus on the action or the decision. The value of this practice is twofold:

- ✔ You can address your shortcomings at minimal cost to your self-esteem.
- ✔ You can gain a better understanding of your strengths and weaknesses, thus reducing the risk of repeating the mistakes.

Looking for the gift

A theme that runs throughout the biographies of successful people is how frequently a failure or a huge disappointment indirectly led to decisions or actions that were instrumental in their ultimate success. You don't have to look at the world through rose-colored glasses to put this into practice. And you don't have to rationalize. If you're taken off a project that has consumed your days and nights for months, look for other opportunities in which you can focus your time and energy. If you've been fired, take the opportunity to reexamine your career goals and make sure you're on the path you want be.

However difficult it may be, don't dwell on what you've lost or given up; focus, instead, on what you hope to gain in the future.

Reaching out when you need to

Failures are frequently accompanied by deep feelings of shame and embarrassment. Some people who've experienced setbacks have a tendency to shut out the world. But taking a cue from the coping patterns of resilient people, becoming a hermit is the one thing you don't want to do. On the contrary, this is the time to rely on the people who are part of your support system: family, friends, and mentors. These people are there to help you, but you have to ask for their assistance. Talk with a former mentor or an instructor from school to boost your spirits and if necessary, help you develop some career strategies. Colleagues, family members, and friends can also add perspective and emotional support.

In some instances, such as a layoff, you may want to attend a support group or participate in an online chat session with others who have experienced similar situations. A career setback may also be a good time to broaden your network by participating in organizations, trade associations, or other community groups — any group that will value your contributions. By getting involved, you'll not only elevate your confidence but also meet people who may be able to help you in your career.

Learning from mistakes

You've probably heard this advice so often that you may not appreciate just how powerful it is — and how easy it is to lose sight of when you're recovering from a recent setback. Remember, however, the critical difference between acknowledging mistakes and learning from them. *Acknowledging* means that you're aware of how you erred. *Learning* means that you're able to take that knowledge and put it to productive use the next time you're in a similar situation. Painful as setbacks can be, they can also be a valuable learning tool. They can enhance your sense of self-awareness. You can't grow until you understand yourself better, and if you don't understand your limitations, you'll never work on them. If you underestimate your strengths, you can't fully capitalize on them.

Reevaluating goals

Setbacks and failures are natural junctures — opportune times to reexamine goals and gain some insight into how committed you are to those goals. Professional actors know that when auditioning, there's a distinct possibility that someone else may get the part. And I've often heard it said that the more successful the actor, the greater the number of parts he or she didn't get. One of the things you may discover when reevaluating your goals is that the ultimate objective is still reasonable, but that the steps or timetable need adjusting. You may have tried to accomplish too much, too soon. That's good feedback, and you need it if you want to keep moving ahead.

Getting back on track

As soon as possible after any career setback, shift your focus from what went wrong to the specific steps you can take right now to get yourself moving forward again. The key here is to set up specific action items rather than general goals. If, for example, you've failed to receive a promotion, make sure you know what's required to earn that advancement, such as assuming more responsibility, acquiring additional skills, and so on. If you need to take a course, set a deadline for signing up. If you need to learn more about what's going on in the company, schedule a series of informational interviews over the next two or three months.

Part III
Working Well with Others

The 5th Wave   By Rich Tennant

"The pay's not great, but where else can you get a retirement plan that will last for eternity?"

In this part . . .

In today's business environment, how you work and communicate with others can make or break your career. This part outlines the best practices of successful leaders and team players and provides the tips you need to communicate effectively regardless of your position. You also discover the trade secrets of networking in order to form mutually beneficial relationships that can last throughout the course of your career.

Chapter 11

Managing Your Boss

*A*t first glance, the title of this chapter may strike you as ludicrous. How do you manage someone whose responsibility is to manage you? But there's no misprint here, and there's no trick to this chapter. It's all a question of how you define the word "manage."

Managing with respect to your supervisor isn't simply telling someone what to do. It means doing your best to make it easier for your manager to manage you, even though the two of you may not see eye to eye on many of the issues that are relevant to your job.

Don't get the wrong idea. Managing your boss isn't the same thing as kissing up. Nor does it oblige you to act like the proverbial doormat, catering to your supervisor's every whim, putting up with abuse, or compromising your integrity. It simply means that, throughout your career, you may find yourself working for people whose competence you may not respect, whose lifestyle you may not approve of, whose approach to managing you may not agree with, and whose demands you may sometimes consider unreasonable. Forgetting for the moment whether these perceptions are justified, your ability to achieve your career goals depends a great deal on how you cope with these situations. Make no mistake about it. How well you work with your boss has more bearing than any other factor on your ability to put your skills, knowledge, personal attributes, and motivation to the most effective use in your job — and more bearing as well on how much you learn in your job and how much satisfaction you derive from it.

This chapter outlines strategies you can adopt to establish and maintain a productive, harmonious, and mutually-beneficial relationship with your manager, even when the two may not be ideally suited to work with one another.

You also get a look at what an ideal boss-worker relationship may be like (don't get too excited, though, because there's no such thing). You gain insights into those factors that significantly affect the quality of the relationship you have with your supervisor. And you get real-world advice on how to deal with the most common types of problem managers.

Envisioning the Perfect Boss

If you were to ask a random group of employees to describe the ideal manager, the specific profiles would undoubtedly differ from one respondent to the next. Most people, though, would use the same broad range of criteria. To one degree or another, they would like to work for people who are:

- **Consummate professionals:** Outstanding bosses are highly competent people who know their stuff and conduct business in a manner that earns the admiration and respect of their colleagues.

- **Inspiring leaders:** By being fair-minded, reasonable, courteous, and respectful, the best managers set an example that employees want to follow. Such supervisors are usually easy to be with and even fun to be around.

- **Good communicators:** The ability to give clear, specific instructions and explain objectives is critically important to the team's success.

- **Effective motivators:** Great bosses are quick to praise when you do a good job, and patient and constructive when you make mistakes. They're interested in you as a person — and, in particular, in your career growth — and look for ways to support your professional development.

- **Advocates for their staffs:** Successful managers are sensitive to their employees' need to balance work and home responsibilities. Such supervisors are willing to go to bat for an employee, when necessary.

If, for any reason, your current boss or, for that matter, anyone with whom you've worked in the past, doesn't score a perfect ten in all the attributes just described, don't be too surprised. There's no such thing as the perfect supervisor — and for a logical reason. All managers (yourself included, if you happen be a supervisor) suffer from the same shortcoming: They're human beings. Consequently, they share with every member of the species (excluding you, of course!) the same foibles and imperfections. Remember, too, that if you work for a large organization, you're probably only one of several people who report to your manager, and each undoubtedly has a different definition of the ideal boss — so no supervisor could be perfect for everyone. Finally, you can't overlook the fact that most bosses have supervisors of their own and may have the same gripes about management as you do.

If you're unhappy with certain aspects of the relationship you currently have with your manager, the initiative to make things better has to come from you, not your boss. You may be fortunate enough to have the kind of manager who is willing to work as hard as you to make the relationship mutually beneficial. But the boss-employee relationship is, by its very nature, uneven.

No one, of course, expects you to work in unhealthy, unsafe, or abusive conditions. But after you get beyond these basics, the fact remains that your manager's wants, needs, and priorities take precedence over yours. In other words, you need to think of your boss as a client or customer. If you have a problem accepting this role, you may want to consider working on your own. Even then, though, you'll find that success will still require you to subordinate your own wants, needs, and priorities to those of someone else — your clients and customers.

And here's one more thing to keep in mind as you read through this chapter: The adjustments you make in order to meet the needs and wants of most managers won't be as overwhelming as you may think. On the contrary, it often takes very little effort to prevent the most common sources of tension and frustration that can arise between you and your boss. The thing is, you have to know what to do — and when to do it.

Understanding Your Sphere of Control

The first thing you need to do to become better at managing your manager is to recognize those elements of the relationship that you have the power to control. What you can't control, of course, is your supervisor's basic personality — a tendency, for example, to swear a blue streak when something really serious happens, such as a busy signal with his Internet service provider. You don't have much control, either, over the quality of standards your manager has set. And there's little you can do to change the personal relationship that may exist between your boss and his or her manager.

But here is what you can control — to a reasonable extent, at least:

- ✔ **Your attitude:** If you approach the relationship with a positive attitude, you'll have an easier time dealing with problems when they do arise.

- ✔ **Your commitment:** Try to do your job as well as you possibly can, despite conditions that may make things difficult for you. The pride and professionalism that result will help carry you through hard times.

- ✔ **Your effort:** Strive for a better understanding of your boss's expectations and the standards by which your job performance is judged.

- ✔ **Your reaction:** When you and your boss disagree, do you make matters worse, or do you seek compromise?

As you may well expect, the amount of control you can actually wield in any of these areas varies considerably from one situation to the next. But the suggestions in the following sections will hold you in good stead in just about any manager-employee relationship.

Getting off to a good start

It's critical that you and your boss get off on the right foot together. A big part of this challenge lies in chemistry: how easily your personalities mesh. Among the factors that contribute to good chemistry are similarities in backgrounds, similar values, and a similar sense of humor (you laugh at the same jokes). It doesn't hurt, either, to share a passionate concern for the fortunes of your local sports team or a deep involvement in the same hobby ("Oh, I didn't know you had an ant farm. What a coincidence!").

But even if the chemistry between the two of you is great, you still need to make sure at the very beginning of your work relationship that you share a common understanding of the following job-related issues:

- **Your basic responsibilities:** What's expected of you and where does your job fit into the scheme of things, based on your company's strategic goals?

- **Values and standards:** What is the basis for measuring your job performance? Does your manager have his or her own standards in addition to those of the firm?

- **Work process:** Particularly with respect to projects you and your manager will be working on together, what are the processes that shape work flow and efficiency?

- **Basic rules and procedures:** What are the formal rules that affect performance? Are you encouraged to introduce innovations in procedures or are you expected to do everything strictly by the book?

Don't underestimate the importance of reaching accord on each of the issues just mentioned, however fundamental they may seem. A mutual understanding of these matters can go a long way to preventing many of the problems that underlie troubled manager-employee relationships.

Checking on progress

It is up to your boss to determine job expectations and evaluate your performance, but you can't always count on clear communication. And although the two of you discussed objectives at the start of your work relationship, you may need a refresher meeting from time to time. You may want to take the initiative and ask your manager directly for specific guidelines and feedback on these issues.

But the challenge doesn't stop with simply asking questions. After you find out what's expected of you, you need to have confidence in your ability to meet those expectations. And if, for any reason, you're not sure, figure out and communicate to your boss what additional support or resources you need.

It's never a good idea to conceal from your boss any shortcoming that may prevent you from meeting a particular expectation. You're much better off telling the truth and expressing a willingness to take the necessary steps to get up to speed as soon as possible.

Looking at the big picture

Whenever you're asked to handle a new task or project, make sure you understand not only what you're being asked to do, but why (from your boss's perspective) it needs to be done a certain way and how it fits into the mission or strategic goals of your company and your department. You may not need this information right away (it may be more practical in many instances to schedule a meeting at which you can get the clarification you need). The point, though, is to establish yourself early on as an employee who does more than simply follow instructions. You need to be a true problem-solver — someone who actively seeks to make your supervisor's job easier.

The more you know about your manager's job and its inherent pressures, the more you can ease those pressures — and the more valuable you become as an employee. You can gain these insights by asking good questions and by observing and growing from day-to-day events.

Here's a list of some of the key aspects of your manager's world worth noting:

- ✓ **Scope of responsibility:** Knowing the different aspects of your manager's job helps you understand how your job relates to and affects those roles.

- ✓ **Number of direct reports:** The more people who report directly to your boss, the more independent you will probably need to be.

- ✓ **Your boss's boss:** By finding out more about your boss's manager, you gain insights into why things may need to be done a certain way.

- ✓ **Overall career ambitions and life goals:** Your supervisor's personal priorities and goals can influence his or her ranking of business priorities.

- ✓ **Career and company history:** This knowledge gives you a better sense of your boss's clout and experience.

- ✓ **Technical or industry knowledge:** The level of technical knowledge (apart from managerial expertise) has important implications for communication. You may need, for example, to use less jargon in e-mails or memos, or you may need to significantly increase your technical understanding just to anticipate his or her needs.

✔ **Outside pressures:** By becoming aware of your manager's personal pressures (apart from the job), you can be prepared to offer additional support during especially difficult times.

Making communication count

No relationship can flourish without good communication, and the relationship you have with your boss is no exception. Regularly scheduled meetings and discussions are a big help, of course. But just as important as the frequency of your communication is the quality — the ability for you to talk *to* one another rather than *at* one another.

The following are the most common barriers to good manager-employee communication and some ideas for overcoming them:

✔ **Divergent perspectives:** There's a basic misunderstanding of roles, responsibilities, and priorities.

Remedy: Find a copy of your job description and ask your manager if you can meet to discuss the possibility of updating it. Just be sure that you're not trying to define every little task you do; remember that the biggest part of your job is doing whatever you can to help your company succeed.

✔ **Lack of availability:** It's very difficult for the two of you to stay in touch, especially when you're not working together in the same place.

Remedy: Try to set up a regular system of communication, whether it's daily e-mails, voice mails, or tele- or videoconferences. Make a commitment to staying in touch on a regular basis.

✔ **Personality differences:** Little quirks and idiosyncrasies prevent the two of you from feeling at ease in each other's presence.

Remedy: You don't have to like everything about your boss to work well together; you just have to focus on the task at hand.

✔ **Different work styles:** You and your boss are like the odd couple — for example, one person is very outspoken while the other is quiet or reserved.

Remedy: Adapt as much as you can to his or her style, especially in stressful times. Neither of you needs to change completely, as long as you remember that you can reach the same goal from different approaches.

✔ **Chaotic environment:** External circumstances in the workplace impinge on your ability to help one another stay informed or share new ideas.

Remedy: The important thing is to make time on a regular basis for quality communication. Consider scheduling a weekly meeting in a conference room or an offsite location where distractions will be minimized.

In light of these barriers, you may need to take some time to decide how best to handle the communication aspects of your job. Much will depend on your boss's preferences. Some managers prefer face-to-face meetings while others favor memos and e-mails. Some supervisors want exhaustive detail. Others want just the facts. Figure out which style of communication your boss prefers and adapt your style accordingly.

Adjusting your work style

The way you prefer to do things may not necessarily coincide with how your boss likes to work. But as long as neither of you fall into extremes (you do your best work at 3 a.m. with loud music blaring in the background; he does his best work at 3 p.m. in an environment as silent as a tomb), you should be able to find common ground.

Keep in mind — and it's a point that can't be emphasized enough — that you need to do most of the accommodating. After you've worked for someone for a month or so, you should have a fairly good idea of his or her basic operating style. And you should also be able to adapt to those patterns without making monumental changes in your own working habits.

Here are some areas to think about:

- ✔ **General working style:** Does your manager prefer a highly structured schedule or is she prone to do things in a more impromptu, spontaneous manner? (Knowing this helps you determine how often — and when — you need to meet with your boss to discuss issues.)

- ✔ **Computer smarts:** Does your boss use and understand the same applications that you use? (Knowing this helps you determine how much time you have to spend preparing or translating electronic communications or projects.)

- ✔ **Progress reports:** How much information (from your manager's perspective) is too much? (Knowing this helps you determine how often to keep your boss apprised of what you're doing and how much detail to provide.)

Undoubtedly, as the two of your work together more and more, you will become increasingly adept at making the adjustments that, in turn, make life easier for your boss. It's important, however, that you remain observant and continually adapt your work style as necessary.

Adapting to your boss's personality

Apart from inviting your supervisor to a personally tailored presentation on how to develop a better personality (not a good career move), you can't do much about the personality characteristics that differentiate you from your manager.

But with thought and effort, you can usually prevent those differences from mushrooming into a source of conflict and frustration. Here are some suggestions on how to deal with this issue:

- **Don't be judgmental:** Remind yourself that nobody's perfect — not even you.

- **Don't assume it's your mission in life to change your supervisor:** You may not like his or her habits, but you need to work around them.

- **Try not to internalize:** Don't automatically assume, if your manager is moody or grumpy, that you're the cause. Oftentimes, a manager with this demeanor is not selective — he or she is likely the same way with everyone.

- **Find out your manager's *flash points:*** Do your best to steer clear of the attitudes, subjects, actions, and events that irritate him or her.

- **Set your own boundaries:** Decide how you yourself want to be treated and model that behavior in your interactions with your manager. And be willing to cut your supervisor some slack in pressure situations.

Meeting of minds

The following are seven ways to get the most out of the meetings you have with your boss:

- **Do your homework.** Research the agenda before the meeting and bring with you any documentation or materials that may be relevant.

- **Take notes.** Always bring something with which to take notes — an electronic organizer or pen and paper.

- **Seek clarification**. Make sure you understand not only the task you're being asked to perform but also the rationale behind the task. (This doesn't mean, of course, that you question every instruction. But knowing the objective of any project helps you make better decisions.)

- **Offer your undivided attention.** Do your best to keep the meeting as interruption-free as possible. Stay focused and attentive, regardless of how often your boss allows the meeting to be interrupted.

- **Don't be a hero.** Ask for guidance on priorities. If at any time during the meeting you sense that you're being asked to take on more tasks than you can comfortably handle, request extra help.

- **Clarify.** If, after the meeting, you're uncertain as to your responsibilities, make a quick call to clarify. Another option is to send an e-mail in which you outline what, from your perspective, were the key points of the meeting, and request feedback.

- **Stay positive.** Regardless of how much pressure the two of you are under, try to go into the meeting with a positive outlook.

Dealing with Problem Managers

Judging from the number of books and articles that have been written about problem bosses, you may be led to believe that the workplace today is infested with supervisors who are overbearing, insensitive, petty, indecisive, manipulative, and in general, all but uncivilized.

That's an exaggeration to be sure. Nonetheless, it's no secret that some managers are more difficult to work with than others. The sections that follow offer a brief description of some of the commonly voiced complaints about supervisors today, along with some suggestions on how to make the best out of the situation.

As you read this section, keep in mind that the advice is deliberately general. The dynamics of a manager-employee relationship can be highly complex, and what works in one situation may not work for you. Keep in mind, too, that if the problems you encounter with a supervisor go well beyond the fact that he says "tomato" and you say "tomahto," the only solution may be to find a different job in the same company or leave the organization altogether. At the very least, however, do everything within your power to make the relationship work.

"My boss is too controlling"

Some managers have a hard time letting go. You know the type: They're not comfortable unless they know everything — absolutely everything! — that's going on around them and they need to be involved in every decision, no matter how inconsequential. If they had their way, they would probably like to tell you how many times to blink while you're working at your computer.

The good news is that whatever faults they may have, managers driven by a strong need to control tend to be highly responsive and concerned — and often quite competent. You can find out a good deal from bosses like this — if only they would give you enough room to learn things on your own. You can't grow or even do your best work when someone insists on looking over your shoulder at all times or wants to be consulted on every decision. ("So how many times should I blink?")

How to respond: The key thing to remember about these types of bosses is that the majority of them can't help themselves. They've been controlling things for so long and in so many areas of their life that their habits are ingrained. They also may be afraid that they themselves will fail if they don't catch your mistakes before they happen. In order to make any progress with such a boss, you have to do it gradually.

Here's a strategy you may want to try:

1. **The next time you're assigned a task, break it down into individual steps, and zero in on one or two of those aspects of the task that are relatively simple and that you know for certain you can do on your own.**

2. **Go to your boss and, as tactfully as you can, ask to be given responsibility for those tasks.**

   Assure your manager that you'll run everything by her and allow plenty of time for necessary changes.

3. **After proving yourself in those areas, you can use the same strategy in subsequent assignments, gradually broadening your sphere of responsibility.**

This is an excellent strategy to follow if you like your job and it looks as if you're going to work for your current manager for a long time. The success of it, however, depends on your ability to deliver on promises. Any failure on your part could reinforce your boss's tendency to micromanage.

"My boss is too wishy-washy"

Complaints about supervisors being too wishy-washy usually relate to the following behaviors:

- ✔ **Indecisiveness:** A reluctance to make decisions can be especially frustrating when the lack of a decision affects your ability to meet tight deadlines.

- ✔ **Hesitancy:** The boss is slow to take a strong stand when your department or team is unfairly criticized or unduly burdened by senior management.

- ✔ **Lack of support:** An unwillingness to go to bat for you when you're looking for a promotion or making a request (telecommuting, for example) that needs more than a rubber-stamp approval.

- ✔ **Vagueness:** The manager is unable to articulate clear objectives and precise deadlines and has difficulty providing specific, constructive feedback about job performance.

How to respond: One good thing about indecisive bosses is that they don't put too much pressure on you — not directly, anyway. However, wishy-washy supervisors can be frustrating to work for, regardless of their intelligence and affable disposition. Their lack of backbone can interfere with your ability to do your job well.

But before you mount any specific strategy designed to light a fire under an indecisive supervisor, first make sure that he or she has the authority to make the decisions or communicate the information you need. Otherwise you're wasting your time.

If your manager turns out to, indeed, have the power but doesn't like to exercise it, here are three suggestions:

- **Recommend with confidence.** Whenever you need your boss to make a decision — especially a tough or complex one — offer alternatives along with your recommendation. Instead of asking, "What would you prefer that I do?" Ask the following: "There are three things I can do: A, B, or C. I believe that B is the best option (and explain your reasoning). Do you agree?" Reassure your boss that you're confident about your recommendation and that you've done your homework.

- **Encourage constructive feedback.** If your boss never gives you any negative feedback, it's not necessarily because you're doing a great job. Your manager may be afraid to hurt your feelings and affect your work performance. If you suspect this may be the case with your supervisor, you may need to go out of your way to assure your boss that any negative feedback will not result in bruised feelings.

  If you adopt this strategy, of course, you have to be careful not to react defensively if your manager is less than successful in delivering negative feedback.

- **Communicate your deadlines.** In many instances (though certainly not always), you can prompt indecisive managers to take action by indicating deadlines for the decisions you need.

  One word of caution when using this approach. Don't push too hard. Mild pressure can sometimes work with an indecisive manager, as long as the two of you have an otherwise good relationship. But if you push too hard or force your manager to make too many decisions at the same time, you run the risk of damaging the relationship.

"My boss makes unreasonable demands"

Before you can develop an effective strategy for dealing with a supervisor who, as you see it, makes unreasonable demands, you need to take a close look at those demands and make sure that they are, in fact, unreasonable.

If the demands are directly related to your job, the best — though not necessarily the easiest — thing to do is to sit down with your manager and make a list of *performance objectives,* things that you need to accomplish. If after doing so you see a gap between what's expected of you and what you believe you can accomplish, make your case and do your best to get some additional support or assistance, such as a project professional to help during peak workloads.

A good way to strengthen your case before such a meeting with your manager is to create a detailed activity report over a specific period — two weeks, for example. This type of documentation serves as a powerful illustration that you simply don't have enough hours in the day to complete all the tasks you've been assigned.

Demands that fall outside the realm of your official job description are trickier to handle. Some bosses see nothing wrong with asking employees to run errands for them and have no compunctions about calling you at home — at almost any time — with requests that could easily be handled during business hours. Are such requests unreasonable? It's hard to say. It depends on the kind of job you have, the relationship you have with your manager in general, the frequency of the requests, and how your ability to perform your job is affected by these requests. In the end, you have to determine for yourself if you're being taken advantage of.

Here, again, an activity report may help. Start documenting the unreasonable requests, how much time they consume, and what impact, if any, these activities are having on your ability to meet other expectations. By doing this for a month, you'll have some solid documentation to support your point of view. Remember to use tact when discussing this situation with your boss. In business, it's not so much what you say, but how you say it, that separates success from failure.

What's important here, above all, is an open mind. Requests considered unreasonable in one environment may well be considered reasonable in another organization. You need to understand the norms in your company and decide whether you can live with them.

"My boss is a tyrant"

The good news about managers whose behavior is often hostile and offensive is that they are a vanishing breed. (They're now known as *dinosaurs.*) True, in certain industries — show business, in particular — it's taken for granted that if you work for certain high-powered and highly talented individuals, you'll have to put up with ballistic temperaments (although you're often well-paid for the privilege of working for them and basking in their glory). Generally speaking, though, few companies today will (or can afford to) tolerate abusive behavior from anyone.

The bad news is that if you're cursed with a supervisor who is prone to tyranny, excessive rage, or other forms of unacceptable and abusive behavior, your options are limited. You can try to talk things out with your manager (see the "Talking things out" sidebar) and let it be known that you don't appreciate the way you're being treated. But people — highly successful people, in particular — who behave in irrational, unacceptable ways aren't necessarily receptive to reasonable discussions about their shortcomings (which, of course, is one of the things that makes them so difficult). You can instead, complain to senior management and request a change to another department, but that strategy could also backfire. If senior management doesn't take any corrective action and word about your complaint gets back to your boss, his or her tyrannical behavior is likely to intensify, not diminish.

Talking things out

Regardless of how much difficulty you're having at work with your manager, you always have the option of improving the relationship through one or more heart-to-heart discussions. Unless you have been trained to do so (and even then, it's rarely easy), discussing problems with a person face to face can be difficult. And when the person with whom you're discussing these matters also happens to be your boss, the stakes are higher — and the difficulty intensifies.

Deciding to have such a discussion with your boss is no small matter. It's a decision you need to make carefully, keeping in mind that if the talk doesn't go well, you may have made a bad situation that much worse. If you're still game — and if you think there's a chance you can work things out — here are some suggestions:

✔ **Establish the right mindset.** You're not likely to get very far in any heart-to-heart discussion with your manager if your only reason for the meeting is to vent or dredge up everything that you find wrong with the relationship. The better approach is to forget about who's right and wrong and focus instead on the issues at hand: how your ability to do your job is being affected and what specific changes may improve the situation.

✔ **Clarify objectives.** After you dispense with the greetings, get to the point. Let your boss know what you hope to get out of this meeting: a better relationship. Emphasize that you're not simply there to blow off steam, vent, or criticize. Your goal is to find ways that the two of you can work together more harmoniously and more productively.

✔ **Emphasize the positive.** Before you discuss what aspects of your relationship need improvement, talk about what's working in your professional relationship. You may want to start out with something along the lines of, "I really appreciate the interest you've shown in my work, and I really like the fact that you seem to notice when I've done a good job." After you've started on a positive note, it's usually easier to move on to more delicate issues.

✔ **Share some of the blame.** Even if you're convinced that you've done everything humanly possible to be a good employee, be open to the possibility that you may be contributing to the problems. Concede from the start that your manager may dislike certain things about you and express a willingness to talk about them.

✔ **Communicate your needs.** Instead of dwelling on your boss's habits and traits, articulate your needs. Let your boss know, specifically, what you need — and what you may not be getting right now — to meet his or her expectations. Be prepared to back up any assertions with examples that illustrate the business implications of what's currently lacking in the relationship. Talk about what you could accomplish if things were different but avoid complaining about what you're unable to do right now.

✔ **Practice patience.** Regardless of how well it goes, don't expect any summit meeting with your manager to produce overnight miracles. If it achieves nothing more than a foundation for future meetings and establishes a level of communication that hasn't existed before, you've succeeded. Give the process some time. But also be prepared for the possibility that your boss may not be receptive to change and may respond angrily to your efforts. If you always err on the side of caution and tact, you can minimize the chances of this occurring. But if your boss responds angrily, the one thing you know is that you've done your best. You can't do any more than that.

To come to grips with this quandary, you need to ask yourself two questions:

✔ **What do you stand to gain by hanging in there?** It may be the money you're earning (more, perhaps, than you could earn elsewhere with a more understanding boss). It may be the opportunity to do something you wouldn't otherwise be able to do or work with someone who, apart from a disagreeable personality, has a great deal to teach you. Or it may be a credential that you need to move forward in your strategic career plan. If these goals are important to you and you can't achieve them elsewhere, you may decide that the tradeoff you're making is worthwhile (for a while, at least). This realization in and of itself may help you cope more effectively with the pressures.

✔ **Can you adopt coping mechanisms that will help get you through the tough times?** Clearly, you need a thick skin if you work for a tough boss, which means that you can't allow yourself to take it personally when your manager starts to blow off steam. It helps, too, to have a sense of humor. And most important, perhaps, you need to become more attuned to the day-to-day moods of your manager and adjust your behavior accordingly.

In the end, however, the question of whether you can work for a truly difficult boss comes down to your own personality and tolerance. Here's a simple test: If you get a knot in the pit of your stomach as soon you walk inside the front door of your office, you're probably not in a place that's good for you in the long run, regardless of how much money you're making or what you're learning.

Chapter 12

Winning Ways to Manage Effectively

*O*n the surface, you may think that your ability to achieve your career goals in today's business environment is mainly up to you: You map out a strategic plan, you make career decisions that are in sync with the broad outlines of a plan, and you perform successfully for each new job you fill or each project you work on.

But unless your line of work is one in which you operate pretty much on your own (you're a composer, for example, or a writer), your success in any given job situation also depends on your ability to manage other people.

In this chapter, you get a crash course in the basics of effective management, with special emphasis on the challenges that every manager is up against in a workplace undergoing warp-speed changes. You gain insights into the often-talked-about but not always easy-to-distinguish difference between being a good *manager* and being a good *leader*. You find out how to recruit and hire the best people. Finally, you're introduced to the key skills of excellent managers, and you get specific advice on those aspects of management (for example, how to motivate an underperforming employee) that many people find troublesome.

For even more detailed information, check out *Managing For Dummies* by Bob Nelson and Peter Economy and *Coaching & Mentoring For Dummies* by Marty Brounstein. (Both books are published by IDG Books Worldwide, Inc.)

Looking at Management Today

As a manager today, you not only face the same challenges that all managers have historically faced, you also have to meet these challenges in a workplace in which the traditional principles of effective management have shifted.

The basics of managing people still apply:

- ✔ You need to be well organized.
- ✔ You need to have good communication skills.
- ✔ You need to be able to motivate the people who work for you.

The difference, however, is that you now have to apply these skills in the face of new circumstances. If you manage in a typical company today, for example, some (if not most) of the people who report to you may have alternate working arrangements: they work part-time, work flextime, or telecommute two or three days a week (see Chapter 8 for more on these options). If you want to have a heart-to-heart with them, you can't simply walk down the hall and poke your head inside their cubicles.

There's a good chance, too — especially if you're working in an industry in which the workload can vary considerably from one month to the next — that some of the people you manage are consultants or contingent workers. Or perhaps you lead a work team and oversee employees who report to other managers.

What all these changes mean is this: Being a successful manager today involves much more than getting the work done. Yes, you and your team must still achieve objectives in a timely, cost-effective fashion. But if the only reason that the work is getting done is that you — along with maybe one or two key people — are putting in 15-hour days, your management skills may need improvement.

Don't get the wrong idea. Being a skilled manager doesn't necessarily guarantee that you're not going to work as hard or as long as you're now working (thus giving you more time to work on your tan or your golf swing). Instead, it means that you will spend less time on the details of tasks and more time focusing on higher-level, competitive and strategic challenges. It also means that you provide a work experience that is sufficiently interesting, challenging, and rewarding. Keep in mind that a big part of your company's ability to attract and retain committed, high-performance employees lies in the opportunities for professional growth and development. Management style figures prominently in this challenge.

Exploring the differences: Managing versus leading

Implicit in this new management imperative is a distinction with which you are undoubtedly familiar. It's the difference between managing and leading.

This difference — which has been the subject of countless books, seminars, and articles — can sometimes be difficult to define, particularly because so much overlap exists between the two roles. Essentially, the distinction lies more in philosophy than it does in specific management techniques. To make the transition from manager to leader (even if you're leading only one or two people), you may need to reframe some of your basic perceptions about management. You need to recognize that, as a leader, you must do more than simply pass along orders from above and ensure that these orders are implemented. You also have a responsibility to inspire the people who work for you and create a sense of energy and commitment.

Rating your leadership abilities

You need to do more than simply read about the basic principles of leadership to gain the necessary knowledge and make the transition from manager to leader. You need to evaluate your own practices and then improve your day-to-day habits.

The following exercise consists of 20 statements, each of which embodies one or more of the principles that underlie effective leadership. Using a scale of 0 to 5 (5 being an accurate description), rate the degree to which each statement accurately describes your current approach to managing. When you're finished with the test, look at any statements rated a 3 or below. These are aspects of your leadership skills that need improvement.

___ I have developed a clearly defined vision of my department or group, and I have communicated this vision to everyone who reports to me.

___ I have developed an action plan with objectives supporting the vision and have explained that plan to my group.

___ The people in my group understand my values; that is, what I stand for. I go out of my way to make sure that my job performance and management style are consistent with those values.

___ I take time to make sure that each person understands his role, recognizes his value to the organization, and collaborates with me to establish performance standards.

___ I don't hesitate to give the people in my group meaningful responsibility, and I provide the resources and support they need to meet that responsibility.

___ I've done my best to create an environment that fosters enthusiasm, cooperation, and high performance.

___ I spend a good percentage of each week focusing on the higher-level issues that can directly impact the company's competitive edge.

___ I do everything I can to help people develop, grow, and realize their professional ambitions, even if it means that, by doing so, they may leave my team.

___ I'm not afraid to express my concerns to upper management if I feel that people on my team are being treated unfairly or if they are inadequately rewarded or recognized.

___ I acknowledge that I don't always have the right answers, and I seek and accept the advice of people who have more experience and expertise, regardless of their rank.

___ Whenever I'm confronted with a tough issue, I meet it head on, dealing with it as decisively and expeditiously as possible.

___ I freely share my expertise and experience with my group, without any fear that such sharing threatens my job security.

___ I'm willing to take prudent risks when the benefits for the organization and my group outweigh the potential for failure.

___ I'm able to make tough and important decisions without worrying excessively about others' perceptions or approval.

___ I keep my word. If I make a promise or commitment to someone, I do everything humanly possible to follow through on it.

___ I don't get defensive when people express doubts or have questions about a decision I've made or an initiative I've recommended. I see it as part of my role to convince people — without relying solely on rank — that a decision or initiative has merit.

___ When I give people responsibility to perform a task, I allow them an opportunity to perform it in the best way they know how. I don't second-guess them if they don't perform the task the way I would have.

___ I recognize that not everyone is motivated by the same desires or ambitions and I adjust my leadership style accordingly.

Whenever I'm communicating one-on-one with someone on my team, I devote my complete attention and do my best to understand the ___ concerns that underlie her comments.

I encourage creative problem solving and reward risk takers. When mis takes are made, I look at them as opportunities for everyone to improve ___ rather than behavior that needs to be punished.

Rating your total score:

- ✔ 90 or higher: Stellar leadership abilities
- ✔ 80 to 89: Excellent
- ✔ 70 to 79: Good but could be better
- ✔ Below 70: Room for improvement

Spelling Out the ABCs of Effective Management

If you're looking for advice on how to manage or lead more effectively, you have plenty of options, from downloading free articles on the Internet to registering for executive seminars that can cost as much as a mid-sized automobile. Essentially, the keys to effective management are contained in a handful of core principles. The following sections give you a look at what you may call the ABC guide to management.

A = Adapting and adjusting

Every manager has his or her own style of managing, and that's okay, as long as you can adapt to the individual needs and personalities of the people on your team to maximize their contributions. Some of your employees may flourish when you give them a great deal of autonomy. Others may require closer supervision. Some may let you know right away when they're not comfortable with some aspect of your managing style. Others won't say a word — until you coax concerns from them. To thrive as a manager, you need to be able to make the subtle adjustments that can mean the difference between employees who simply show up and employees who make a difference.

B = Building value

This principle is the cornerstone of everything you do as a manager. *Building value* means incorporating strategic messages into every objective you set —

whether you're creating a work plan for your group or having a heart-to-heart with an underperforming employee. Your role is to communicate that employees drive their individual career successes as well as the company's success. You need to explain how their actions positively impact the organization's goals and objectives. That's a lofty message, admittedly, and it's not always easy to make the connection in every instance. The trick is to build this message into everything you do, as often as possible.

C = Communicating

The communication you have with your employees must go well beyond providing instructions for a particular job. You need to have an open, honest, and two-way flow of information between you and your staff members. And that means you have to be equally concerned about your listening skills and your ability to articulate ideas and long-range vision. The goal is to encourage and respond to input from your employees.

D = Delegating

If you're not delegating — that is, assigning responsibility to others — you're not managing. Delegating is, in fact, the very essence of managing. But you need to know how to delegate, which means matching the right tasks with the right people, based on the strategic needs of your department and the capabilities of your staff members. And you have to remember, too, that the challenge of delegating doesn't end when you've assigned the task. You need to make sure that you're providing a person with the authority, knowledge, and resources to accomplish the objective.

E = Energizing

Energizing is another word for motivating — managing your staff members in a way that fosters commitment and enthusiasm. These qualities can mean the difference between mediocre and good performance and good and exemplary performance. Contrary to popular belief, you don't have to be a spellbinding orator or a psychologist to motivate people. You simply have to take the time to find out what is important to them and do your best to help them achieve those objectives.

Hiring the Right People

Half the battle of effective management is finding people who share your vision and commitment to excellence and want to work together toward a common goal. It takes a lot of time, patience, and focus to recruit and retain the best employees. But it's an investment that pays critical dividends — and it's an investment you must be prepared to make. The following sections give you some suggestions on how to do it.

Thinking strategically

Instead of viewing hiring as "filling a vacancy," focus first on the strategic needs of your group, department, or business. Then ask yourself what combination of skills and expertise is required to meet those needs. You may find that the best person isn't one individual but instead a combination of resources, such as two part-time employees (each with different skills). Or you may need to reorganize the work flow and hire a contract employee for a special project.

Making the job description accurate

When developing the job descriptions, draw a clear distinction between responsibilities and qualifications. Responsibilities are the tasks or duties for which an employee is accountable. Qualifications are the combination of knowledge, skills, and attributes that are necessary to do the job well. Make sure that any experience or credentials you list as qualifications are absolutely necessary for the job, as opposed to preferred standards of achievement that have no real bearing on job performance (an advanced degree, for example).

Casting a wide net

Every hiring initiative should include a disciplined, well-thought-out recruiting strategy. The goal of that strategy is not simply to attract a large number of applicants but to attract quality applicants. Some options worth considering include:

- ✔ **Employee referrals:** Encourage employees to refer friends and relatives and offer incentives to staff. (Be careful, however, that you carefully spell out the particulars of the incentive program.)

- ✔ **Network referrals:** Ask other professionals in your network for candidate referrals. Be as specific as possible when you're telling people what you're looking for, and make sure you trust the source of a recommendation.

- ✔ **Online postings and job boards:** Be sure to list employment opportunities on your organization's Web site, as well as on staffing firm sites and online job boards. For more details on Internet recruiting, get ahold of my book, *Human Resources Kit For Dummies* (IDG Books Worldwide, Inc.).

- ✔ **Classified advertising (print):** Don't overlook regional newspapers or professional journals and do take the time to write an ad that will attract the right candidates.

- ✔ **Recruiters:** Check out recruiters personally and look for firms that specialize in finding people with the talent and skills you need.

Setting up a screening system

The simplest method for sorting candidate resumes is to decide who warrants a brief screening interview (usually completed over the phone) and who doesn't. After you've screened applicants, decide who warrants a face-to-face interview. Your overall objective is to limit the number of interviewees to only those people who are strong candidates for the job.

Getting the most out of interviews

Extracting key information and insights from an interview is an extraordinary challenge — especially when savvy job seekers go out of their way to showcase strengths and camouflage their weaknesses. Don't make the mistake of underestimating the difficulty of the interview process. Here are some suggestions:

- ✔ **Make time.** Set aside at least 45 minutes or an hour for each interview and do your best to schedule the interviews during a period in which you're not going to have to deal with frequent interruptions.

- ✔ **Prepare carefully.** Familiarize yourself with the applicant's background. Decide ahead of time which areas you want to focus on during the interview and which questions you're going to ask.

- ✔ **Put the candidate at ease.** Disregard any advice you may have heard about gaining insight into a candidate's personality by testing his or her reactions to uncomfortable circumstances. This method says more about you than the candidate. You'll be able to elicit more candid responses by creating a casual, comfortable interview environment.

- ✔ **Ask open-ended questions.** Ask questions that require more than a "yes" or "no" answer and provide some insight into how the candidate thinks or solves problems. Instead of asking, "Are you detail-oriented?" ask, "Can you give me some examples of situations in which your attention to detail made a significant contribution to a project?" As often as you can, ask questions to prompt the candidate to reveal the way he thinks and operates.

✔ **Coordinate your questions.** Ask the candidate many of the same questions that you plan to ask his or her references. That way, you can compare the answers. If a reference tells you something significantly different than what the candidate tells you, follow up with the candidate for an explanation.

✔ **Be systematic in the final decision.** Whether you're making the decision by yourself or with others, always set up some reasonably systematic way of evaluating applicants. You need to measure their perceived strengths and weaknesses in conjunction with the position's key requirements. The simplest system is to rank (based on its relative importance to job performance) each of the hiring criteria and then rate candidates on a scale of 0 to 5 (5 is the most qualified) in each area. For some jobs, you may want to administer a test to help you evaluate particular skills that are relevant to the position.

✔ **Check references yourself.** Yes, it can be time consuming and often frustrating to get former employers to tell you anything other than name, rank, and serial number for a candidate, but its worth the investment. You'll usually get better results if you handle the reference checking yourself and if you don't limit your efforts to former bosses. Try to talk to a candidate's coworkers or professional colleagues. Keep in mind that you're looking for input that either confirms or challenges your impressions of the candidate.

To hire or not to hire?

Avoid the following six pitfalls when making your final hiring decision:

✔ **Carelessness:** Don't rely solely on your memory. Take diligent notes during interviews so that you can review them when making the final decision.

✔ **Lack of perspective:** Try not to attach disproportionate importance to a candidate's ability to handle himself during an interview. (Remember, savvy candidates know how to camouflage weaknesses.)

✔ **Underestimating the importance of enthusiasm:** If a candidate can't demonstrate enthusiasm during the interview process, don't make the mistake of thinking that he or she will be able to muster enthusiasm for the job itself.

✔ **The halo effect:** Don't allow one particular aspect of a candidate's background (the fact that she went to an Ivy League school or, like you, has a pet boa constrictor) blind you to all the obvious reasons why she shouldn't be hired.

✔ **Too many chefs:** It's okay to seek input from relevant parties, but try to limit the number of people who have a say in the final decision. Otherwise, you'll end up with a candidate who, instead of being the best, is the least objectionable.

Managerial Charisma: Eight Keys to Inspiring Better Performance

If there's one overall responsibility you have as a manager in today's workplace, it is simply this: to do everything in your power to inspire people to realize their full potential as employees and as individuals. You don't have to conduct yourself like a professional sports coach or have movie-star charisma to inspire extraordinary performance. But you yourself have to be motivated and you have to work at conveying that energy and commitment. The following sections give you some guidelines.

Creating an inspiring vision

You hear so much about "vision" these days that you may wonder whether you need to spend years in the desert meditating on the mysteries of management. Not quite. But there's a reason that vision has become so important today: The workplace demands it. To flourish in the global marketplace, companies need their employees to take initiative and assume personal responsibility for meeting the needs of customers. Staff members — not just managers — need to find new and more efficient ways to handle day-to-day operations. And if employees are going to rise to this challenge, they need something to believe in and rally around. They need an ideal to which they can aspire.

True, it's usually up to senior management to create a vision for the company as a whole. But all managers need to instill a sense of higher purpose in their staffs. If you're a technology manager, for example, the vision may be communicated in terms of responsiveness to the business needs of the rest of the company. If you're managing customer service staff, the vision may be superior customer satisfaction, as measured by an independent source. You have any number of options, depending on your line of work. What's important is that you recognize the importance of a vision, that you take the time to outline a vision, and that you inspire your staff to rally around it.

Clarifying roles and responsibilities

By providing this information, you can make everything else you do as a manager that much easier. To work together effectively, everyone in your group must understand his or her responsibilities and how performance is evaluated. The essentials are as follows:

✔ **Job descriptions:** Make sure that everyone who works for you has a detailed job description.

✔ **Understanding one another:** Give each person a clear sense of what others do and how the team functions.

✔ **Questions:** Create an environment in which everyone feels free to discuss confusion or doubt about roles and expectations.

✔ **Conflicts:** When conflicts arise, let responsibilities and expectations be the starting point of discussion.

Setting stretch goals

Good motivators place more confidence in the people they manage than the employees may place in themselves. Follow their example. Encourage those who work for you to set goals that stretch their skills and abilities. Help them develop professionally in ways they may not have been aware were possible. Be sure to provide a supportive environment and be there to coach and mentor if your employees run into problems. People will begin to discover for themselves that, hey, they're a lot smarter than they thought. Their job performance will begin to soar, and your job as their manager will become a lot easier and more fun.

Coaching your team

Nearly all successful leaders in business today understand the value of turning followers into leaders. The role they envision for themselves goes beyond supervision; they also see themselves as mentors and coaches. They take the time to get to know each person they manage and, in particular, to understand the career ambitions of their staff.

Here are some other suggestions on how to become a coach:

✔ **Getting to know you:** Find out early on what each of your employees' professional aspirations are and keep those ambitions in mind when you're assigning tasks and offering feedback.

✔ **I'm here to help:** Encourage your employees to seek your guidance whenever they're running into problems. And when they take you up on your offer, make sure you listen, empathize, and do your best to help them work things out.

✔ **Let's grow together:** Create a development plan with each employee and establish milestones. Let the person take the steps needed to gain new knowledge and develop new skills, but offer your assistance in overcoming any obstacles.

Realize that some people may want to move on to another company to reach their career goals. You'll be a better coach if you help them grow professionally to reach those aspirations than if you hold them back in an effort to keep them on board. If you stifle an employee's opportunities, you may receive a letter of resignation sooner than later.

✔ **Different strokes:** As long as people are demonstrating the right attitude and making progress, don't expect everyone to advance at the same speed. Some people are quick studies; others may be slow but steady, after they get comfortable. Don't impede the learning process by showing impatience.

Solving problems together

Whenever problems arise that affect your department as a whole, resist the temptation to fix it quickly yourself and impose the solution on others. Employees will always be more enthusiastic about initiatives to which they themselves contributed. Instead of saying, "Here's what I think you should do," when people come to you with problems, try asking, "What do you think we ought to do?" Here again, you don't want to make this strategy a pointless exercise. If you ask people their opinions, you have an obligation to consider what they tell you and explain your rationale, if you don't agree.

Showing your gratitude

When your staff or team members do a good job, let them know — and always sooner than later. You can show your approval in any number of ways, and it doesn't always have to be with a monetary reward. A "thank you" via e-mail, a public acknowledgement at a team meeting, a private word of thanks — these simple gestures can carry powerful motivational significance, as long as the praise is warranted and genuine.

Remember, it's virtually impossible to overpraise people who are doing a good job. But in order for praise to have any effect, it must be heartfelt and warranted. If you get into the habit of praising people indiscriminately simply as a way of making them feel good and without any real justification, you weaken the impact of praise you offer when it's been truly earned.

Making decisions

You don't want to get a reputation among your staff members for being arbitrary and impetuous, but you also don't want to slow down the workflow through indecisiveness. When big issues arise, be diligent about gathering the facts and soliciting input. But after you've thought things through, don't procrastinate: Make the decision.

Launching a mentoring program

Your company may already have a mentoring program in place, but be sure to encourage your team or department to participate. In most of these types of programs, junior employees are paired with more advanced, experienced workers. It's possible that such relationships may already exist informally. Frequently, however, new employees can be reluctant to ask for help because they're embarrassed, and experienced staff members can be hesitant to offer help for fear of interfering. By encouraging mentoring as an established process, you eliminate these problems and create a more collaborative and more productive atmosphere.

Grooming Your Successor

Assume for a moment that you've been offered a job that you've always wanted, but with one condition: You have to find someone who can do your current job as well as, if not better than, you. Assume, too, that someone in the department seems to be a likely candidate for this but still needs some help — and mainly from you.

The phrase *succession planning* sounds at first blush as though it belongs in a book about the British monarchy, but there's no misprint here. Succession planning, which means grooming someone to take over your job, has now become a key concept in organizational development — and not only at the CEO level. Conventional wisdom, of course, may lead you to think that by grooming someone to take over your job, you are, in effect, cooking your own career goose — that is, undermining your leverage and creating a scenario that may someday cost you your job. ("Gee, Frank. You've done such a great job training your staff, we don't really need you anymore.") But not so. You and your company will likely find the following benefits in succession planning:

- ✔ Companies that encourage managers to groom their own successors almost always have an easier time meeting their staffing needs because they're able to fill key positions by promoting from within. They don't have to worry as much about the departure of key managers, which disrupts productivity.

- ✔ The fact that you've taken the time and energy to develop your staff members means that your own chances of promotion improve. Senior management at your company doesn't have to be concerned as they may otherwise be about the void that may be created if you were to be promoted from your current job.

- ✔ Grooming your successor gives you and your company an insurance policy of sorts in the event something unexpected happens that forces you to take an extended leave.

✔ The more responsibility your staff members are able to assume, the more time you can spend on higher-level strategic issues that enhance the productivity of your team or department and increase your visibility in the company.

A recent survey conducted by Robert Half International in conjunction with the Financial Executives Institute found that while 82 percent of the CFOs polled in the survey reported that they themselves had not been groomed for their current position, two-thirds of them were actively grooming their successors. This trend also seems to be taking hold at other levels along the corporate ladder — and for reasons that relate to both the productivity of the company and the career progress of individuals.

The following are a few key principles for succession planning:

✔ **Hire smart.** Whenever you have the opportunity to add new people to your staff, incorporate into your hiring criteria (in addition to the requirements of job itself) the qualities and attributes that will allow that individual to accept greater responsibility down the road. And without necessarily tapping someone as your heir apparent, try to identify as many people as you can who, with the right leadership, can conceivably fill your role.

✔ **Let star employees fly solo.** Staff members who are bright, observant, and highly motivated should be able to learn a great deal by osmosis; that is, by observing how you deal with the various challenges of your job. But you shouldn't rely solely on passive learning. Make sure that you have a clear idea of what's required to be successful in your job (other than your own irreplaceable brilliance!) and take the time to determine how much of a gap exists between those attributes and the skills and abilities possessed by the person or people you're grooming. Delegate as much as possible, allowing your staff members an increasing amount of autonomy as they gain new skills and knowledge. Work with them individually and as a group to set performance goals and establish criteria to determine progress in those areas that are most critical.

✔ **Avoid the cloning pitfall.** It's natural to expect the person or people you're grooming to follow your lead in most aspects of the job you currently hold, but keep in mind that the same performance objectives can be achieved in a variety of ways. Focus your grooming efforts on objectives and values, as opposed to style, giving your staff members an opportunity to determine for themselves how they handle a particular task. Their style of working and managing may differ from yours, but as long as those differences don't affect the quality of the work, it benefits neither you nor them to insist that everything be done your way.

Keep in mind that one of the cardinal rules of succession planning today is to make sure that while you're grooming your successor, you, too, are taking steps that prepare you to go to the next level. Make sure that you're acquiring or developing abilities that will qualify you for higher-level jobs. And work with your manager — or your mentor — to provide you with whatever additional help you need to position yourself for that move.

Handing Off: Keys to Delegating

Delegating is often described as a manager's number-one tool — one of the first skills emphasized in a management training program. Delegating isn't an exact science, however. You have to recognize that some tasks are easier to delegate than others and that some people can accept responsibilities better than others.

Breaking bad habits

If you're a card-carrying micromanager (and you know who you are), you need to change your ways. Start small. Draw up a list of all the tasks you perform and break them into roughly three categories:

- ✔ A: Tasks that you are absolutely, totally, irrefutably convinced only you can do
- ✔ B: Tasks that someone else may be able to do well (though not as well as you, of course)
- ✔ C: Tasks that you're absolutely, totally, and irrefutably convinced don't require unusual skills or knowledge

Start by delegating C-level tasks and gradually incorporate B- and A-level responsibilities. Be sure to reevaluate your list from time to time. As you begin to delegate more and become comfortable with the process, you may find that your list has fewer A-level tasks and many more B- and C-level items.

Providing specific instructions

When you delegate, take some time to make sure the person is aware of the following key points:

> ✔ The ultimate objective
>
> ✔ Why it's important
>
> ✔ The deadline(s)
>
> ✔ The measurements of success

If you're not sure you've communicated all this, send a follow-up e-mail or memo outlining the information.

Trusting others

Delegating, by definition, presupposes that you have confidence in the ability of another person to do the job. If you lack that confidence, you shouldn't be delegating that particular task to that particular person. And if you're hesitant to delegate any tasks to any of the people who work for you, it means one of two things: You're either hiring the wrong people or you have an excessive need to control.

Offering support

Be sensitive to the difference between delegating and dumping. When you *dump,* you simply assign a task without concern for time, skills, or resources. When you delegate, you and the employee determine what's needed to complete the task, and you provide the necessary support.

Allowing for growth

Delegating should be an ongoing practice. As an employee demonstrates an ability to assume greater responsibility, delegate more and grant him or her additional autonomy. Doing so will make both of your jobs more interesting, exciting, and fulfilling.

Making Meetings More Effective

Here's a quick mental exercise for you. Think back to the last two or three meetings you attended as a participant, not a leader, and answer the following questions:

✔ Was it absolutely necessary for me to be there?

✔ Was it easy to maintain interest or did most of the discussion have little bearing on what I do in my job?

✔ When I felt the need to say something, did I get an opportunity to do so and did people listen and pay attention?

✔ When the meeting was over, did I feel as though my time was well spent?

Now put yourself in the shoes of the people who attend the meetings you lead, and ask yourself how they would respond if you were to ask them the same questions. If you're not sure how they would answer, here are ten suggestions:

✔ **Make the meeting count.** If there's no compelling reason for the meeting to be held, don't schedule it. Every meeting should have a purpose that everyone can relate to and support — even if it's simply to bring people together for some old-fashioned brainstorming or team-building exercises.

✔ **Hold it in a suitable place.** The conference room down the hall may not always be the right place for every meeting. Be sure to select a room that's well lit, spacious, and equipped with facilities to accommodate everyone. But if your goal is to brainstorm out-of-the-box solutions to a particular problem, consider moving the meeting offsite to produce a more creative environment. Be open to new locations for special circumstances.

✔ **Limit the list of invitees.** When deciding who should attend the meeting, ask yourself the following two questions:

 • Whose job or area of expertise will be affected by the topics of discussion? (Don't be too confining when you're making this determination.)

 • Is there anyone else whose insight, experience, or expertise (regardless of position or rank) can provide input?

Be sensitive to the potential for bruised feelings. If someone on your staff doesn't meet either of these criteria but may feel slighted if not asked, explain the purpose of the meeting and let him or her decide whether to attend.

✔ **Create a written agenda.** An agenda is simply a rough outline of the proposed discussion and is particularly helpful when covering three or more topics. Consider priorities when you're creating the agenda and deal with the most important items first. That helps ensure that you don't spend too much time discussing the flavor of punch for next month's party at the expense of resolving a current crisis with a $2 million project.

✔ **Start — and end — on time.** Unless you have a very good reason for doing otherwise (a power blackout, for example), start the meeting on time. If people can arrive 15 minutes late and find that the meeting hasn't started yet, they don't have an incentive to arrive on time for future meetings. It's equally important to end the meeting on time. If important matters still need to be discussed but time has run out, offer participants a choice. The discussion can continue with those who are able to stay, or another meeting can be scheduled for all participants at another time.

✔ **Encourage participation.** Not everyone is equally articulate or comfortable expressing his or her views at meetings. So it's up to you as the facilitator to guide the discussion and solicit input from people who would otherwise be quiet.

✔ **Keep everyone on target.** Hard as it may be when you have a creative group of staff members, be sure that everyone remains focused on the issues that are on the agenda. If new ideas crop up that require a significant amount of time for discussion, consider rescheduling the topic for another meeting. While you don't want to inhibit creativity, you need to make sure that objectives for the meeting are achieved.

✔ **Take notes.** Make sure that someone takes notes on the discussion, particularly any items that require action or a decision. Meeting notes are a further reminder of what needs to be done and they provide a summary of the discussion for those who can't attend.

✔ **Monitor the success.** Let your staff members know that you want their feedback on how to make the meetings more productive and effective (and no need to call a meeting for this). Be willing to accept the possibility that what worked in the past may not work under present circumstances.

✔ **Pay attention to group process.** Try to monitor how smoothly the group interacts and gets along. If someone on the team seems upset by the direction of the meeting, meet with him or her one-to-one to discuss concerns. But if you're not happy with the dynamic overall, consider bringing in an outside facilitator to provide new ideas or resolve conflicts.

Conducting Performance Appraisals

Some organizational authorities don't have flattering things to say about the way formal performance appraisal systems are administered — and with good reason. Managers, generally speaking, don't like the paperwork that many appraisals require and they have difficulty delivering constructive criticism.

On the other hand, everyone agrees that employees need regular feedback through a reasonably formal process that serves as an objective basis for promotion and merit raises. The following sections give you some suggestions that may help you make the best of an important — but not always easy-to-deal-with — issue.

Viewing it as a process

Rather than thinking of a performance appraisal as a periodic event, see it as a year-round process in which the formal appraisal is simply one of a series of steps. The chief advantage — and it's a significant one — is that the official evaluation, when it comes, will be less tense and more productive. Because you communicate openly throughout the year, the annual appraisal simply serves as a reminder of issues previously discussed and is a springboard to future action.

Partnering for results

Involve the employee as much as possible in establishing goals and the criteria for success. People perform much better when they have a say in their objectives and understand expectations.

Explaining the process

Make sure that employees know the extent to which appraisals determine bonuses or raises. They should also know what recourse they have if they don't agree with an appraisal.

Offering specifics

Provide specific examples when critiquing poor work performance and discuss behaviors, not attitudes. Instead of saying, "You didn't try as hard when you were working on the last project," (that's an interpretation) spell out what actually happened: "The last report you submitted failed to mention two key points."

Asking for input

One technique that many management experts recommend for performance appraisal meetings is to allow an employee to provide a self-evaluation that offers his or her views. The advantage of this approach is that the employee is prompted to review strengths and weaknesses before the meeting and is not, therefore, surprised by your feedback. This technique also allows you to gain insight into how the employee evaluates his or her performance, and lets both of you clarify expectations.

Managing Underperformers

You know who they are and you may have one or two of them working for you. They do their job, but barely — just enough to get by. They lack commitment to their work and it shows in the quality. You could, of course, fire such a person, but that's not always the best option. The following sections offer some strategies.

Discussing the issues

Maybe you've already tried this before, but you may want to consider trying it again: Schedule a one-to-one discussion with the employee. Define the problems and provide specific examples. Express, as tactfully as possible, your displeasure and give the employee a chance to explain. There may be some issues you're not aware of — friction within the department or pressures at home.

Developing a plan

Make sure the underperforming employee understands his role, your expectations, and the impact his contribution can have on the success of your department or company. Rather than simply issuing a "shape-up-or-ship-out" option, get the employee to develop his own "get-back-on-track" strategy.

Assigning a mentor

If the person doesn't already have a mentor and is relatively new to the department, see if you can pair her with an experienced leader. As with all mentoring arrangements, find someone who knows the ropes, enjoys mentoring, and whose personality is a good fit with the employee's.

Counteracting boredom

If you suspect that a big part of an employee's problem is boredom, look for ways to make the job interesting without disrupting workflow and without alienating other employees. Find out from the employee what additional tasks he may enjoy.

If you manage a large group of people, think twice before you offer a reward to any underperforming employee. By providing rewards to these employees, you run the risk of alienating those who perform well but don't get rewarded.

Dealing with Dismissals

Dismissing an employee is, by far, the most stressful aspect of a manager's job. Sure, you can justify the decision, but that doesn't make it any easier to tell a person that his or her services are no longer required. So don't delude yourself into thinking that you can handle this extremely difficult task in some easy way. There aren't any. But the following sections offer you some suggestions to help you make a difficult process as professional as possible.

Deciding to act

Employees should be given every reasonable opportunity to become proficient at their jobs. And if they're not measuring up, they should receive feedback and guidance on how to improve. But if you've provided that information and opportunity to improve, and the employee — for whatever reason — still doesn't achieve the objectives, you need to take decisive action. The sooner you act the better. Employees who can't fulfill their responsibilities or whose behavior is disruptive can create problems for you, their coworkers, and the company.

Delivering the news

Dismissing an employee is one task that should never be delegated. If you're the person's manager, break the news in person. Be tactful and sensitive, but get to the point. Any explanation of why the person is being terminated should be brief.

Following a disciplined procedure

Many companies outline specific procedures for terminating an employee. These procedures can protect your company from legal action and can make things easier for you and the employee. Typical procedures include the following:

- ✔ **Documenting:** Document the behavior, poor performance, and prior performance-counseling discussions that lead to the decision to terminate an employee.

- ✔ **Planning your words:** Plan your agenda in advance of the meeting and think about exactly what you will say. Say only what is necessary to deliver the news and potentially respond to simple questions. This is not the time to review ancient work history or debate your decision.

✔ **Delivering the news:** If at all possible, deliver the news first thing in the morning or at the end of the workday — ideally, after most of the employees have gone home. Make sure that another manager is present when you deliver the news so that you can prevent claims that you said something you really didn't say during the discussion.

✔ **Making arrangements:** Provide a severance check, pro-rated salary due, expense reimbursements, or outplacement arrangements at the time of the dismissal.

✔ **Safe-guarding access:** When you deliver the news, request that all security-related items, such as keys, passwords, or company credit cards be given back immediately. Alert your information technology department (if appropriate) to discontinue the person's access to the network or equipment.

✔ **Returning equipment:** Make specific arrangements for the return of any company-owned equipment (computer, vehicle, and so on).

✔ **Accompanying the employee:** Accompany the dismissed employee to retrieve his or her personal effects.

✔ **Taking precautions:** If you have any reason to suspect (based on the employee's personality or past behavior) a violent reaction to the news, take reasonable precautions, such as having another person in the office with you.

Chapter 13

Pulling Together: Making Teamwork Work for You

● ●

In This Chapter

▶ Looking at high-performance teams

▶ Getting off to the best start on a new team

▶ Leading an effective team

▶ Creating virtual teams

▶ Finding solutions for teams in trouble

● ●

*T*eamwork has been a core value in American life ever since colonial times, and it's a value that virtually every organization has historically tried to foster in its workforce. But it's only been within the past 20 years — and largely because of competitive pressures in the global marketplace — that the actual dynamics of teamwork have become an integral part of the day-to-day work practices in many American companies.

It's true, of course, that team-oriented work practices have not always been a rousing success in every organization that has tried to adopt them. In fact, one of the harsher lessons many companies learned during the 1990s is that the power of effective teaming requires more than pulling together a group of employees and labeling them a "team." American culture celebrates individual achievement, and traditional work practices and reward systems aren't always in sync with the conditions that promote successful teams. What's more, many people don't fully appreciate — until they themselves are part of a team on an important project — how difficult operating in a truly collaborative fashion can be.

Clearly, though, the trend toward teamwork is intensifying throughout the workplace. Recent surveys show that more than two-thirds of major American companies have integrated elements of teaming into various aspects of their operations. And senior management in these companies seem committed to the practice. In a recent survey conducted by Robert Half International, more than 80 percent of chief financial officers in *Fortune* 1000 corporations asserted that self-managed teams will increase productivity in the decade ahead. And when the Work in America Institute asked a group of members representing 100 leading American companies what research topics would have the most value to their companies, 95 percent indicated, "teamwork — creating and sustaining team-based organizations," as the highest priority.

What does this trend mean to you and your career strategies? Simply this: Unless you've been blessed with a trust fund with a total asset figure that includes at least two commas, you may have a tough time achieving your career goals without a team-oriented mindset. What's more, in light of the nature of work teams today, you need to be able to function effectively as not only a member of a team, but also as a team leader.

This chapter focuses on the skills and attributes you need to possess to perform effectively in a team-oriented environment. You get a look at what teamwork really means when applied to critical business functions. You gain insights into the qualities that differentiate high-performance teams from teams that fail to realize their potential. You get advice on how to make a meaningful contribution to a team, regardless of what role you're playing: leader or follower. And you pick up tips on how to avoid the common barriers to successful teamwork and what to do if those barriers materialize.

Understanding Work Teams

Before you can begin to adapt to a team-oriented environment, you should have a general idea of the overall concept. A good starting point is to familiarize yourself with the sometimes-confusing terminology that surrounds teams. Here's a look at the most common teamwork terms and their meanings:

- ✔ **Work team:** Any group of employees (usually no more than 15 and rarely part of the same department) who have been pulled together for the purpose of working together on either a temporary or permanent basis in a specific function.

- ✔ **Project team:** A specific kind of work team, formed to handle a particular project or problem, such as the introduction of a new company-wide benefits package. (Project teams are sometimes called *steering groups* or *task forces.*)

- ✔ **Cross-functional team:** Any team — project or otherwise — made up of people from different departments or specialties. (Cross-functional teams are often created as part of quality initiatives and are sometimes formed to foster collaboration in companies with a history of interdepartmental tensions.)

- ✔ **Self-directed teams:** Work teams that have been given significant autonomy in such areas as budgeting, scheduling, or hiring.

These definitions can't be taken too literally. The categories overlap and each has numerous variations. Depending on the project or the company, for example, a project team may work together for either a few months or for more than a year or two. That team may have little or no authority to make key decisions or it may have so much autonomy that it operates, in effect, as a company within a company. Teams can also vary significantly with respect to size, makeup, and the extent to which members are able to work exclusively for the team (as opposed to dividing their responsibilities between the team's mission and their regular jobs).

But regardless of their form, all work teams face the same fundamental challenge: channeling the knowledge, talents, and efforts of individuals into a collective force whose output is significantly greater than the sum of its parts. The very concept of teams is based on the premise that a group of people working together with a wide range of skills and perspectives achieve far more than individuals working independently toward the same collective goal.

Gaining Insight from High-Performance Work Teams

Making measurable contributions (as either a leader or team member) presupposes that you recognize and embrace the qualities that differentiate high-performance work teams from work teams in general. A growing number of organizational researchers and business reporters have been investigating these qualities over the past decade, with enlightening — though hardly surprising — results. The teams that have been the focal point of this research represent a variety of industries, from professional sports teams to the military to business. But research shows, in general, that high-performance teams, regardless of their field or mission, share similar practices. And although the challenges faced by these teams may not mirror the obstacles faced by other teams, it's a good idea to familiarize yourself with their practices and use them as a benchmark for your own future team efforts.

Inspiring a sense of mission

High-performance teams are almost invariably driven by a deeply rooted sense of mission. Each has its own particular goals, depending on the type of work it does. The mission may be to win the Super Bowl, save the lives of accident victims, develop a new software application, or rescue comrades whose planes have crashed behind enemy lines. Whatever form they take, however, the goals that unite high-performance teams are always broad enough and inspiring enough to transcend the individual aspirations of team members. Workers on high-performance work teams view their jobs as a calling, not just a means of earning a living, and are usually willing to work long hours and make other sacrifices to achieve the team goal. That shared sense of mission becomes the glue that holds the team together, enabling it to weather storms and overcome obstacles that would weaken the resolve of less committed teams.

Orchestrating a strong team ethic

Members of high-performance teams subscribe without reservation to a team ethic. They are able — and willing — to subordinate their own aspirations and ambitions to the collective goals and interests of the team. Individual expertise counts, of course. You can't have a high-performance team unless its individuals have the skills and knowledge required to perform their jobs exceptionally well. But individual expertise isn't enough to ensure outstanding successful team performance. Members of these teams are invariably more concerned about team success than with their own achievements. In an interview with *Fortune* magazine, cellist Sadao Harada of the Tokyo String Quartet said, "We don't think about who gets to show off their great sound, their great technique. We must project as one and put forth the quartet's musical personality."

Fostering good chemistry

Chemistry refers to how members of a team get along with each other — at least during the time that they're working together. You probably won't be surprised to discover that in high-performance teams, chemistry isn't just good, it's phenomenal. True, individuals who spend enough time working together to overcome challenges do, as a matter of course, bond with one another. But the chemistry found among high-performance teams goes beyond the conventional boundaries of team spirit. There's typically a powerful sense of family — individuals are concerned about and look out for one another.

The chemistry that pervades high-performance teams manifests itself in numerous ways, but particularly in the ease with which team members communicate. You can see this quality primarily during team meetings. Even when a hierarchy exists (as is the case of a hospital or a military unit, for example), people speak their minds spontaneously. No one seems preoccupied with saying the wrong things or making mistakes.

One reason that communication can be so open is that the members of high-performance teams trust one another, and this eliminates many of the barriers that reduce the effectiveness of other teams.

Examining the popularity of work teams

The following are four reasons why work teams have become one of the key trends in American business over the past decade:

✔ Everything else being equal, a well-organized team usually outperforms individuals working independently toward the same goals.

✔ Small, project-oriented work teams are much more flexible than large groups. They can meet more frequently, communicate more intimately, and change directions more quickly, should the need arise.

✔ Team projects, when managed well, provide members with a sense of comaraderie and accomplishment that they may not get from their regular jobs.

✔ Thanks to advances in information technology, geography is no longer a barrier. Teams in many companies today consist of employees who work in locations throughout the world and maintain communication through e-mail and teleconferencing.

Developing discipline

High-performance teams recognize how inherently difficult it can be for individuals with different backgrounds, skills, and temperaments to work toward a common goal. Consequently, these teams adhere to disciplined processes expressly designed to reinforce the team ethic. High-performance teams take time, especially at the start of a project, to develop protocols — a certain way of doing things. Process dictates how meetings are conducted, how responsibility is shared, how information is communicated, and how conflicts are resolved.

What Does It Take to Be a Team Player?

Just about everyone at some point has been part of a team or a group effort. So you would think that adjusting to the demands of work teams would be relatively easy. Not so. To be a productive member of a team, you need to be able to do something that doesn't come naturally to most people. On the one hand, you need to be as productive as you would be if you were working on your own, handling your job in the way you and your manager see fit. On the other hand, you need to work within team-oriented rules, protocols, and work practices. It's possible, for example, that you're one of those 11th-hour persons who does his best work when the crunch hits, but that working style may be counterproductive within a group. Or it's possible that you've never been comfortable delegating key tasks that directly affect your work, which means that it's not going to be easy for you to enter into the kinds of trusting relationships that underlie successful team performance.

But why dwell on the negative? The truth is, if you are like most people, you're fully capable of becoming an active, productive member of a team, as long as you give the process a chance. You hear a lot of talk these days about the importance of developing team skills. But the ultimate skill in teamwork — the ability to collaborate with others — has more to do with attitude and mindset than it does with technical proficiency. You have to recognize that while you may indeed be making certain compromises or sacrifices by virtue of working as part of a team, you're accomplishing a great deal more. You get a chance to forge relationships that will last beyond the process. You have an opportunity to learn from others, incorporate new skills, and experience one of the supreme pleasures of life: sharing an accomplishment with others.

Understanding the basics of team smarts

It's four o'clock in the afternoon and you've just received a phone call from your manager who wants to see you in her office. Your first reaction is, "Uh, oh, what did I do now?" But when you walk into the office, you find your manager as upbeat and positive as ever. Within seconds, you know why she has summoned you. A new project team is being formed to handle a major new initiative and she has recommended you as a member.

Should you feel proud? Yes. And if you've never participated in a small, performance-driven work team, you may have a little anxiety. But the following guidelines can help you overcome any concerns and become a productive member of the team.

Embracing the opportunity

Recognize this as an opportunity for both personal and career growth. Keep in mind that your ability to secure good jobs in the future could well depend on your success in a team-oriented environment.

Coordinating with your manager

Chances are, your supervisor is the one who asked you to become part of a team. Discuss the assignment with your manager and get clarification on the following two questions:

- ✔ How does this assignment rank in priority with current responsibilities?
- ✔ Will you need any additional support from coworkers or staff to meet all of your responsibilities?

Use this opportunity to find out as much as you can from your manager about the nature of the assignment, the people with whom you're going to be working, and any suggestions on making the experience a success.

Understanding the team mission

Make sure (even before you attend your first team meeting) that you understand the objective of the group and, more important, get excited about that mission. And even if the mission isn't something about which you can be passionate, identify certain goals within the process that will keep you motivated and focused.

Leaving your biases at home

If you've been asked to join a cross-functional team (made up of people from different departments), you're probably going to be working with people who may not think, act, or communicate the way you do. Keep an open mind and don't make snap judgments. The person sitting across from you, regardless of rank or position, may possess the quickest and most creative mind in the company.

Beginning with flexibility

Demonstrate as early as possible your willingness to be flexible and support the group. It's okay to let others know what your skills are and what you would prefer to work on, but be prepared for the possibility that when roles are assigned, you may not end up with tasks you wanted. Give the process time. Roles in most teams tend to be fluid — dictated more by the needs of the objective rather than a particular structure. So even though you may not like your role at the start of the project, your responsibilities may change as the project evolves.

Respecting the process

Show respect for the team process by faithfully and enthusiastically adhering to disciplines and procedures. Don't underestimate the importance of little things, like being punctual for meetings and contributing to discussions. And be prepared to resolve disagreements and conflicts in a rational, collaborative, and consensus-driven manner. Some of the best minds in an organization can detract from their great ideas by dominating the meeting or being negative toward other ideas. Above all, be accountable. Keep in mind that, as a team member, your successes — and your failures — impact the group.

Communicating for success

Be sure to update appropriate team members as often as possible. Sometimes, just knowing that you're still waiting for a given piece of information can allow another team member to better manage his or her responsibilities.

Sharing the glory

Group success in a work team takes precedence over individual achievement. You may be tempted at times to feel that you're pulling people along and not getting credit for it. But chances are, without that support, you wouldn't be as good as you are. Find ways to help teammates become more productive and focus on group successes, not individual achievement.

Allowing chemistry to build

No group of individuals, no matter how compatible they are, can hope to achieve unity and synchrony overnight. Team spirit evolves naturally as you work together, overcome obstacles, and achieve success. Don't try to rush the process.

Succeeding as a Team Leader

What do you do when your success as a team member leads to your nomination as leader of a new team being formed? The chance to lead a work team is a great opportunity for both personal and career growth. But the fact that you've done exceptional work as a team member doesn't necessarily prepare you for the challenges of team leadership.

The basic responsibilities you have as a team leader are similar, at root, to supervisory responsibilities, but team leadership embodies unique challenges. For one thing, the people on your team may not report to you, which may blur the lines of accountability. You may need to help them balance team responsibilities with day-to-day tasks. And if you're managing a cross-functional team, you may find yourself surrounded by people who know far more about certain aspects of the project than you.

None of this means that you need to reinvent your personality or pursue an advanced degree in team management in order to be an effective team leader. Be aware, however, that you probably have to make some adjustments to your normal management style. Take a look at the following sections for some suggestions and Table 13-1 for an overview of how to succeed as a team leader.

Table 13-1	Do's and Don'ts for Team Leaders
Exceptional team leaders do	*Exceptional team leaders don't*
Listen attentively to every contribution.	Pass judgment or comment negatively on members' ideas and comments.
Encourage thinking outside the box; play devil's advocate.	Tell the team what needs to be done.
Propose solutions.	Act like an expert.
Prepare for the meeting.	Dictate all arrangements; set the agenda in stone.
Think of themselves as coordinator or guide to the team.	Manipulate the situation to benefit themselves.
Use visual aids to track progress.	Fail to share input from supervisors.
Bring all team members into discussion with open-ended questions.	Let team members pass the buck on making decisions or contributing to discussions.
Ensure that meeting objectives are achieved.	Contribute more than their share.

Understanding your role

Effectiveness as a team leader begins with an appreciation of your role. Your function as a team leader isn't so much to supervise or manage the project but to facilitate a process that capitalizes on the contributions of everyone involved. This involves more than delegating. Responsibility in the typical work team is much more broadly shared. You may still have to exercise authority from time to time, but if you're doing your job well, it won't be necessary to do so. Your job is to help team members understand their roles and keep everyone on track.

Securing management support

As the leader of a work team, you typically serve as a liaison between senior management and the team itself. Your success in this sometimes-tricky task depends largely on your ability to request and respond to support from senior management. The earlier you address the issue of management support, the better it will be for you and your team members in the long run. Few things will sink the morale of a work team more quickly than a suspicion that the group efforts are neither supported nor appreciated by senior management. Among the critical issues to discuss with senior management as early as possible are the following:

- **Mission:** What is the mission of the group and how does that mission relate to the company's strategic goals?

- **Resources:** What resources (financial, staffing, and so on) are available for the project?

- **Deadlines:** What are the key deadlines of senior management that relate to or affect the team?

- **Autonomy:** How much autonomy, if any, does your team have, particularly with respect to budget, personnel decisions, and reward mechanisms?

- **Your role:** How much autonomy do you have?

- **Progress reports:** How often should you provide updates to senior managers?

- **Kick-off announcement:** Is a member of senior management available to address the group at a kick-off meeting, thereby reinforcing management's support?

You may not always be able to secure as much clarification as you'd like. But unless you have good reason to believe that your team's mission can't be achieved without that support, be prepared to work with what you have. Do your best to inspire the team to log in some early successes. After the team has begun to prove its worth, you can usually count on additional support.

Picking the right players

You won't always have an opportunity to assemble your own team, but if you're given that chance, take advantage of it. Here's what to do:

- **Develop a skills list.** Think through the nature of the project and list the expertise and abilities needed to complete the project successfully. If you're in doubt about what's needed, seek the help of others in the company who may have been involved in similar projects.

- **Research prospective members.** Find out as much as you can about the background and expertise of every prospective team member before nominating them.

✔ **Consider team experience.** Everything else being equal, choose people who've already proven themselves as effective team members.

✔ **Avoid potential personality conflicts.** Unless an individual possesses a rare expertise that's critical to the team, don't select anyone who may be too self-centered or disruptive.

✔ **Seek recommendations.** Ask others in your company for recommendations of people who would be well suited for the project for which you're responsible.

✔ **State the mission.** Prepare a general statement of the team mission and objectives before interviewing anyone, and use it as the basis of your discussions.

✔ **Check with managers.** Before you select anyone, check with each individual's supervisor to ensure that a potential team member can commit the necessary time and effort for the project.

Creating the right environment

Conventional office layouts aren't always conducive to team-oriented efforts. People are often separated into small, private work areas with no convenient place for everyone to gather as a group. If that's the case in your organization, explore opportunities to overcome this limitation. Here are some down-to-earth possibilities to consider if your current work environment lacks a suitable place for group meetings:

✔ Work out an arrangement with senior management to hold your meetings in a corporate board room (assuming your company has one)

✔ Convert an existing office (a *large* office) into a meeting space

✔ Consider the possibility — on occasion, at least, and if you have the budget for it — of renting a meeting room in a local hotel or community center

Getting off to a great start

You get only one opportunity to launch a team-oriented effort, and you want to make the most of it. Make sure the people who attend your initial team meeting not only understand the team's mission but also get excited about the project and their opportunity to contribute.

Some organizational experts recommend that you incorporate so-called team-building activities — exercises, contests, and games — to help people get acquainted with one another. If the project you're working on is important and members don't know one another, these activities can help break the ice. If you don't have any experience in creating and running team-building activities, find someone in your company who does or bring in an outside specialist.

In addition to fostering team spirit, you need to accomplish certain critical objectives. Above all, you need to communicate to everyone why the team has been formed, what the mission is, and how this mission relates to the strategic goals of the organization. If at all possible, try to get someone from senior management to affirm the project's importance and inspire members.

The amount of detail you provide during this initial meeting about individual roles and responsibilities usually depends on the size of the group and the scope of the project. In significant, long-term projects, it's usually a good idea to outline the various categories of roles and skills and then allow the group to assign specific tasks and responsibilities. With smaller teams, you can usually handle this aspect of the process more informally, through group discussion. If you have specific people in mind for particular roles, you can offer suggestions. Otherwise, let the group decide for themselves who's going to do what.

Here are some other points that relate to the first meeting:

- ✔ **Be prepared:** Don't schedule the first meeting until you've made all the necessary preparations and assembled all participants.

- ✔ **Schedule Q & A:** Allow sufficient time in the agenda for questions and clarifications.

- ✔ **Show team spirit:** Exemplify through your own behavior the spirit you want the team to embody.

Communicating the vision

Nothing you do as a team leader is more important — and, in some situations, harder to do — than conveying a sense of mission. You have to be careful, of course. Not every business goal is endowed with a kind of higher purpose, and that's where the challenge comes in. You need to clearly define the strategic implications of the project. For example, if your team is coordinating the launch of a new benefits package, explain how benefits affect employee satisfaction and, therefore, retention.

Drawing up a charter

Even if your team will only function for a few months, create a charter. This document articulates the team's mission and sets down the ground rules of how you're going to work together. You should have a general idea about these ground rules, but the ultimate document should reflect collective input and have buy-in from everyone in the group. After the document has been completed, run it by senior management. If, for some reason, certain aspects of the charter aren't approved, revisit those issues with your team and try to work out a compromise upon which everyone can agree.

Motivating your team

Regardless of what team-building activities you may schedule during the early stages of the project, the interpersonal dynamics of your team — how everyone works together — should be an ongoing concern. Your time and effort on this particular aspect of the project depends, of course, on how well the group interacts. Keep in mind, however, that the qualities that underlie effective teamwork aren't self-sustaining. You have to constantly nourish and reinforce them. Consider the following suggestions:

- **Find reasons to celebrate.** Whenever there's a reason to celebrate (someone's birthday, a milestone reached, and so on), do so — even if it's as simple as bringing in a plate of cookies during lunch hour.

- **Accentuate the positive.** Even when things aren't going smoothly, do your best to keep the mood upbeat and positive. Always try to begin each team meeting with a summary of what's been going right before you address concerns.

- **Reinforce the mission.** Sometimes team members can get so caught up in the details of the project that the big picture becomes fuzzy and enthusiasm wanes. Find new ways to remind everyone how the tasks at hand support the ultimate team objective.

Getting everyone involved

If the team you lead is typical, you're going to deal with a wide range of personalities, temperaments, and working styles. Without being too intrusive, make sure that no individual dominates or in some way diminishes another's contributions. A constant challenge for team leaders is that top performers do, by choice, take on more responsibility than others. This isn't necessarily a bad thing just as long as others don't relinquish their own involvement or accountability. During team meetings, be aware of who's doing most of the talking. And without suppressing the enthusiasm or involvement of the most vocal participants, take measures to elicit ideas and responses from everyone else.

Avoiding micromanagement

Micromanaging isn't good practice under any circumstances, but it's particularly ill-advised when you're heading up a work team. So even when members of your team are under the gun or struggling with a particular task or issue, offer support but resist the impulse to step in and do the job yourself. Individual problems that crop up should always be viewed as team problems and, as much as possible, should be resolved through team processes.

Collaborating by remote

Thanks to advances in communication technology, people don't necessarily have to work the same hours, report to the same office, or be based in the same region in order to be productive members of a team. Consequently, some communication among members of a team will likely take place over the phone, through e-mail, via teleconferencing, or with video-conferencing. While you may have an easier time creating and sustaining a strong sense of teamwork when the members have the opportunity to interact in person, in the absence of face-to-face communication, the following suggestions can help:

✔ **Regular meetings:** If feasible, try to schedule — at least once per month — a meeting that everyone attends, regardless of working arrangements.

✔ **Communication protocols:** Emphasize to every member of the group the importance of communication and sharing information on a regular basis. Document your agenda and write up notes on the meeting for all members. Use teleconferences and e-mail regularly to supplement monthly meetings and provide important updates.

✔ **E-mail etiquette:** Impress upon everyone the importance of thoughtful, tactful e-mail messages.

✔ **Supporting software:** If the project warrants it, look into software packages, such as Microsoft Project, that have been expressly designed for collaborative efforts.

Getting a Team Back on Track

Even the best teams can lose their edge, and it's during these periods that you get a chance to prove your skill as a team leader. The one thing you don't want to do is overreact. Teams, like individuals, have good days and bad days, and you can't expect every meeting to go smoothly or every task to be completed without any glitches.

On the other hand, if you notice a definite pattern of declining performance, something is clearly wrong — and you need to get to the root of it. Here are some suggestions:

✔ **Revisit the mission.** Has something happened — a change in senior management, for example — that may have weakened the team mission? Speak with members individually to make sure that everyone is still committed to the initial goals. If you sense some hesitation, call everyone together to explore ways to rekindle some of the lost fire.

✔ **Clarify roles.** Even though you may have done it before, check to make sure everyone understands his or her responsibilities and is able to meet those expectations. If you notice a pattern of confusion, gather everyone together for a meeting to clarify roles and accountability. If you have the authority to do so, speak with any individuals who no longer feel committed to the project and allow them the option to leave the team.

✔ **Review the process.** Consider how well team members are adhering to the processes that were originally set into place. If protocols are slipping, review them with the team and consider revising any steps as necessary.

How healthy is your current team?

Ask yourself the following eight key questions to help determine whether your team is operating at peak efficiency:

✔ Does everyone understand and embrace the mission of the group?

✔ Is everyone clear about his or her role and how that role affects others and the group's mission?

✔ Does everyone on the team really want to be there — and do they convey their enthusiasm?

✔ Are team members able to discuss problems and challenges openly and

constructively without becoming defensive or impatient with one another?

✔ Are protocols in place to govern basic processes, meetings, and conflict resolution? Do team members respect them?

✔ Has senior management expressed its belief in and support of team objectives?

✔ Is there a genuine sense of cooperation among the team members?

✔ When problems crop up, do people band together (as opposed to pointing fingers)?

Chapter 14

Mastering the Art of Communication

· ·

· ·

The ability to communicate effectively is a fundamental skill, yet one that many people struggle with. You have to express your thoughts clearly and concisely with people who may have only a vague understanding of your specialty or who may work in offices halfway around the world. Communication skills in general — and writing skills, in particular — are no longer simply an advantage to getting ahead in business; they're a necessity. And now that so many business operations and projects are team-based and cross-functional, you also need to communicate persuasively, influencing the thoughts and actions of people without pulling rank or issuing ultimatums.

This chapter covers the key communication skills that you need to master for success in today's business world, regardless of your occupation. You get new insights into what effective communication really means (and there's far more to it than simply expressing what's on your mind). You also get solid advice on what most communication experts consider the weakest skill: the ability to listen. And you get suggestions on how to overcome a writing phobia, timely advice on how to beef up your presentation skills, and insights into the ultimate communication skill — the ability to persuade.

Defining Good Communication

On the surface, communication seems to be a simple concept. It's about conveying a message through the spoken or written word. So, what's the big deal?

It's this: Communication — effective communication — is a two-way process. The fact that you've expressed an opinion or explained information means only that you've expressed or explained what you wanted. It doesn't necessarily mean that anyone paid attention to your message or understood it. And it doesn't mean that the person with whom you've communicated will respond the way you want.

To communicate effectively, you need to be concerned not only with what you yourself want to say or write but also with how you deliver that message. True, you can't control every factor that affects how others receive, interpret, and ultimately respond to your messages. If you're a technical specialist, for example, you can't help that many of the people with whom you communicate don't share your level of technical sophistication and think that bandwidth refers to wedding rings. And you can't control the possibility that during a meeting, a coworker may be distracted by thoughts of his horrendous morning commute.

What you can control, however, is your response to the obstacles you face as a communicator. Above all, you need to recognize that effective communication requires focusing on the needs and mindset of others. This means that at the same time you're thinking about what you yourself want to say or write, you need to consider your audience: who they are, what they care about, and how they will likely interpret your message. To put it another way, effective communication has as much to do with mindset and attitude as it does with speaking and writing skills.

Understanding great communicators

If you watch television interview shows, you've undoubtedly noticed that some guests are more interesting and enjoyable than others. You may have wondered what qualities set them apart from the guests who make you want to reconsider your cable subscription. Subject matter, of course, plays a large role: If you're not interested in professional football, you're not likely to listen intently while the Super Bowl MVP describes the touchdown pass he threw in the last three seconds of the game. But some people are able to express themselves in ways that capture and sustain your interest, regardless of the subject matter.

Scholars, linguists, and behavioral scientists have been looking into the question of exceptional communication for years. And although no one has yet devised any formula to become a master communicator, experts have isolated certain qualities that are shared by people who know how to communicate effectively. Here's a brief look at some of these qualities and why they're so important.

✔ **Articulating ideas:** An articulate person expresses ideas coherently and logically. Whether in conversation or in writing, the key points and their importance are unmistakable and stated clearly, directly, and simply. The ability to do all of this, of course, presupposes two skills:

- A mind that's disciplined and orderly enough to organize thoughts

- Sufficient command of the language to verbalize those thoughts in a way that can be easily understood

As the economy moves from product-based businesses to idea-based businesses, it is crucial to have the ability to articulate ideas and concepts effectively.

✔ **Understanding the subject:** Effective communicators have a solid grasp of the topics about which they speak and they have noticeable confidence in that knowledge. You rarely catch effective communicators offering opinions they can't defend or verbalizing purely for the sake of hearing their voice. And this means that the communicator builds credibility.

✔ **Communicating interest:** Good communicators are passionate about what they're saying or writing. Their enthusiasm is genuine, obvious, and often infectious. They don't have to feign interest and excitement in what they have to tell you. On the contrary, that interest and excitement is what fuels their desire to communicate. And it also fuels a desire of others to listen.

✔ **Focusing on others:** Many people have short attention spans and may not pay attention unless they are personally engaged throughout the communication process. That's why highly accomplished communicators tailor their messages to the needs of the audience, without compromising the integrity of the message.

These four attributes — articulate expression, expertise, enthusiasm, and audience-oriented delivery — are the cornerstones of success for every medium of communication, from simple e-mails to elaborate presentations.

Listening for Information

Because listening appears to be a subconscious action, it may seem odd to consider it a communication skill over which you have control. Most communication experts agree, however, that the root of misunderstandings and communication breakdowns isn't necessarily poorly stated ideas or information. It's typically poor listening habits.

While being a good listener helps ensure that you understand what other people are trying to tell you, listening skills also figure prominently in your ability to establish rapport with and gain the trust of the people with whom you communicate. You've undoubtedly experienced how annoying and frustrating it can be to convey information to someone who appears distracted or uninterested by what you have to say. And if you want to avoid being the source of frustration for others, take a look at the following sections for information on some of the most important principles of effective listening.

Focusing on the moment

To be a good listener, you have to be willing — and able — to focus your full attention (yes, full attention!) on the speaker, in spite of everything that may be going on around you. This principle holds true whether you're talking one-on-one in a quiet room, sitting across from someone in a noisy restaurant, or participating in a teleconference. Sure it's possible to get the gist of what people are saying and listen with half an ear, which means that you can access your e-mail, sort papers on your desk, or figure out what lottery number to play while another person is speaking. But this is precisely the kind of habit that often prevents you from retaining most of what you hear, and it signals to other people that you don't really care about what they have to say. You may be able to get away with this once in a while, but over time, people will be less likely to share important information or ideas with you because you are typically unreceptive. Give your full attention to the speaker for the duration of the conversation. If you can't spare the time or energy, reschedule for a time when you can.

Waiting your turn

Many people have a bad habit of talking before the other person has finished his thought. This impulse can be especially hard to fight if you're impatient or you don't agree with what you're being told. Good listeners, however, are usually able to restrain themselves. They don't interrupt. Nor do they feel obligated to complete other people's sentences for them. Most people don't come by this discipline naturally: They have to work at it. Recognize, before any words leave your mouth, that interrupting people in mid-sentence is not just impolite, it's also extremely disruptive. By interrupting, you may miss an important piece of information that would've been conveyed, and the person may lose his train of thought. You have to force yourself — at first, at least — to restrain the impulse. After you've developed the habit of not interrupting, you won't have to work as hard to stifle the urge. And you usually find that people stop interrupting you, as well.

Engaging in the conversation

You undoubtedly know people who offer no indication that they're listening to you as you speak. (You may begin to wonder if they're just sleeping with their eyes open.) Take this lesson to heart when you're on the receiving end of a conversation. Of course, you don't want to go overboard to assure people that you're attentive. There's no need to respond to every statement with a comment that indicates your understanding ("I see what you mean. I see what you mean. I see what you mean."). But don't go to the other extreme either, which is to sit there silent and expressionless. Engage in the conversation. If you agree with a point, nod. Be sensitive to your overall body language. Remember that your posture and facial expressions communicate a message as clearly as the words you speak.

Keeping an open mind

If you've already decided, long before the other person speaks, that you're not going to hear anything interesting or relevant, you're not likely to pay much attention to what is said. And it won't take too long for the other person to notice your indifference. Don't prejudge. Accept the possibility that everyone with whom you communicate has something important or useful to say to you. More often than not, you'll be pleasantly surprised at how much you can discover.

Taking time to respond

No law of communication compels you to respond milliseconds after another person has finished his sentence. On the contrary, it's usually better to wait a few seconds to fully absorb and distill what you've been told and then formulate a thoughtful response. Don't worry about the moments of silence that occur when you stop to think about what you're going to say. As long as the pause doesn't drag on too long, it doesn't disrupt the flow of conversation. (Besides, silence always seems longer than it actually is.)

Paraphrasing for clarity

If you're not sure what the other person is trying to say, don't feign understanding. Ask for clarification. And if you still aren't sure, try paraphrasing — repeating what you think they said using your own words. Paraphrasing can not only help avoid misunderstandings but can also assure the other person that you're listening attentively. Be careful, though, that you don't overuse this technique or put words in people's mouths. Begin by saying, "So, are you saying that . . . ." And always follow your paraphrase by asking the other person to affirm or correct your assumption.

Delivering Presentations

The further you advance in your career, the more likely you'll be called upon to deliver group presentations, whether for external customers or managers within your own company. The good news is that the basic ground rules of communication don't change simply because you have numerous audience members. But you do need to overcome any anxiety you may have — and most people have at least some — about speaking in front of a group. You also may have to work to engage everyone in the group.

Many large companies offer presentation-skills training as part of management development programs for employees. If this opportunity isn't available at your firm, consider joining a public speaking group, such as the local chapter of Toastmasters International. You get an opportunity to work with a communication professional who can offer helpful feedback and suggestions. And with the help of video, you can gain some insight into the aspects of your presentation style — such as posture, gestures, or voice — that may need improvement. In the meantime, the following sections give you a summary of the principles that are stressed in most of these programs.

Dealing with anxiety

Unless you've had years of experience speaking in front of large groups, the prospect of delivering a presentation can be unnerving. Even if you know and like the people in your audience, you may be a little nervous. It's a perfectly natural reaction; most people feel the same way. However, there's no foolproof solution. If you're an introvert by nature, you may never be as comfortable as an extrovert in front of a group of people. But this doesn't mean that you can't become an effective presenter. You simply have to find a way to get through those first few presentations to gain confidence and further develop this important skill.

Here are some tips on how to begin the process:

✔ **Know the material.** Make sure you know your material inside and out. The more confidence you have in your presentation, the less you may worry about saying something stupid, which is one of the reasons so many people avoid public speaking.

Don't try this at the office

Here are six surefire ways to convince people that you're not the least bit interested in what they have to say:

↙ Finish their sentences for them. (They'll appreciate the help!)

↙ Start thinking about your reply before the other person has finished talking. (Your response is probably more interesting than his or her statement anyway.)

↙ See how many other tasks (balancing your checkbook, working a crossword puzzle, reading Shakespeare, and so on) you can do at the same time you're having a conversation with someone over the phone.

↙ When you're in a restaurant, keep your eye on the door to note who walks in and where they're seated.

↙ Drum your fingers on the table, roll your eyes, and look at your watch as often as possible.

↙ Go online and check the weather report during a meeting in your office.

↙ **Allow for nervousness.** Rather than trying to completely suppress your anxiety, accept the butterflies in your stomach as part of the game and try to channel that nervous energy into your presentation.

↙ **Practice, practice, practice.** Try to give yourself as many opportunities as possible to hone your presentation skills and develop confidence with groups with whom you feel comfortable (family members, for example).

↙ **Maintain perspective.** Keep in mind that the nervousness you feel is never as noticeable to your audience as it is to you.

And, remember that no one expects you to be Jay Leno or David Letterman.

Preparing for the event

The last thing you want when delivering a presentation is a surprise — about anything! So be sure to research all aspects of the event well in advance. Here's a list of questions to help you get started:

↙ What's the purpose of the talk?

↙ Who's going to be in the audience, and what will they expect?

↙ How much time is allotted?

↙ Where will the presentation be held?

- ✔ What audiovisual equipment (if any) is available?

- ✔ Will there be time for a question-and-answer period?

- ✔ How will the seating be arranged: conference- or auditorium-style?

And on the day of the presentation, you also want to avoid unnecessary surprises. Here are a few additional tips:

- ✔ If you're relying on information stored electronically, carry a back-up disk.

- ✔ Make a contingency plan. For example, if you're using a computer, prepare a set of standard overheads, just in case something goes wrong.

- ✔ Arrive early to make sure that the audio and video equipment is working. Also, check the lighting and heating or air conditioning. Take the time to do a quick run-through of your presentation.

Thinking strategically

As soon as you have a general idea of the event and what's expected of you, direct your attention to the strategic aspects of the presentation. Keep in mind that your goal in many presentations isn't limited to conveying information — you may also need to convince members of the audience to take action. So before you start to organize the content of the presentation, focus on the following questions:

- ✔ What do I want the people in the audience to do as a result of having heard my presentation?

- ✔ What key thoughts will the audience need to take away from the presentation to prompt this response?

- ✔ What perceptions or attitudes may already exist among the audience that may make it difficult to convey my message?

- ✔ How much do members of the audience know about the subject of my presentation?

- ✔ What sort of relationship do I have with the people who will be in the audience? Do they know me well or is this the first time many of them have seen or heard me? How important is it for me to establish my credibility?

Tailoring the presentation

The same message delivered in exactly the same way by the same person to two different groups can result in diametrically different responses, depending on the make-up of the audience. So when you're putting together your presentation, you need to account for backgrounds, interests, and goals of the audience. For example, if members of the group include coworkers who may not be well-versed in your specialty, avoid using jargon and acronyms that may not be familiar to them. And, when you're making a presentation to senior managers, do your best to explain how your topic relates to or impacts the company's bottom line.

Starting out right

Within 30 seconds of your opening, your audience should know two things:

- ✔ What you're going to tell them
- ✔ Why it's important to them

If you can do so naturally, begin your presentation with an anecdote or background information that breaks the ice and establishes rapport. But don't use gimmicks or let the opening drag on too long. There's nothing wrong with beginning your presentation by introducing yourself, stating your purpose, and letting your audience know what you want them to take away from the presentation.

Making a personal connection

The best and simplest way to establish rapport with your audience is to be yourself, as long as you're at your enthusiastic and energetic best. Try to envision yourself simply conversing with people, not giving a speech.

Here are some additional tips:

- ✔ Move around the stage casually and comfortably.
- ✔ Smile.
- ✔ Make eye contact with many people in the audience throughout the presentation.
- ✔ Smile.
- ✔ When appropriate and relevant, use examples from your own experience to reinforce key points and help the audience better relate to your message.
- ✔ Smile.

✔ Make your key points as audience-oriented as possible. When citing features or important information, let your audience know why these aspects are beneficial to them. Instead of saying, "The new software will improve efficiency," say something along the lines of, "With this new software, you will be able to process twice the number of claims in the same amount of time."

✔ Smile.

Focusing on a few key points

The success of your presentation doesn't depend on the amount of information you cover, but on your ability to group that information into two or three memorable points. Ask yourself the following question: "What two or three concepts do I want people to remember after my presentation?" Make sure that most of the information you deliver is linked to these key points.

Simplifying visuals

Thanks to the versatility and power of presentation software packages, you don't have to hire an outside specialist to develop visuals that add impact and interest. Be careful, though, not to go overboard. Just because software packages offer you a choice of 700 different fonts and twice that many graphic symbols doesn't mean you have to use them all in one presentation. If you're going to create your own slides, keep them simple. Use one or two fonts and don't clutter a slide with too many words or images. And if you're not sure of your judgment in this area, find someone in your company who has a background or expertise in graphic design. (See the "Maximizing visuals" sidebar for more specifics on using visual aids.)

Wrapping up

If the first 30 seconds of your presentation is the most important part of your presentation, the last minute is a close second. Organize your talk so that you finish the formal part of your presentation at least ten minutes before scheduled. This enables you to take some time to summarize the key points and invite questions from the audience. (See the "Q & A: Fielding questions with ease" sidebar for further details.) And your audience will retain more of the information you present because they won't be nervously looking at their watches as you race to complete the talk.

Presenting with style

How you present yourself is just as important as how you present the information. Your gestures, facial expressions, voice — each of these affects the impact of your message and the audience's interest. The best way to enhance your presentation style is through practice, practice, and more practice. Consider signing up for some professional coaching that enables you to watch yourself on videotape so that you can get feedback on those aspects of your presentation style that may need some work.

If you can't afford coaching, arrange to have yourself videotaped by a friend or family member. Here are some questions to ask when you review the tape.

- **Posture:** Did you establish and maintain good posture throughout the presentation? (Or did you shift your weight back and forth from one foot to the other?)

- **Eye contact:** Did you make eye contact with the majority of the audience (as opposed to burying your eyes in your speech or looking at only a few people)?

- **Hand gestures:** Were your gestures natural and relaxed and without any distracting nervous habits?

- **Voice quality:** Did you project your voice and generate energy and enthusiasm? Did you vary the pitch and volume of your voice at appropriate times to avoid a monotone effect?

- **Facial expression:** Did you smile enough and appear relaxed?

Maximizing visuals

Are you going to design your own visuals for your presentation? Great! You don't need to be Michelangelo to do a respectable job, but you need some basic skills and a reasonably sophisticated eye. Keep in mind the following points when working with the most commonly used presentation software:

- Create a master slide that dictates the background and basic color scheme of each slide in the presentation. This allows you to use the same general layout for each slide.

- Rely on short headlines and bullet points as opposed to lengthy sentences for the text.

You don't want people reading the slide; you want them to listen to you.

- Limit the number of fonts to two or three at most. Use one for headlines and the other for body copy. Be consistent on every slide.

- Make sure the type is large enough for the audience to read. A 24-point sized font is typically a good choice.

- If you lack confidence in your judgment, request assistance from a graphic designer.

The Write Stuff

If you were to give most people in business a choice between walking across a bed of hot coals or spending an entire day writing, many of them would choose the coals. That's because, to many people in business, writing is a painful, arduous exercise.

Understanding the basics

If, for some reason, you don't have much confidence in your ability to use proper grammar or choose the right words when writing, take some time to brush up on the basics. Purchase any of a dozen or so do-it-yourself grammar and usage books and set aside 15 minutes a day for about two weeks. Don't let yourself be intimidated. Just remember that grammar isn't rocket science; it's taught to children. After you've mastered the difference between "affect" and "effect," the rules for "its" and "it's," and the logic behind using "that" or "which," you won't spend as much time agonizing over those decisions when you write. You'll have that much more energy for the important part of writing: communicating your thoughts clearly and concisely.

Setting aside the time

When you're interrupted every five minutes or so, writing can be extremely difficult — or next to impossible. Writing requires enormous concentration,

---

Q & A: Fielding questions with ease

In most presentations, you have time for questions and answers. Here's some advice on how to handle this important and often-overlooked aspect of your presentation:

✔ Let people know at the beginning of the presentation that the last 10 or 15 minutes will be devoted to questions.

✔ If you're speaking to a large group, repeat the question you're asked for the sake of the rest of the audience.

✔ Address your answer primarily to the questioner but make eye contact with others in the audience to maintain their interest.

✔ Keep the answer brief without being curt. If an answer requires a lengthy explanation, cover the main points and offer to provide further information after the presentation.

✔ Do your best to link your answer to any of the key points you made during the presentation.

✔ If you're not sure of an answer, admit that you aren't certain and offer to research it further.

so try to set aside a block of time during the day in which you can concentrate on nothing else. And, if possible, plan to do this at the time of day when you're at your peak.

Beginning with the objective

The first thing to consider before writing any business document is the objective. What do you want to accomplish with what you're writing? Do you want people to change behavior or go along with an action you're recommending? Your objective is a key factor in determining not only the content of the document but also the tone.

Organizing your thoughts

Whether you put together a formal outline or simply jot down some ideas, take some time before you write to list and prioritize the key points you want to convey. This is especially important when you're writing anything that's complex, such as a report, proposal, or detailed memo. By sketching out the most important thoughts, you're more likely to prevent writer's block and are better able to organize the finished piece.

Writing for the reader

Always keep in mind that the people who read your copy may or may not share your understanding and opinion of the subject. And readers are likely to quickly lose patience if they have to reread sentences one or two times to figure out what you mean. Use clear and concise sentences and make logical transitions from one point to the next. Never assume that because you happen to know what a particular phrase means, your reader will draw the same conclusion. Here are some things to consider as you write:

- How familiar are your readers with the topic?
- How familiar are they with any technical terms used?
- Are they interested in the subject or do you need to create that interest?
- What attitudes or preconceived ideas may influence their interpretation and response to your writing? Do you need to counter those attitudes or ideas in your copy?

Rewriting for clarity

Most professional writers recognize how difficult it can be to produce a finished product. They take for granted that they need to rewrite the same document several times to revise and enhance the copy.

You'll find writing much more enjoyable — and get better results — if you follow their example. When writing your first draft, concentrate mainly on conveying your thoughts. Don't worry (for the time being, at least) about spelling, punctuation, or word choice. If you're not sure what word you want to use, leave it blank with an underscore so that you can later insert the right word. When you write your second draft, smooth out the transitions and address any reader concerns or questions. Make each draft a fine-tuned version of the previous copy, and you'll save yourself a considerable amount of energy in the long run.

Stating the point

Let readers know as soon as possible — in the first or second sentence — the subject of the document and how it's relevant to them. (Pretend that you only have ten seconds to catch the reader's attention. State the most important information at the start so that readers know why they need to continue reading.) Although it may not strike you as the most creative way to start, a reliable way to introduce the information is something along the lines of, "Attached is a copy of the most recent report on customer satisfaction that includes specific comments about your service department." Depending on the situation and the relationship you have with the reader, you may want that statement preceded by a short personal message or a sentence that makes a connection with the reader ("At last week's staff meeting, you asked for recommendations on improving our workflow.").

Controlling the length of memos

The unwritten rule in many companies is that no memo should ever exceed two pages — and ideally, it should never be longer than one page. So you need to get maximum mileage out of every word you use and be equally disciplined in the number of ideas you present.

Here are some additional guidelines:

> ✔ **Summarize, if necessary.** If you're convinced that you can't do justice to your subject in one or two pages, begin with an executive summary — a brief synopsis of why you're writing, why it's important, and the key points that will follow.

> ✔ **Make one document for one subject.** Review the outline or brief sketch of ideas that you developed before writing. Are all the key concepts related, or would it be better to prepare two or more memos to address all the issues?
>
> ✔ **Don't over-inform.** If you write frequently to the same person, get feedback to help you decide what is necessary and what isn't.
>
> ✔ **Edit, edit, edit.** Try to eliminate (and it's a gradual process) patterns of expression that require five or six words to communicate what could easily be said in one. For example, instead of "In the event that we decide . . ." write "If we decide . . . ."

Writing in plain English

You can't be as casual or colloquial in business communication as you are when chatting with your coworker down the hall. But you don't have to go to the other extreme, either. It's not necessary to write in an ultra-formal style, using big words and long, convoluted sentences. If you wouldn't be comfortable using a particular word or phrase when speaking with someone face-to-face, you may not want to include it in your written communication. Again, this doesn't mean that whatever you may say in conversation is okay for a memo. It simply means that the difference between spoken English and written English isn't as vast as some people can lead you to believe.

Proofreading for quality

Regardless of how careful you think you've been while writing your memo, e-mail, or report, always take time to proofread. Print out a hard copy and read the document word by word. You may even want to read it aloud.

Take advantage of the spell-check function on your computer. It can catch mistakes you may otherwise miss, but you shouldn't rely on it entirely. Spell-check doesn't necessarily let you know when you've left out a word or used the wrong word. Errors in spelling, punctuation, or usage can cause readers to question your commitment to quality and leave a lasting, unfavorable impression.

Managing by Consensus

If you work in an environment in which collaboration is an important management value, you will need to become proficient at the managerial process known generally as *consensus building*. In other words, you will have to find out how to get a group of people with diverse interests and varying opinions to come to agreement on an issue or solve a particular problem.

At the same time, you need to encourage individuals to continually offer viewpoints, initiatives, or solutions, regardless of immediate group consensus. If you've never been involved in a consensus-building process, be warned that it's not an easy process to oversee or facilitate, especially when the stakes are high and when the interested parties have strong (and differing) feelings about the best ways to proceed. On the other hand, you don't need a degree in international diplomacy to learn how to guide the consensus-building process. It's mainly a matter of committing yourself to the goal of consensus — genuine support from everyone — and building on each new consensus-building experience.

Here are the key principles to keep in mind:

- **Allowing time for the process:** Building genuine consensus (as opposed to passive or grudging acceptance) takes time, and the further apart the group members are in views and attitudes, the more time you need. You may be under pressure as a manager to get a particular project or initiative underway, but do your best to keep the pressure from short-circuiting the process. Try to get an early start in your consensus-building efforts — well before the project is scheduled to begin.

- **Establishing a shared outcome:** As a facilitator in a consensus-building process, your first priority is to get every member of the group to adopt a shared vision of the outcome — even if the outcome is highly general, such as "everyone agreeing to agree." Establish basic ground rules at the start. For example, everyone agrees to let people express views without issuing a personal attack.

  Also try to formulate some general criteria that will determine an ultimate solution. Without getting too specific, you may want to establish that an initiative can't be undertaken unless it's consistent with the values of your company, doesn't disrupt current practices, or doesn't place an unfair burden on any individual or group. By establishing these types of criteria at the beginning of the process, it will be easier for you to keep everyone on track after discussions get underway.

- **Requesting input from everyone:** Consensus requires that everyone involved has equal time to voice views and concerns. It's your responsibility as a facilitator to see to it that everyone has a say. Don't assume that simply because people aren't speaking up that they are in agreement with the discussion. The last thing you want in a consensus process is passive acceptance.

- **Bringing assumptions to the surface:** The views that group members espouse during the course of a discussion can sometimes be the result of invalid assumptions. So it's important in consensus-building that assumptions be brought to the surface. For example, one member of your group may be opposed to a particular initiative because of his assumption (based on prior experience) that the cost will be prohibitive. If evidence can be presented to alter that assumption, his resistance will usually disappear. If people can discover for themselves that their assumptions are erroneous, they're much more likely to change their position.

✔ **Clarifying viewpoints:** When people air their views, do your best as a facilitator to probe beneath the surface. In other words, get people to do more than simply voice their opinions, encouraging them to set forth the reasons they feel that way. Phrase your questions carefully. Pay attention to your tone, and if you're not absolutely sure of what they mean, ask for clarification so that your probing isn't misinterpreted as an attack on their position.

✔ **Encouraging productive discussion:** Even though it's essential to the consensus-building process that each person be given an opportunity to argue the merits of his view, try not to allow your sessions to turn into debate contests. When people disagree, have them focus more on what can be done to bridge the gap between their views and the opposing viewpoints and less on the merits of their respective positions. A good technique to use is to present suggestions in the form of _what ifs_. If someone, for example, is resisting an initiative because she doesn't believe that senior management will support it, encourage productive dialogue by acknowledging her concern but then ask whether she would feel the same way if she had some reasonable guarantee that the support would be there.

✔ **Monitoring the emotional temperature:** As a facilitator, you need to be able to recognize the fine line that separates the kind of spirited debate that's an essential component of the consensus-building process and the petty sniping that can sink the process. If you sense at any time during your discussions that the emotional mood is taking an ugly turn, take a break, let heads cool, and meet individually with team members who are locking horns. Don't let animosities infect the overall atmosphere.

✔ **Accepting the limitations:** Consensus-building is an important and powerful practice in today's business. You can't expect it to work all the time with every group of people. If you find yourself in a situation where, despite your best efforts, people are still disagreeing about how things ought to be done, you may have to exercise your responsibility as a leader. Make the decision that you and the majority of the group consider the best option, even though others may still have their reservations. Make sure, however, that this step is only a last resort.

E-mail etiquette: Minding your manners in cyberspace

In many companies, e-mail has become the primary means of communication between employees and clients, as well as between employees and their managers. Strictly speaking, of course, an e-mail is nothing more than a business letter or memo sent through cyberspace. But the unique characteristics of e-mail have prompted the need for certain guidelines. Here's a glimpse of some key principles that companies have instituted as part of an e-mail etiquette policy:

✔ **Consider the purpose.** E-mail messages, by their nature, encourage short, quick communication. That's great if you want to remind someone about a meeting but not so effective if you're unhappy with a situation and you have a number of issues to discuss. In short, don't use e-mail to resolve situations that are better addressed over the phone or in person.

✔ **Be sensitive to tone.** Even if you've decided that e-mail is the right form of communication for a particular issue, be sure that your tone doesn't convey the wrong message. Many people write in an abbreviated style in e-mail, using short, clipped phrases or sentences. Be careful that what you write doesn't appear curt or angry.

✔ **Verify compatibility.** If you need to attach any files to your message, check with the recipient to make sure the format can be accepted. And never forward a file that you haven't personally created or scanned to make sure it doesn't contain viruses or objectionable content.

✔ **Use the subject line.** Make sure the subject line effectively summarizes the content of your e-mail. Keep in mind that people may receive a lot of junk e-mail, and if they can't quickly identify the subject or relevance of your messages, it may be inadvertently deleted.

✔ **Break the chain of chain-mail.** Don't burden coworkers and colleagues with chain-letter e-mail. Most people get enough junk mail already. They do not need more. Also, your important e-mail messages will be recognized as such because you won't have a reputation for sending frivolous e-mails.

✔ **Give the recipient a heads-up.** Unless you know for certain that the person to whom you're sending a message regularly checks his e-mail several times a day, call to let him know you've sent a message. It's common courtesy.

✔ **Respond quickly.** If someone has sent you an e-mail, you can assume she's eager for an answer. Try to respond to all e-mail as soon as possible, even if your reply does nothing more than acknowledge receipt and indicate when you'll be able to provide a more thorough response.

Building a Persuasive Case

The ability to persuade — to use communication as a tool for changing the way people think, feel, and act — is universally regarded as one of the valuable skills you can possess in both your business or personal life — and with good reason. While building consensus can be important when leading a group, your ability to persuade may come into play when you need to present your group's proposals to senior management. If you have good persuasion skills, you can exert influence without having to pull rank or throw your weight around, which means that the people who agree to go along with your ideas will be far more motivated to give you the support you need.

The important thing to keep in mind, though, is that persuasion is not the same thing as manipulation. Persuasion, in the true sense of the word, obliges you to act ethically and morally. You don't rely on tricks, ploys, or other deceptive practices to win people over. You don't misrepresent yourself or tell lies. And you take moral responsibility for the action you're asking other people to take. To express the same thought another way, you don't use persuasion to convince people to go along with agendas that you know aren't in their best interests.

The following sections highlight other fundamental principles of persuasion to be aware of and incorporate into your day-to-day business practices.

Defining your goal

Before you can exert a positive influence over others, you must have a clear idea of what, specifically, you want the other person to do, and you need to be committed to that result. A great amount of your credibility (not to mention the quality often referred to as *charisma*) depends on the passion and drive you bring to the agenda that you want other people to accept.

Preparing the case

The case is the argument you build to support your proposal. If you'd like senior management to invest the money in upgrading the computer network you manage, explain why such a decision is in the best interest of the company. The key to making an effective case lies in your ability to do two things:

- ✔ Cite claims and statistics that are relevant to your audience.
- ✔ Back up those claims with solid evidence.

If one of the key arguments you intend to make is linked to cost savings, cite specific and believable examples that give more credence and persuasive weight to your assertion. You may, for example, prepare a chart that tracks the amount of time it takes to perform a critical function with your present set-up and also shows how much less time it would take with a new system. Better still is a chart that translates that time-savings into dollars.

Keep in mind, too, that the bigger the request, the more important it is for you to present solid arguments — and strong evidence to back up those claims.

Acknowledging the other point of view

Never assume that simply because you think the proposition you're offering the other person is a great deal, he or she will think the same way. And be particularly sensitive to how people may perceive the risk involved in what you're asking them to do. If you determine that the proposition involves significant challenges, see if you can build into it specific measures that will minimize risk.

Remaining focused

The ability to persuade assumes you have an ability to keep your impulses (what you may feel like saying or doing at a particular moment) from sabotaging your chances of achieving the goal. You may sometimes find it both bewildering and infuriating that someone you're addressing can't see the benefit of your proposal. But if you allow your frustration to surface, you're likely to put the other person on the defensive and harden whatever resistance you're encountering.

Protecting your credibility

Regardless of your eloquence or the strength of your case, your message will have no merit if your actions in the past resulted in a lack of trust from your colleagues. Keep this principle in mind the next time you're tempted to shade the truth or not be totally forthcoming in order to win someone to your point of view. That strategy may work in the short-term, but shiftiness will catch up to you — and sooner rather than later.

Asking for a raise

Your power to persuade can be extremely helpful when you decide to ask for a raise. In addition to the guidelines in this section, keep the following advice in mind:

✔ **Know your market value:** *Market value* is the salary or overall compensation that people with your background and skills currently earn in jobs that are comparable to yours — taking into account, of course, the cost-of-living differentials in various regions. This is generally the basis of most salary decisions. If you're not sure of your market value, consult a variety of sources. A good place to start is the *Occupational Outlook Handbook* (published by the Bureau of Labor Statistics and available on the Internet at www.bls.gov) or specialized staffing firms such as Robert Half International. Other good sources include industry or professional associations and members of your personal network.

✔ **Pay attention to timing:** The best time to ask for a raise is not necessarily when you need the money. It's when you're most likely to get your request approved. All things being equal, the most opportune time to ask for a raise is after you've done a great job on a high-profile project and have been given additional responsibility. (That's assuming, of course, that you haven't been given a hefty raise within the past few months.) The worst time to ask is when your company is going through rough times, and you know for a fact that other people who've asked for

raises have been turned down. It's also bad timing if your boss is new to the company or department and hasn't had a chance to see you in action.

✔ **Make a business case:** To build a strong business case for the raise, point to your specific accomplishments that have had a measurable impact on your company's ability to compete. (The fact that you need extra money to finance a trip to Europe doesn't qualify.)

✔ **Be prepared to negotiate:** You should have a particular percentage increase in mind when you make your case for a raise, but consider alternate suggestions. Instead of a 15 percent increase, for example, you may agree to 10 percent now and an additional 5 percent in six months. Be open, too, to other ways you can be rewarded, such as a bonus or extra vacation time.

✔ **Have a back-up plan:** Regardless of your confidence, always formulate a back-up plan, just in case. You need two options, depending on the reason your original request is refused. If you're told that the timing is wrong, ask if you may request again at a more appropriate time. Try to find out what conditions would qualify as a better time to approach the subject. If your boss tells you flatly that she doesn't think you deserve more money, find out why. Ask for guidance on what you need to do to warrant the raise.

Chapter 15

People Power: Building Your Personal Network

. . . .

In This Chapter
▶ Taking a look at networking basics
▶ Discovering the keys to successful networking
▶ Getting the most out of your affiliations
▶ Understanding the benefits of volunteer work

. . . .

*I*magine that a few weeks ago — perhaps at a party or a professional meeting or at the home of a friend — you were introduced to a woman, and in the course of your conversation, she let you know that she was a Web site designer who'd recently helped a number of small consulting firms establish an Internet presence. Imagine, too, that this woman impressed you as being intelligent, highly professional, and enthusiastic — exactly the sort of person you yourself may consider hiring if you were looking for help with your site. Now imagine that just this morning, you received a phone call from a friend who works for a small consulting firm and wants to find out if you know of anyone who may be able to help his firm develop a Web site.

I'm sure you get the picture.

This chapter focuses on the process popularly known as *networking* and is best defined, simply, as making professional connections — meeting and establishing relationships with people who could be of help to you in your career.

This chapter provides the basic principles of successful networking. You discover why networking is more important today than ever before as a career management strategy (hint: When people are under as much pressure as everyone is these days to find reliable resources, they rely more and more on personal recommendations). You get solid advice on how to make the most out of the networking process, even if you're not the sort of person who has an easy time introducing yourself to new people. And you get some good ideas about using associations and other organizations to kick your networking efforts into high gear.

As you read through this chapter, keep in mind the following proviso: Networking isn't a euphemism for social climbing or using people, and it's not a one-way process. Your goal when you network isn't simply to accumulate as many names as you can load into your Rolodex or personal digital assistant (PDA). The true purpose of networking is to develop relationships that benefit both you and the person with whom you establish the relationship. This means, above all, that you need to be prepared to give as much as you receive and do as much for others as you would like them to do for you. If you adopt this mindset in your networking efforts and follow through with actions that reflect this way of thinking, you've already created the foundation of a highly successful networking strategy.

What Is Networking, Anyway?

Networking has been part of the business lexicon for quite a while, but the concept is still a source of confusion to many people. Some people, for example, see networking as almost exclusively a job search strategy. You inform as many people as you can about the kind of job you're looking for in the hopes that they — or someone they may know — will hear of an opening and let you know about it before the job is filled.

No question, networking can be a productive way to find a job, particularly when you consider that many good positions are never advertised but are filled through personal referrals.

But networking can be as valuable a strategy in your career development as it is in your job search. For example, in a recent survey of 1,400 chief financial officers that was commissioned by Robert Half International, 80 percent of executives polled said that networking with other professionals has been an important factor in advancing their careers. If you were to ask the same question of professionals in almost every other field, you would get much the same response.

Looking More Closely at the Process

Networking is often described as a skill, but it is more accurately defined as a process. You don't really need highly specialized skills to develop and expand your circle of professional contacts. True, you need to be reasonably comfortable with people — comfortable enough so that you don't become tongue-tied when you're introduced to someone new. But you certainly don't need a life-of-the-party personality. You simply need to be focused, disciplined, and most of all, sincere when you're articulating the help you need. You would probably be amazed — if you're not already aware of it — how helpful people you've never met before can be when

✔ You approach them in the right manner.

✔ You're able to articulate what you want specifically and honestly.

✔ The request you make is reasonable and can be satisfied without an excessive amount of time and effort.

The very worst thing that can happen when you ask someone for help is that the person will say "no," which, when you think about it, is nothing to fear.

Setting up a networking strategy

Successful networking involves two different, though often overlapping, components. The first entails actually building the network: in short, meeting and establishing relationships with an expanding circle of people. The second component is taking advantage of your network contacts when you have a specific need. For example, you may want to tap your network if:

✔ You're seeking a new job or a freelance assignment and you want to add as many extra eyes and ears to your search as possible.

✔ You've identified a company or individual to whom you would like to sell your product or service or approach for a job, and you're looking for someone who can give you a name or, better still, arrange an introduction.

✔ You're looking for someone to either fill a job or take on an assignment for your company, and you want the assurance that comes from personal referrals.

✔ You're trying to help out a friend or family member who is looking for a job.

✔ You've uncovered a job lead and are looking for firsthand information about the company or the individual who may interview you.

✔ You're contemplating a career change and want to talk to people who are in a field that interests you.

✔ You've run into a career-related problem at work and want to talk to others who've experienced similar problems.

Six degrees of separation: A math lesson in networking

You may be familiar with the phrase, *six degrees of separation*. If so, you already grasp one of the key principles of networking, otherwise known as the *ripple effect*.

The premise behind this phrase is this: Everyone on the planet is indirectly connected to one another by a string of friends and relationships that rarely exceeds six people.

Sound implausible? Well, here's how it works. If you've never been to Venice (Italy, not California), it's a safe bet that you've never met any of the gondoliers who work along Venice's canals. According to the six degrees of separation principle, however, you could probably construct a five or six-person link to that gondolier, as in the following sequence: Your friend Jill (1) once dated a man named Phil (2), who, while working in an Italian restaurant when he went to college, met Mario (3), who grew up in Rome and whose closest friend, Michael (4), dated a girl, Teresa (5),

whose cousin — guess what? — is a Venetian gondolier.

In a nutshell, this is how effective networking works. It's not simply who you meet and know yourself that opens doors for you. It's also a factor of who the people you meet and become friendly with know, and who those people, in turn, may know and so on. A single conversation with someone you've met for the first time can eventually result in your name being mentioned in as many as a dozen conversations all over the world — including Venice! Of course, unless you're looking for expert advice on current gondolier practices, your goal will be to become the topic of conversation closer to home and among individuals with influence in your field or profession. The more people you introduce yourself to, the greater your odds for success. A resourceful Web site that helps people network is industryinsite.com.

The actual steps you take to achieve each of these networking objectives vary, of course, depending on your need and on how well you know the person you're approaching for help. Sometimes you ask your network contacts for the help you seek, while in other situations, you may ask them to connect you to someone else.

How you communicate with them — by phone, fax, e-mail, or in person, for example — depends on what specific advice you seek. If you're considering a career change and want to talk with someone in that field about his or her experience, arrange a one-on-one meeting over lunch so that you can spend quality time with that individual. Just be mindful of his or her time and keep the conversation on track. There's no one-size-fits-all strategy. You need to be flexible.

Even when you don't have a specific reason to tap your network of contacts for help, make networking an ongoing process and a top priority. One of the biggest mistakes you can make in networking — and it's a highly common one, unfortunately — is to wait until an urgent need arises before you start to look for people who can help. This doesn't mean, of course, that you need to be obsessed with making every person you meet part of your network (no, there's no need to stand on a street corner passing out your business cards). It simply implies that when the opportunity for making new professional contacts presents itself, you should capitalize on it.

Many career coaches believe so strongly in this principle that they urge their clients to set specific networking goals — say three or four new contacts a month. The rationale behind this advice is that the more contacts you develop and cultivate, the easier it will be to get the kind of assistance you need — when you need it.

The six cardinal rules of successful networking

As with any process, certain networking practices are more likely than others to produce successful results. The following sections highlight six such practices that help you get the best results from your networking efforts.

Making it a priority

Successful networking is rooted in mindset and habit. First, you need to recognize the value of maintaining a broad range of professional contacts to call upon when the need arises and then create a systematic plan for continually expanding this list. Some ideas include the following:

✔ Join and become active in a professional organization for your field industry (see the "Networking through Professional Organizations" section, later in this chapter).

✔ Become a volunteer in a service-oriented organization. You're likely to meet people from all walks of life.

✔ Join your alumni association, read alumni publications, and attend local alumni meetings and reunions to stay connected with your college contacts.

✔ Look for groups that bring together people who share your interests and avocations. If you belong to a church or synagogue, get involved with committees and other functions that put you in contact with other people.

✔ Attend social events — charity benefits, for example — where you're likely to meet professionals in your field or in a field that you may be interested in pursuing.

✔ Join a gym, a softball or bowling league, a runners' or rowing club — any organization that's centered around an activity you enjoy and where you can meet others who share your passion.

✔ Get involved in activities in your own company (volunteering for special projects, for example) that put you in touch with people with whom you don't normally interact.

In each of the preceding examples, the connection you make with others occurs more or less naturally, which is always the easiest and best way to network. Keep in mind, too, that if you were to add as few as four new people to your list of contacts each month, your network of professional contacts after one year would be close to 50! Quite an achievement.

Thinking strategically

While having a broad network is extremely important, it's just as critical that these contacts be targeted. In other words, unless you're running for political office, don't measure the success of your networking efforts on the basis of numbers alone. You're also interested in how helpful these contacts can be with respect to career objectives. In most instances, the majority of people who become part of your network will have a direct connection to your field or industry. Those that don't will likely have strong contacts within the business community at large, which can prove extremely valuable if you're looking to explore a new field. Everyone you meet has the potential to serve as a helpful source of information on your career goals. It's up to you to capitalize on these opportunities.

Developing a winning networking style

Contrary to popular opinion, you don't have to be a born schmoozer or know how to work a room to network effectively, but you do need some basic people skills. The best rule to follow when meeting new people is to be yourself — correction, your *best* self.

Here's a brief overview of some of the basics:

✔ Whenever you're going to be somewhere — an association meeting, for example — where you're likely to meet or be introduced to new people, always try to look your best, as if, in fact, you were being interviewed for a job.

✔ If you're introduced to someone, keep in mind the importance of first impressions. Smile, look the person in the eye, and offer a firm (but not bone-crushing) handshake. Resist the impulse to tell the other person everything there is to know about you. Instead, be a good listener.

✔ When you approach someone for guidance, regardless of how well you know that person, always have a clear idea of how, specifically, he or she can help and make sure that you can articulate your request clearly and concisely. Follow up your request with a brief phone call or e-mail thanking the person in advance for his help.

✔ Keep business cards on hand at all times. If you're going to be at a convention or a professional meeting, take along an extra supply.

Another suggestion: If you're in the job market, consider having more than one type of business card. One version may simply list your name, address, phone number and specific area of expertise, without mentioning the company you're with. Another may identify your current employer.

✔ When you're introduced to someone for the first time and the two of you clearly share some professional interests, ask for a business card. If he or she doesn't have one, get an e-mail address so that you can stay in touch.

✔ Become skilled at using small talk to break the ice with people you've been introduced to for the first time before you begin asking them questions about their work. Some usually reliable openers include asking the person how long he or she has been involved with the organization or how they happen to know the individual who introduced you.

✔ Until you get to know someone reasonably well, avoid discussing controversial topics — politics and religion, in particular.

✔ Do your best, without being too intrusive, to find out some basic personal information about the people you plan to contact: whether they have children, pets, their personal interests, and so on, and ask about these things when you meet with them.

✔ Make sure you're able to describe who you are and what you do in less than 15 seconds. And don't be afraid to be creative when you're describing your work. Instead of "I'm an office manager," you may say, "I wear many hats, but I'd say my strongest suit is keeping our department on track!" This tells the person you're both organized and flexible and gives him or her a better mental image of who you are, other than a job title alone.

Keeping track of contacts

Develop a system for managing your contacts. An alphabetized file box of 3 × 5 index cards can do the job, but a simple database is much more efficient. Just remember to keep your files backed up. When creating the database, remember to set up a sufficient number of fields so that you can use a variety of criteria as the basis of your search when you're looking for help in a given area. Here's a sample listing of possible *fields* (that is, information you want to obtain about each contact) to get your started:

✔ Name, address, and all ways of reaching the person, such as e-mail, cell phone number, and so on

✔ Job title or area of responsibility

- Employer
- The industry in which the person works
- Professional or social organizations to which the person belongs
- College(s) attended
- People he or she knows (including contacts you have in common)
- Family situation (marital status, number of children, and so on)
- Interests and hobbies
- Comments (how you first met, a general description of appearance to help jog your memory, and so on)

Choosing a mentor

The value of having mentors in advancing your career is beyond dispute. But there's a catch: The mentoring relationship has to be the right fit for both of you. Here are suggestions on how to find the right people to fill this critical role and make sure that the relationship is productive and satisfying for you both:

- **Take the initiative.** The easiest way to establish mentoring relationships is with people you know well and with whom you're comfortable. But don't limit your choice to your immediate circle of relatives and friends, because you may inevitably limit the range of advice and counsel you receive. If you're not comfortable with the idea of introducing yourself to new people, ask your friends to help arrange introductions. Attend events — association meetings or breakfasts, for example — where you can easily mingle with people who already share a common interest.

- **Cast a wide net.** There's no law that says you can have only one mentor. On the contrary, you're better off with a circle of mentors who have expertise in a wide range of areas. When you're assembling your team, look for variety. One of your mentors, for example, may be someone who could counsel you on a technical problem relating to your profession. Another mentor may have management expertise or industry insights. Consider the kind of advice you're likely to need as you advance in your career and make your mentoring choices accordingly.

- **Make learning the key priority.** Assuming the two of you get along reasonably well, your number-one priority when seeking a mentor is how much you can learn. He or she should be more than a cheerleader; instead, your mentor should be someone who can offer guidance and — from time to time — a reality check. You want mentors who are willing to be candid with you and challenge you if they think you're making a bad decision. Keep in mind, finally, that mentors don't necessarily have to be older than you. The key factor in your choice should always be the wisdom and perspective they can offer.

Obviously, you're not going to be able to gather all of this information for every contact, nor should you try to gather it all during your initial meeting. (The last thing you want to do when you first meet someone is play the role of interrogator.) You can acquire much of this information from the person's business card or from things you pick up during the conversation. Chances are, too, you'll be adding new bits of data with each new meeting or phone call or on the basis of articles you may read in a business journal or alumni publication.

Why go to all this bother? For several reasons. First, the more you know about people, the easier it is to converse with them: You have a much broader range of topics to discuss. The real value of such a database, however, emerges when you're trying to decide which people among your circle of contacts are best able to solve a particular problem or give you a particular piece of information.

Here's an example: You read in your local newspaper or a professional journal that someone who holds a key position in a company you would like to approach for either a job or an assignment is active in a particular organization — Big Brothers, for example. With a well-stocked database, you could run a quick search for Big Brothers, and come up with three or four names of people who are also active in that group and who may, in fact, know the person with whom you want to get in touch. Think of how much time you've saved by not having to call people randomly to find out if they're members. You can also use the database to generate labels for a mailing to your professional contacts to announce that you're moving or changing companies.

Being willing to give as much as you receive

The more you're willing to give in your networking efforts, the more you're likely to receive when you need assistance. But giving involves more than simply responding when people come to you with requests. It also means being alert to ways in which you can be of help, even when people haven't specifically asked for it. Here are some suggestions on how to put this critical principle of effective networking to good use:

- ✔ Keep an eye open for information that may interest different individuals on your contact list and send it off to them with a brief note. This could include everything from a relevant newspaper clipping to an article you read online.

- ✔ If you're unable to fulfill a request or answer a question for someone, offer an alternative — perhaps the name of someone who could help.

- ✔ If you're introducing two people whom you know, help break the ice by suggesting what the two of them may have in common and why they may benefit from talking to one another.

> ✔ If you've given someone the name of a person to contact, follow up with that person to let her know to expect the call. Get in touch a week or so later with the person who made the request to see if your contact was helpful and to see if he or she needs any additional guidance.

> ✔ Don't underestimate the value of being a good listener. It's often the one thing people who call on you need most.

Staying in touch

After you've established a relationship, don't allow the time and effort it took to make the connection go to waste by losing touch. If you're not meeting with or talking to people every five or six weeks or so through the normal course of business activities or through organizational involvement, give them a call or send an e-mail just to say hello. Some other good ways of staying in touch include the following:

> ✔ **Set aside time every month to read through your alumni association or professional association publications.** If you discover that someone has changed jobs, been promoted, or received a reward, drop them a note of congratulations.

> ✔ **Set aside some time every few months to go through your list of contacts.** If you haven't heard from one of them for a while, drop a short line to let them know that you're thinking of them.

> ✔ **Keep current addresses of people you know who've moved to another city.** If you're going to be visiting that city for business or pleasure, get in touch with them and see if the two of you can get together to catch up.

The ten deadly sins of networking

A list of things you should definitely avoid doing in your networking efforts:

✔ Making promises you know you are incapable of keeping.

✔ Making promises you're capable of keeping but then failing to keep them.

✔ Having a hidden agenda: For example, you call someone and announce you have a question you want answered when what you really want is a favor.

✔ Using someone's name as a door-opener without first clearing it with the person whose name you're using.

✔ Not being considerate — that is not taking into account when you ask someone for help how difficult it may be for them to provide that help and being resentful when they don't respond quickly enough.

✔ Discussing business at inappropriate times, such as at a wedding or sports event where the other person may be doing his best to forget about business.

✔ Not showing your appreciation (a phone call or card) when someone has done you a favor.

✔ Putting persistent pressure on people who've agreed to help you.

Networking through Professional Organizations

You may be hard-pressed to name any arena that represents a more productive way to expand your range of business contacts than by joining a professional organization — and for obvious reasons. Nearly everyone who joins a professional organization does so for the same reason: to network. So you have no reason to be shy about introducing yourself at association events. Everyone has the same agenda.

The main decision you need to make is which organization represents the best use of your time, all things considered. The choice may not be as apparent as you think, especially if your schedule is already jammed with both work and personal commitments. Here's a general look at the different types of organizations you can join — and what you can expect to get from your affiliation.

✔ **Occupation-specific organizations:** Any group made up primarily of people in one particular line of work. Many of these organizations are national or international in scope, but have state, regional, and local chapters that meet periodically (usually, once a month), send out newsletters, and often invite guest speakers to meetings. Some occupation-specific groups are made up purely of local people who meet informally. The main advantage of affiliating yourself with an occupation-specific group is the feeling of fellowship and community that comes from sharing ideas, experiences, and concerns with people who face the same day-to-day challenges as you do. These groups are also a good way for you to keep up with what's going on in your field and to find out from someone you know what it's like to work for a particular company.

✔ **Industry-specific organizations:** Industry-specific organizations bring together people who work in the same field but in different capacities — everything from finance to sales to information technology. Almost every industry is represented by such a group, and as with occupation-specific groups, industry organizations typically have national and international governing bodies with regional and local chapters. Typically, too, these organizations hold annual events, such as national meetings and conventions. How much value you can derive from affiliating with an industry association depends primarily on whether your long-term career ambitions are focused on that particular industry and how important it is for you to connect with others in your field. Becoming active in these organizations increases your visibility — and can enhance your attractiveness as a job candidate.

✔ **General business:** Almost every community has at least one — usually more — association made up of business people and professionals from a variety of industries and occupations. Typically — but not necessarily — these organizations are better suited for professionals in certain fields — insurance, for example — in which customers cut across a broad section of businesses and occupations. Depending on the community and on the makeup of the membership list, these organizations may be a fruitful source of career-related contacts for you.

✔ **Interest- or cause-specific business organizations:** *Interest-specific* (sometimes called *cause-specific*) organizations bring together people in the same area who are linked by a common interest in a particular business-related issue. It may be a redevelopment project in your city or an educational initiative sponsored by business leaders. An attractive feature of these groups is that their membership usually includes local business leaders.

In light of the number of options (and assuming you don't have the sort of schedule that frees you to attend association meetings every night of the week), you need to be selective when deciding which association to join. Some suggestions to help you narrow the field are as follows:

✔ Before you join a group, make sure you get a clear sense of its mission, its activities, and if possible, its membership list. Arrange to attend a meeting to see whether the affiliation makes sense for you.

✔ Get a clear idea, before you join, of the time commitment involved. Some organizations — Rotary Club, for example — let you know up front that they're only interested in members who are willing to attend regular meetings and be involved in key functions.

✔ Do some research — use your network sources, for example — to find out which organizations the most successful people in your field belong to. Favor those organizations over others.

✔ When deciding which association to join, envision what you may be doing if you were to become active in the organization and give thought to whether that activity is likely to help you in your career.

If you join an organization and have an opportunity to get involved in special projects or committees, let your expertise be known but also try to get involved in activities outside of your job description. You'll develop new skills and challenge yourself, both of which benefit you professionally. For example, if public speaking isn't usually your strong suit, volunteer for a project that involves speaking before a group. If you'd like to learn more about marketing or special events, sign up for the association's promotions committee.

Six ways to get over your networking phobia

As you can well imagine, networking doesn't come easily to people who are basically shy. If you fall into this category, the following suggestions can help you push past the anxiety:

✔ **Start where you feel comfortable.** Initiate your networking efforts with relatives and close friends — people with whom you already feel comfortable. Ask them to arrange introductions for you.

✔ **Make networking calls when your energy is highest.** If you're doing your networking by phone, try to do most of your calling during those times of day when you feel the most energetic and upbeat.

✔ **Know what you want to say when calling.** Prepare for each call by having your opening statement (a 10 to 15 second description

of who you are) memorized and a list of key points handy. Don't be embarrassed about asking for assistance. And always ask early on if the person has the time right then to talk to you.

✔ **Take time out to recharge.** Plan your schedule so that you have periods to collect your thoughts and prepare for a big networking event.

✔ **Get help from your friends.** If networking really isn't your strong suit and the idea of approaching a complete stranger is truly terrifying, try to persuade a friend (someone who's more naturally gregarious than you) to accompany you, and work the room together.

Volunteering as a Networking Option

The idea of using volunteer work as a way to enhance your career may strike you as being a little, well, self-serving. But it doesn't have to be — if you're genuinely committed to the purpose of the organization you join and are willing to work hard to fulfill your commitments to the group. In other words, the contacts you make as a result of your volunteer efforts should always be a secondary (albeit important) consideration — a bonus. Can you make meaningful contacts through volunteer work? Absolutely. And volunteer work can do something else for you as well (quite apart from boosting your spirits): Depending on the organization you join and the kinds of jobs you do, you can use volunteer experience to develop job skills that can be of help to you in either your current or future job.

Still, your priority in any volunteering effort should be the mission of the organization and the well-being of the people you're serving. Indeed if these priorities aren't at the top of your radar screen, it won't matter whether you get an opportunity to meet and connect with people who can be valuable to your career. If anything, your lack of commitment will work against you.

Choosing an organization

After you've decided that you want to — and can afford to — set aside a portion of each week or each month for volunteer work, consider the following factors in your decision about which organization to join.

- ✔ **The mission:** How strongly do you believe in the goals and vision of the organization?

- ✔ **The commitment:** How much time and effort does the organization require of its volunteers? Are you in a position — in light of your other responsibilities — to meet those requirements? (For example, will you be required to complete special training?)

- ✔ **The nature of the work:** What will you actually be doing — and how much will you enjoy or be able to learn from it?

The Internet is an excellent resource for investigating volunteer opportunities (see the "Online sources for volunteer groups" sidebar for more information). You can also talk to friends and coworkers to find out which organizations they volunteer for and what it's like to be involved with those groups.

Online sources for volunteer groups

If you're interested in finding out more about volunteer opportunities in your area, the Internet is, by far, your best option. Here are three sites that are particularly helpful.

- ✔ **VolunteerMatch** (www.volunteermatch.org): This site serves both organizations who are in need of volunteers and people who are looking for volunteer opportunities. Search criteria lets you narrow your options on the basis of such factors as how far you want to travel, what kind of commitment (ongoing or one-time) you're willing to make, when you're ready to start, and in what area(s) you want to get involved. You're then given a list of organizations that match your interests, with links to those organization's Web sites.

- ✔ **Idealist** (www.idealist.org): Idealist describes itself as the most comprehensive directory of not-for-profit and volunteering resources on the Web. It's geared not only to people who are seeking volunteer opportunities, but also for those looking for jobs in the not-for-profit sector. The most notable feature of this Web site is its international scope.

- ✔ **Suite101.com** (www.suite101.com): Volunteerism is one of hundreds of topics covered in this multifaceted Web site, and it's a good place to get your bearings. After you enter the key words **get involved**, you're given a variety of options, including a list of links to related sites on the Web.

Getting the most out of the experience

Assuming you're genuinely committed to the cause, the networking benefit you derive from volunteer work is primarily a function of what you're actually doing, how involved you are, and who you're meeting in the process. Here are four suggestions on how to benefit the most from using volunteer work as a networking strategy:

✔ **Start close to home.** If you work for a large company, chances are it has already established a relationship with one or more not-for-profit agencies and chances are, too, that members of your firm's senior management may serve on the boards of some of these organizations. By getting involved in that same cause and by volunteering to head committees or fund drives, you can gain visibility in your company that you may have difficulty gaining through the normal course of your job.

✔ **Don't be put off by requirements.** Difficult though it may be to believe, some organizations are as choosy about whom they accept as volunteers as companies are about the people they hire. The better volunteer organizations want to make sure that they're not going to disappoint the people they serve. So don't get defensive if the organization asks you a lot of questions about your motives and time. And be prepared in some instances — if the assignment involves working with children, for example — to provide references or to agree to a criminal background check. The organizations may be legally bound to demand such checks.

✔ **Don't over-promise.** Carefully consider any commitment you make, and if you're going to err, do so on the side of caution. Give the organization a realistic sense of your availability.

✔ **Look for learning opportunities.** Volunteer work provides a variety of opportunities to get involved in activities and develop skills that are new to you, which could be valuable in your career. Whenever possible, try to position yourself for these kinds of assignments.

Part IV
Taking a Non-Corporate Approach

The 5th Wave   By Rich Tennant

ROSCOE CONTEMPLATES SELF-EMPLOYMENT

In this part . . .

Are you ready to go it alone? Do you want to find out how to be successful apart from a traditional corporate career ladder? If you're interested in making your mark as an entrepreneur or consultant, this part will help you evaluate the options and select the path that's right for you. You also get solid advice on increasing your visibility and recognition as an independent professional.

Chapter 16

Going Out on Your Own

*I*f you're like most people and you work for someone other than yourself, you have probably wondered (at least once) what your life would be like if you were your own boss. Would you make more money, take more pleasure in your work, have more time for family and leisure interests, live a more interesting lifestyle, and advance more quickly in your career? Assuming the answer to one or more of these questions is "yes," how do you make the leap to self-employment without jeopardizing your financial security?

This chapter helps you answer these and other questions about the opportunities for self-employment, as either a consultant or entrepreneur. You gain insights into whether you have the necessary mindset to go it alone. You also get a better understanding of what it takes to be a successful entrepreneur, independent contractor, or consultant. And finally, you get some solid advice on making the transition from full-time employee to independent worker.

Determining whether Self-Employment Is Right for You

The good news for people considering self-employment is that the opportunities are tremendous. More than ever, firms are relying on outside sources — independent contractors, consultants, and entrepreneurs — to handle operations and assume responsibilities that were once the exclusive domain of full-time employees. Years ago, the career options for independent contractors or consultants were somewhat limited. But today, virtually every profession has opportunities for self-employment — from project attorneys to interim CFOs to brand-marketing specialists. And thanks to advancing technology such as PCs, faxes, e-mail, voice mail, and teleconferencing, self-employment is both an attractive and realistic career option.

But before you get too excited about the opportunities for self-employment in today's marketplace, you need to be reasonably sure that it's the right career move for you. Going out on your own is by no means a routine career decision. You're not simply changing jobs, moving to a new company, or relocating to another part of the world. You're making a significant and fundamental shift in your lifestyle, and you want to be absolutely sure that you're doing so for the right reasons.

The first step is to view the options as objectively as possible. Don't allow dissatisfaction with your current job to bias your thinking. It may well be that you're miserable at the office, working for someone who makes Attila the Hun look like Mother Teresa. But self-employment may not be the answer. You should first consider the possibility of another full-time job with another manager or employer. So before you assume that you're destined to fly solo, you need to reexamine your career goals so that you can make a strategically sound decision that will enhance your career. (See Chapter 2 for more information on strategic career plans.)

Researching your options

To find out firsthand what life will be like when you're your own boss, talk with others who have chosen a similar career path. Use your professional network of contacts to arrange informational interviews with other entrepreneurs or consultants, and ask about the day-to-day joys and hassles. (For more details on informational interviews, see Chapter 3.) Try to speak with someone who's in the same line of work and has a similar size of business as you plan to develop. For example, if you're planning to be a management consultant for not-for-profit organizations in your region, you may want to contact other management consultants who cover the same-sized territory.

Research business matters that relate to self-employment. Access Web sites or read articles in trade magazines that discuss legal, financial, and personnel issues that affect independent workers. How will you need to report your tax information? What charges and costs can be considered business expenses? What licenses or credentials do you need? Will you have difficulty getting medical insurance? How do you make arrangements for employee benefits when you only have one other person assisting you? Find out as much as you can about these and other matters so that you don't have to encounter as many surprises down the road.

Unmasking the myths of independence

Working independently clearly has advantages that aren't always available as a salaried employee, but it's not a good idea to over-romanticize the lifestyle. The four following sections identify widely held perceptions about self-employment — and the truths behind them.

You'll make more money when you work for yourself

Maybe yes, maybe no. Yes, you usually have more control of your financial picture when you're your own boss. You can set your own fees (depending on what the market will bear) and, assuming there's enough work, put in as many hours as you want.

On the other hand, you don't always get the same perks you have when working for an established company. (Although, if you're a consultant working with a staffing firm, you may have access to many of the same benefits as a regular, full-time employee.) You're often responsible for your own health insurance, travel expenses, phone bills, and so on.

You don't have to worry about office politics

True, if you're an independent contractor, you can always pick and choose your assignments to avoid situations that seem too politically charged. But remember that all business is driven by relationships. If you're not sensitive to the political environment within the companies you do work for, you run the risk of committing blunders that could prevent you from getting their business in the future. And you also increase your chances of creating unnecessary problems after you're actually working with a company. In some ways, you may need to be more politically astute as an outsider than you would as an employee.

You don't have to answer to anyone but yourself

If you're working for yourself, you can certainly run most aspects of your business or practice the way you see fit. But if you want to be successful, you also have to adapt your practices to the needs of your clients and customers. Their priorities and deadlines become your priorities and deadlines.

You'll have more time for yourself

Being self-employed clearly gives you greater control over your time, but it doesn't necessarily mean that you're going to be working fewer hours than you were in your last job. And if you work out of your home, it's often difficult to separate your personal life from your business life. You can have more time for yourself, but you need to be very disciplined to make sure that it happens. Check out *Home-Based Business For Dummies,* by Paul and Sarah Edwards and Peter Economy (IDG Books Worldwide, Inc.), for great tips on working from home.

Testing your I.Q. (independence quotient)

A number of factors determine success, especially for someone who's self-employed. Next to talent, the most important ingredient is your mindset. You won't know for certain, of course — until you've actually been on your own for an extended amount of time — whether you're temperamentally suited for the challenges of self-employment. But if you know yourself fairly well, you can gain an accurate sense of whether working independently is a viable option for you. The following set of questions can help you gain insight.

Implicit in each question is one or more of the attributes typically found among successfully self-employed individuals. Keep in mind that this test doesn't assess your technical ability or expertise. It's simply a way of helping you measure your inclination for working independently. To take the test, read each statement, and using a scale of one to five, rate how accurately each statement describes you (five means it's a very accurate description). When you've finished the test, find someone who knows you well (perhaps a family member or close friend) and ask that person to rate you using the same questions.

_____ I am, by nature, a highly independent person, and I enjoy working without a lot of contact with coworkers.

_____ I find it easy and enjoyable to adjust to new environments, new people, and new situations.

_____ I can make important, strategic decisions that affect the future of my business without spending much time second-guessing myself.

_____ I handle stress well and can quickly prioritize.

_____ I have a great deal of energy and am prepared to devote nearly all of my time and efforts to establishing my business.

_____ I have a strong passion for my field and for the business I plan to develop.

_____ I can deal with periods of financial instability or pressure.

_____ I'm a good problem solver, and I enjoy the challenge of developing innovative solutions to problems that may frustrate other people.

_____ People who know me well describe me as resilient. I don't give up easily, and rejection doesn't discourage me.

_____ I'm not afraid to aggressively market myself or my product or service. I can establish a realistic dollar value for my work and feel comfortable demanding that fee from clients or customers.

Understanding your score: If your total score was 40 or above (and if your answers were truthful), you're probably well-suited to self-employment. If you scored 20 or below, a career as an entrepreneur or independent contractor may not be for you. However, you may want to consider working as a consultant with a staffing firm (see "Exploring the Benefits of Consulting" section, later in this chapter).

Linda Miller

Linda Miller isn't one to let obstacles stand in her way of pursuing a dream career. With some junior college education and professional skills training, she decided to open her own business, Pine Mountain Day Spa, and then expand her operations with a bed-and-breakfast — which she was told could never happen. She also pursued her goals in her mid 40s, when most people are seeking more stability in their career life. But she says she would've become an entrepreneur years ago had she known then what she knows now. And Miller recognizes that her maturity and insights have been key to her success.

✔ **On finding your dream career:** "Do your research and detective work. Your new career must be your passion! It has to be as important as air, food, and water."

✔ **On overcoming obstacles:** "If you come up against a wall, go over, around, or through it — whatever it takes! I have two uncles who went broke twice before they became very successful businessmen. They gave me some excellent advice: 'No' is just a word. It means you probably are talking to the wrong person; go speak to someone else. Failure is just a tool: It teaches you to avoid making the same mistake twice."

Building the Foundation for Successful Self-Employment

Okay, you're reasonably convinced that, with hard work and dedication, you can be successful working on your own. If you're like most people who've gone this route, you'll find yourself dealing with new and sometimes unanticipated challenges, learning some of your lessons through trial and error. You may make some false moves. But if you remain focused, you can gain insight from your mistakes and become stronger because of them. In the following sections, I highlight seven key principles to keep in mind as you get started.

Adopting a business mindset

Even though you may be a one-person operation, the mere fact that you're in business for yourself obliges you to adhere to certain fundamental business principles. Command the respect of your clients by viewing your work or service as a real company. If you consider yourself "just a consultant," you will project that image in your interactions with firms. Work especially hard to meet all deadlines, but if for some reason you can't, save the personal excuses. No business professional would tell a client that the brochure was delayed because his dog chewed through the power cord to the PC. As a self-employed professional, you are the CEO of your business.

Setting up an efficient base of operations

Whether you intend to rent an office or work out of your home, take the time to design and set up a workspace that gives you the privacy you need as well as the comfort you'll enjoy. (See Chapter 8 for information on setting up a home office.) There's no need to go overboard — not at first, anyway. Focus on the basics: enough desk area to avoid clutter, good lighting, and an ergonomic chair. Make sure that you have a computer, fax machine, and phone line specifically dedicated to your business needs.

Keeping a tight lid on your expenses

The one comment rarely heard from anyone who's gone out on his own is that it took less money than initially expected to get the business up and running. So even if you have a decent-sized nest egg to support your efforts, keep a watchful eye on how you spend your money. Before you spend any sizeable amount, ask yourself the following two questions:

- Is the expenditure absolutely necessary to start or maintain the business?
- Is it possible to buy the same product or service for less money without compromising quality?

Be especially careful about making long-term financial commitments. For example, before you invest in cutting-edge equipment, try to get by with just the basics or consider renting equipment on a month-to-month basis. You'll pay a little more in the short-term, but you'll be much better off if, for some reason, you decide that self-employment isn't for you.

Projecting a professional image

Without going to extremes (no need to augment your wardrobe with Armani suits or designer accessories), do your best to project a professional image. Pay attention, in particular, to the little things that can either enhance or diminish your image in the eyes of potential clients. Give your business a name. Get outside help (if you think you need it) to make sure your stationery and business cards look professional. And even though you can dress any way you choose when working at home, pay attention to your attire when running errands during the day. You never know when you're going to run into a current or future client or customer.

Organizing yourself

When you're just starting out in your own business, organization can seem like a low priority. Heck, you're too busy trying to find new clients and customers, let alone do the work you've already been contracted to do. But there's nothing more important to your initial success than ensuring your easy access to information — particularly client information. Efficiency can make the difference between landing — or losing — a client's account. Remember that without others to file your documents or provide background research on industry trends and events, you'll need to do all of this yourself. Be sure to schedule at least an hour or two per week to keep yourself up-to-date.

Avoiding the eggs-in-one-basket pitfall

Too much of a good thing can sometimes cause problems when you're self-employed. It's generally a good thing, for example, when a client or customer is so satisfied with your services that they request more and more of your time. But the downside is the possibility that unexpected events in that company — a business reversal or change in personnel, for example — could result in the loss of this account, putting you into an immediate cash crunch. (Remember, there's no such thing as severance pay for the self-employed.)

It's certainly to your advantage to have major accounts, but be aware of the risk if any one of your customers constitutes more than 30 percent of your yearly revenues. If that's the case, reserve a certain percentage of those fees for investment in a stable market account or savings option. Think of it as a security blanket. You'll sleep better at night.

Coming up for air

Working for yourself can be all-consuming. So it's in your best interest to establish routines that ensure a balance among work, personal relationships, and your health.

If you're working all day in your home office, schedule some structured breaks and set aside at least one or two days a month to meet friends for lunch. Get involved with professional groups and attend their activities. It will be a good break from your day-to-day tasks and could help you make contacts that lead to new business.

And one way or another, try to set aside at least a half-hour each day — before or after work — for some form of physical exercise, even if it's nothing more than a brisk walk around the neighborhood. It will help keep both your mind and your heart healthy.

Choosing the Life of Independence

The fastest-growing niche in self-employment consists of people known variously as independent contractors, consultants, or project professionals. These are specialists who earn their living by working on a project-basis for different companies as opposed to working full- or part-time for one company. And although no hard-and-fast definition exists for each term, for the purposes of this chapter, I distinguish between independent contractors and consultants or project professionals. *Independent contractors* are those who find their own work, market their own services, and provide their own benefits. On the other hand, *consultants* or *project professionals* are those who work through a staffing firm, which helps them secure new projects, market their talent, and — in many cases — offers them access to health and life benefits. But whether you're an independent contractor or consultant, you're still independent — it's just a matter of choice.

The motivations that lead independent workers to choose this career option vary widely. Some people choose to be independent contractors because they already have established business contacts that they can pursue as clients. And some choose to work as consultants through a staffing firm so that they can devote more time to their particular area of expertise while the firm lines up future projects. But either way, independent workers — regardless of their specific career path — have much in common. They're drawn to project work because of the freedom it gives them to choose their assignments and to devote more time to their families or personal pursuits. Project work also offers professionals a way of expanding their experience by working with many different companies, thus enhancing their marketability. And for veteran business professionals — people who've been in the workforce for 20 years or more — project work provides an excellent way to ease the workload or prepare for semi-retirement.

Avoid jumping too quickly on the bandwagon. Opportunities for independent workers are indeed on the rise, and the trend shows every sign of continuing in the years to come. But it would be wrong to conclude that simply because you're good at what you do as a salaried employee, you have what it takes to succeed on your own. The basic challenges of the work may be the same, but the pace and the pressures are different. As a consultant, for example, you have to be able to jump into the thick of things and begin to produce results from day one. And if you're an independent contractor, you also need to devote part of your time to landing your next assignment, and the one after that, and so on. The bigger challenge for consultants and independent contractors is that with each new project — assuming it's with a different company or for a different boss — you have to adapt your work style. However talented and knowledgeable you are, you need to be flexible enough to meet the needs of different types of managers in different work environments — and enjoy the process.

Creating a personal mission statement

To help ensure that your decision to go out on your own is in the best interests of your career and personal goals, write out a personal mission statement — assuming you haven't already done so. That statement articulates your career goals (the kind of work you want to do and where you eventually want to go in your career) and your values (what's most important to you in your work). Along with your mission statement, list your personal goals: how much money you eventually want to make; the kind of lifestyle you want to live; and the time you want to devote to your family, intellectual growth, and leisure pursuits. By writing down this information, you're in a better position to decide whether your career and personal goals are well served by self-employment. If you continue down the career path of consulting, you'll be able to refer to your mission statement often and make sure that your career is still on track.

Choosing projects strategically

Assuming you can afford to be selective, try not to base the assignments you accept on money alone. Be aware of the opportunities each project may offer in building new skills or broadening your experience and remember that your marketability as an independent worker is directly linked to your experience and expertise. The more experience you have, the easier it's going to be for you to get new work — and, more important, to be selective about those assignments. Keep your eye on the marketplace and revisit your personal mission statement when considering any new project. Just as an organization ensures that all operations strategically support the corporate mission, make sure your projects are strategically linked to your personal mission statement.

Observing local customs

Even though you're not, technically speaking, an employee of any company for which you're working, you still need to adhere to that firm's values and standards — all the more so when you're onsite. Observe the corporate dress code, and if you're going to deviate, always dress up, not down. Steer clear of office politics and coffee-break gossip. And be especially considerate of full-time employees you work with or see on a day-to-day basis. (If you've been given authority over certain employees, be flexible. Instead of giving orders, make requests.)

Transitioning to self-employment

Whether you're just starting out as a consultant, independent worker, or entrepreneur, it may take you anywhere from several weeks to six months before you find your first assignment or make your first sale. In all likelihood, then, you're going to need a transition strategy — a plan for making sure there's food on the table until your business or practice begins to generate cash flow.

Before you quit your day job, here are some suggestions to consider:

✔ **Get your personal finances in order.** Before you walk away from a regular paycheck, create a financial safety net for yourself. (You may have to postpone that trip to Bali you've been considering.) Many self-employment experts recommend that you accumulate at least six months of living expenses before you branch out on your own. This advice may seem conservative to you, but the rationale behind it is sound. When you're just starting out, the last thing you need are personal finance pressures.

✔ **Lay the groundwork while you're still employed.** If you can do so without breaching confidences, compromising your integrity, or affecting your work performance, try to lay the foundation for your career move while you're still working. This may mean working evenings and weekends for a while. However, if your new business will be in direct competition with your current employer, the one thing you shouldn't do is aggressively pursue customers. Instead, take care of the many preliminary issues of self-employment (setting up your home office, investigating loans, creating your business plan, and so on). Your goal should be to do as much as you can ahead of time so that you can hit the ground running.

✔ **Don't burn bridges.** Even if you're unhappy in your current job, try to leave on a positive note. Assuming you're not going to be competing with your soon-to-be-former company, you may be able to work out an arrangement to consult or work part-time until your business is established. Even better, try to retain your former employer as your first client.

Working as an Independent Contractor

No factor will have a greater impact on your success than the quality of your work. Do good work for enough people and you win in two ways:

✔ You'll have a large and constantly growing list of satisfied clients.

✔ You'll find that you're getting business by word-of-mouth.

But there are a few extra things to do when you choose to work as an independent contractor that can add to your success. Here are some tips:

- **Get the most out of your network.** If you're like most independent contractors, you're not going to have the resources or, in many instances, the time to market yourself on a broad scale. You're going to have to rely instead on word-of-mouth and personal contacts. One of the first steps to take is to send an e-mail or note to everyone in your personal network, announcing your availability as an independent contractor. And don't stop there. Be sure you make networking an ongoing priority — even when you're knee-deep in assignments. Networking isn't just something you do when you need a job. It's something you do to enhance your long-term career prospects. (See Chapter 15 for more on networking.)

- **Do your homework.** Always try to get an accurate picture — ahead of time — of what you may encounter when working with a new client. Find out as much as possible about the strategic goals of the company, the people you're going to be working with and for, and the corporate culture. If you're unfamiliar with the industry, use the Internet, your contacts, or your local library to get up to speed as quickly as possible.

- **Clarify the mission.** Before you dig in to any new project, make sure that you and everyone else involved agree on two critical issues:

  - The overall objective of the project

  - Your role in that objective

  Be sure that you have a clear understanding of how — and in what time frame — you're expected to contribute. If possible, put these expectations in writing. In most instances, the person who hired you will have mapped out a fairly detailed game plan already, which is usually good news — providing, of course, that it isn't built around unrealistic expectations. If you believe that the overall project plan is unrealistic, express your concerns early on and offer an alternate plan.

- **Manage your time.** Sometimes you may be brought on board to handle a particular project, but little by little, you're assigned other, unrelated tasks. If these extra projects or details interfere with your ability to complete the original assignment, be sure to meet with the person who hired you and get clarification on priorities. And if those tasks fall outside your area of expertise, don't attempt to fulfill them just to earn the consultant-of-the-year award. Make a realistic judgment of whether you can handle the jobs effectively, and if you can't, let your project manager know. You'll save time and energy for both of you.

Exploring the Benefits of Consulting

More and more professionals are choosing — for a few or all of their project assignments — to work with specialized staffing firms that focus on their particular industry. Here are some of the advantages of becoming a consultant with a staffing firm:

- **Marketing your talent:** The one area of self-employment that can be the most daunting and time-consuming is self-promotion — finding more work. But even if you don't mind the responsibility of marketing yourself, you can work with a staffing firm to help find projects that you wouldn't otherwise hear about. They have established networks and contacts in the community. The ultimate benefit to you is a steadier and more reliable stream of income.

- **Accessing benefits:** Many specialized staffing firms offer their working consultants the opportunity to access benefits (such as healthcare, dental and vision plans, and holiday and vacation pay) that are traditionally available for regular, full-time employees in the corporate world. Some firms even provide advanced, computer-based training and skills enhancement programs for consultants free of charge. You can maintain your independence while enjoying the perks of a full-time employee.

- **Offering market-savvy advice:** A specialized staffing professional who places consultants within your industry can be a valuable source of information. If you're interested in project work, you can arrange an appointment with a placement specialist in most firms without paying a fee or any other obligations. You'll gain insight into how marketable you are as a consultant and what skills you need to enhance to land the best assignments. Many staffing firms will test you (again, for no fee) to determine your proficiency in key areas.

- **Getting freedom of choice:** Working with a firm doesn't preclude you from pursuing and accepting assignments on your own. You always have the option of declining any assignment. However, you can't expect to be offered new opportunities if you're constantly turning down work.

Growing the Business: From Independent Worker to Entrepreneur

If you're good at being an independent contractor or consultant and you know how to handle clients, chances are good that one day you're going to wake up and find yourself with an interesting problem: You have more business than you can handle on your own. You now have an important decision to make. Do you continue to fly solo or do you grow the business — that is, become an entrepreneur?

As you may have guessed, there's no right or wrong answer to this question. It's mainly a matter of your personal objectives and career goals. The main thing to keep in mind, however, is that you can't have it both ways. After you commit yourself to a growth strategy, you need to be prepared to make fundamental changes in your outlook, routine, and mindset. Here, in brief, are the issues to consider:

✔ **Does the business have room to grow?** The answer to this question depends mainly on you. More specifically, it has to do with how important a role you need to play in developing business and generating revenues. It may well be that your success as an independent contractor is rooted in skills and attributes that are unique to you. If that's true, you're not going to be able to expand the business unless you can find a partner. (Of course, you could clone yourself — but that's a completely different kind of growth strategy.) The key point is that, to grow a business, you need a business model that doesn't rely entirely on you.

✔ **Am I ready to change roles?** To succeed as an entrepreneur, your main focus has to be growth. This means that if you want to expand the business, you're not going to have as much time to do the actual work (whatever that work may be). You need to devote more time to the business aspects of what you do. Ironically, then, if you truly enjoy your profession, you may have a hard time making the adjustment from independent contractor to entrepreneur. Carefully consider whether you're ready to make this change. If the idea of growing a business isn't inherently exciting to you, you probably won't enjoy being an entrepreneur. The alternative is to partner with someone who has the entrepreneurial spirit and can parlay your skills, expertise, and track record into a bigger business.

✔ **How will I finance the growth?** With rare exceptions, you can't build a business unless you're prepared to make a capital investment. How much money you need depends on the business you're in, how big you want to become, and how quickly you want to expand. One way or the other, though, you have to determine the source for the extra money: business revenues, your own personal resources, a bank, and/or outside investors. Each of these options has its pros and cons. Before you make any decision, get advice from your accountant or a small-business advisor.

✔ **What's my hiring strategy?** You can have a terrific business concept and be a bright, shrewd, and ambitious entrepreneur. But without the right employees, your road to business is going to be bumpy. Don't underestimate the difficulty of finding and keeping good people — especially in a tight labor market. And remember to staff according to your growth. After you decide to build your business, make sure you have a realistic strategy for handling the influx of work, if indeed your dreams of rapid business expansion quickly materialize.

So You're Sure You Want to Be Your Own Boss . . .

Regardless of how motivated you are to set up your own shop and how psychologically well-suited you may be to the challenges of self-employment, you still have work to do before you print up business cards. You have to analyze the marketplace. You need to make sure — before you quit your job — that a viable market exists for the product or service you're offering. The key question is, are there enough potential customers or clients in your region to generate the amount of business you need?

Yes, your ability to attract and keep clients will depend to a large extent on how good you are and how hard you work. But, nonetheless, the marketplace needs to be considered a force unto itself. You could be the greatest, hardest-working dog trainer in the world but still not be able to scratch out a living (excuse the pun) if everyone in your neck of the woods is a cat person. Your expertise notwithstanding, there would simply be no need or market for your service, regardless of how low you set your fees. And even if every third person in your town owns a puppy — in other words, there is a large market — you still need to take note of how many other trainers are competing for the same business. Assuming your potential customers already have plenty of options (a safe assumption, usually), ask yourself why someone would choose your product or service over the other available options.

Conducting market research

The best way to get a sense of the marketplace for your particular specialty is to do what major companies do before launching a new product or service: conduct market research. No need to hire an army of outside specialists — you can do your own digging, which means talking to as many sellers or buyers as you possibly can. *Sellers,* of course, are the people who are currently earning their living doing what you hope to do. *Buyers* are potential clients or customers.

Chances are, you have personal contacts in both categories — perhaps through your job or your affiliation with a professional association. Otherwise, you may have to rely on your personal network to provide names and arrange introductions. In either case, don't be shy about asking for advice. It's possible that some of the people — sellers, in particular — may not be eager to talk to you out of fear that you may discover their secrets and become a competitor. However, when approached properly, most people will give you their honest appraisal of how the marketplace works and what you need to do to establish yourself. Here are some of the questions you should ask:

✔ **Questions for sellers:**

- How competitive is the market overall? Does supply exceed demand or vice versa?

- How *segmented* is the market? (In other words, is everyone offering the same fundamental product or service, or are there a variety of niches, each with its own needs and characteristics?)

- What criteria do buyers typically use when selecting a product or service provider?

- What are the standard fees?

- Typically, how long does it take for buyers to make up their minds? (The technical version of this question is, how long is the selling cycle?)

- How much time and effort do sellers typically have to spend marketing and selling their services?

✔ **Questions for buyers:**

- What criteria do you use when selecting a product or service provider?

- What do you consider a fair market price for this product or service?

- After you realize that you want or need this particular product or service, how long do you typically spend deciding upon a provider?

- What would motivate you to switch from one provider to another?

Developing a business plan

You may be under the impression that a business plan is something that only concerns entrepreneurs who want to make a ton of money.

Think again. Everyone — yes, everyone — who opens a business should take the time to write a business plan, regardless of how modest his or her career goals. The plan doesn't need to be a literary masterpiece, and it doesn't need to be more than three or four pages in length. But more important than the document itself is the actual development process. Drafting a business plan forces you to address the issues that are essential to success. And it greatly reduces the risk of making poor decisions. Get a copy of *Business Plans For Dummies,* by Paul Tiffany and Steven Peterson (IDG Books Worldwide, Inc.), for the lowdown on developing a top-notch business plan.

If you don't know how to develop a business plan, don't worry. You can go online and download a template. (Go to your favorite Internet search engine, type **business plans**, and you'll be guided to the appropriate sites.) You can also purchase software packages that walk you through the process step-by-step. And you can find small-business consultants who, for a fee, can help you develop the document. Regardless of the option you choose, you'll need to address the same general issues. Here's a brief summary of some of the key questions you'll need to answer.

Be sure to consider both the best- and worst-case scenarios in each of the following categories so that you can make your plan as realistic as possible:

- **The core business:** What product or service will you offer clients and customers? Are these products and services already developed or are they in the process of being developed? What will be the structure of your business: sole proprietorship, partnership, or corporation? (To get assistance in answering this last question, talk to an accountant or financial advisor.)

- **Market:** To whom will you offer your services or products: companies or individuals? Are there certain segments — based on industry, region, pricing considerations, or other factors — that you'll target? Is that market growing or shrinking?

- **Business vision:** What do you ultimately want to accomplish? Do you want to remain a one-person shop; create a boutique-type business that caters to specific, well-defined needs; or do you want to become the next *Fortune* 500 company? Do you want to provide products or services to a handful of clients or a wide range of customers?

- **Financial goals:** How much revenue do you hope to generate through your business or practice, in both the short- and long-term?

- **Investment requirements:** How much money is required to get your business up and running? And what will be your monthly operating costs?

- **Labor needs:** How many people other than you are needed to carry out the basic operations of your business? What skills will they need? Is there a labor pool in your area that can supply the need? If so, how do you intend to recruit, train, and pay them? Can you partner with other entrepreneurs to fulfill clients' needs?

- **A unique selling proposition:** What aspect or aspects distinguish your product or service from your competitors? Is it price? Quality? Speed? Innovation?

- **The marketing plan:** How do you intend to market and sell your services? Will you use direct mail, the Internet, advertising, direct selling, or a third-party selling agent? Who will coordinate the effort, and who will be in charge of implementing the actual marketing plans?

- **Location:** How much office space will you need? Where will you be located? And, if you're going to be operating somewhere outside your home or apartment, what will you have to pay for rent?

✔ **Competitors:** Who are your competitors (for example, the individuals or companies currently hired to do the same kind of work)? What are their strengths and weaknesses? How long have they been in business? And how strong are their relationships with your potential customers or clients?

Don't worry if you're unable to immediately answer all of these questions. The whole point of developing a business plan is to carefully consider every aspect of your business — before you launch your company.

Finding out more

Many excellent resources offer information and advice on how to become a successful entrepreneur. The following is a selected list of sources, publications, and other services targeted to small businesses:

✔ **Small Business Administration:** The Small Business Administration (SBA) is a federal agency that offers a wide range of programs and services, including training and educational programs, counseling services, and financial aid. To locate the SBA branch office nearest you, look in the Government Section of your telephone directory. You can also call the SBA Small Business Answer Desk at 1-800-U-ASK-SBA (827-5722) or access the SBA Web site at `www.sba.gov`.

✔ **The Entrepreneur's Reference Guide to Small Business Information** (`http://lcWeb.loc.gov/rr/business/`

`guide2.html`): Developed for the U.S. Library of Commerce by an organization known as BEAT (Business Enrichment Advisory Team), this 61-page document (available online) lists and briefly describes more than 170 information sources related to running a small business.

✔ **The Small Business Journal** (`www.tsbj.com/`): Updated weekly, this lively and informative Web site houses more than 100 different articles covering every aspect of small business management — everything from putting together a business plan to designing your own Web page. Site offerings include software, books, and links to nearly 400 sites.

Chapter 17

Going Public with Your Expertise

In This Chapter

▶ Serving up information as a resource

▶ Accessing the media

▶ Getting your name into print

▶ Using public speaking to enhance your professional image

*T*here's a good chance that the very theme of this chapter — self-promotion — makes you a little uneasy. You may be the sort of person who turns red whenever anyone pays you a compliment. You may question, in fact, whether it's really necessary — assuming you're good at what you do — to focus on activities that enhance your image and reputation. You may know or work with people who, in your opinion, are shameless in getting publicity for themselves, and you don't have any desire to emulate their practices.

Well, you can relax. You don't need to reinvent your personality or hire a press agent to follow the advice in this chapter. And I'm not going to try to convince you that self-promotion should take precedence over who you are as a professional and what you do. But this chapter is built around the premise that hiding your light under a bushel isn't a good principle to follow if you have ambitious career goals. Being good at what you do is important. But you can't expect to advance in your career if the only person who knows how good you are is you.

In this chapter, you find out how to spread the word about yourself — but in ways that won't make you feel uneasy. You get advice about how to enhance your reputation and accelerate your career progress through effective use of the media and local lecturing opportunities.

Becoming a Resource

The number of Web sites, periodicals, radio and television shows, and general organizations that provide information and advice has reached staggering proportions. And this explosive increase is welcome news to business professionals who want to go public with their expertise. Unprecedented opportunities exist for people who are reasonably good communicators with interesting or useful information to impart and who are willing to devote the time and energy it takes to capitalize on these opportunities.

But here's some news that may surprise you. The key to becoming a successful expert is, paradoxically, to help others become successful experts — through your information and guidance. By offering information to others, you and your company position yourselves as the leading resource or expert. Stories that are purely self-serving rarely capture the interest of the news media and are therefore unlikely to be noticed by potential clients. You need to provide solid, well-thought-out information that people can actually use.

This is not to say, of course, that you can't draw from your own experience when speaking or writing. On the contrary, your expertise and credibility are the prime reasons someone would be interested in your contribution. It's a matter of balance and emphasis. The content of any publicly offered material should be geared to the interests of the readers, listeners, or viewers. And to reach them, you may need to understand the needs and interests of the middle man — the organization, media outlet, or Web site responsible for disseminating your information.

Contacting the Media

Reporters, editors, news-show producers, and other people connected to the media have an ongoing need for subject matter experts — people they can call upon to shed authoritative light on stories they're covering. Assuming you have the expertise and credibility in a particular field, you can often position yourself as a reliable source and benefit by having your name appear in stories that are read by others in your field. But you also need to keep up your end of the bargain, which means being available to comment if and when the media call you. It's a two-way street: If you want editors and producers to listen to your ideas when you call, you need to help them out if they're working on a story that may not necessarily feature you or your company.

You have to be careful, of course. If you want to reap the benefits of having good connections with the media, you need to be good copy. This is another way of saying that when you are approached for a comment, you're willing to do more than simply reveal your name, rank, and serial number. You need to have something compelling and meaningful to contribute. There's a fine line here: It can be very difficult — if you're not experienced at dealing with the media — to be candid and interesting, but not so controversial that you put yourself in a compromising position. You always run the risk — no matter how well you know the reporter — of being misquoted or taken out of context.

All things considered, however, the pros of establishing a strong relationship with people who work for the media far outweigh the cons. Here are three suggestions to get you started.

- **Get to know the key media specialists in your field.** Whenever you come across articles that deal with your industry or area of expertise, take note of who the writer is and look for opportunities to contact him or her. If you find, for example, that a certain reporter has written a story about your line of business, send additional articles (written by you or other authors) that may be of interest. Good reporters welcome the information and may call upon you when writing future stories. Other ways to develop personal relationships with the reporters who cover your industry or specialty include attending industry functions or using your network to arrange introductions.

- **Become active in professional organizations.** Professional organizations can play an important role in your media strategy. That's because reporters often get in touch with these groups when they're researching stories. If you're actively involved in an association, you may well be the person reporters contact. Participating in industry associations or local business groups also offers you opportunities to contribute to panel discussions and symposia that can interest the press.

- **Contact trade and local publications.** The fact that you've been selected to speak at a local industry awards banquet may not be of interest to the editors of *Fortune* or *The Wall Street Journal,* but it may be the kind of news that editors of local newspapers, business journals, or professional associations will publish. If the town you live in has its own weekly or bi-weekly newspaper or a magazine that focuses on local issues and people, there's probably a section of the publication that focuses on residents who are in the business community. Often, getting your name mentioned in that section requires little more than a simple press release written by either you or a public relations specialist whom you hire. This same principle holds true for most trade magazines, association publications, and alumni periodicals.

Working with the media

Working with the media can sometimes be tricky. Favorable publicity in the right publication can do wonders to enhance your professional reputation. But saying or doing the wrong thing can have the opposite effect. Here are some ideas to help you avoid common pitfalls:

✔ **Get permission.** If you're an independent contractor and will represent the company you work for in any interview, make sure you're aware of the media relations policy of that company. In many firms — especially those in high-profile industries — it's against corporate policy to talk to reporters about any aspect of a company's operations unless you've been specifically authorized to do so. Even then, you're usually expected to clear all statements with the company's public relations department. In some instances, these restrictions aren't limited to issues and topics that are company-related but also to any sort of coverage in which the company's name is mentioned.

✔ **Understand the context.** Before you agree to be interviewed by any journalist — for any reason — make sure you know the focus of the article or broadcast, where it will appear, and what particular angle the writer intends to take. If you have any concerns that your involvement in the article may cast either you or any company with whom you are working in a bad light, politely decline.

✔ **When in doubt, don't say it.** You're probably familiar with the distinction between comments that are *on the record* (you're willing to attribute your name to the statement) and comments that are *off the record* (not attributable). But don't say anything (on or off the record) that you don't want to see in print.

Getting Published

Are you interested in submitting your own full-length article for publication? (No gulping, please.) You don't need a dazzling writing style to meet the editorial standards of most publications or Web sites. But you do need to make sure that the material you submit is accurate, well organized, and clearly written. The less work editors have to do to make your article publishable, the more likely they are to run it and invite you to write more.

If you're a reasonably good writer — and, more important, if you enjoy writing — you're ahead in the game. If writing is an ordeal for you, but you still think you have good information to impart, you may want to explore the possibility of contracting a freelance writer familiar with your industry or area of expertise. It may cost you some money (writing fees can range anywhere from $30 an hour and up), but the career benefits could far outweigh the cost.

The following sections contain advice on how to put the power of the written word to work in your career.

Creating a list of target outlets

The first decision you need to make is which publications or Web sites you think are appropriate for your articles. Start by developing a database of media targets — newspapers, magazines, Web sites, and other outlets. To get a sense of what's available, consult the publication directories found in most libraries and, in some instances, on the Internet. They're usually grouped according to topic and region. If you go to the business publication site on most search engines, you can also find publications grouped according to industry or profession. Be sure to make your database as extensive as possible.

After you assemble your target list, familiarize yourself with each publication or site to get a sense of which ones represent the best potential placement opportunities for you. You should be able to conduct most of your research through the Internet or at any good reference library. But it may also be necessary for you to write the publication for sample copies. As you get to know each outlet, investigate these areas:

- **Target audience:** Who are the typical readers or visitors to the site? In what professions do they work? In what part of the country or world do they live? And, most important, are the readers the sort of people you want to reach: potential clients, customers, or associates?

- **Editorial focus:** What kind of information does the outlet typically offer? How global or regional is it? Is the editorial focus news-oriented, service-oriented, or a combination of both? Are the articles highly technical or written for a lay audience? Remember, the idea is to find a good match between the kind of articles you're qualified to write and the editorial mix of the outlet.

- **Opportunities for contributing writers:** What percentage of the articles are written by outsiders, as opposed to staff members? (The best way to answer this question is to try to match names on the article bylines with those names listed in the masthead. If the vast majority of articles are written by staff writers, the opportunities for contributing writers are not likely to be very good.) The good news, however, is that many local business publications and Web sites have lean editorial staffs and rely significantly on outside contributors.

Developing editorial ideas

Regardless of how well you write and how well you select targeted publications or sites, you still need to come up with ideas that not only serve your own career interests but also capture the interests of editors. (Remember: The idea isn't simply to get an article published. It's to publish an article that can enhance your reputation as an authority in your field.) You never know for certain — not until you've submitted an idea and had it accepted or rejected — how good your ideas are. But you can usually get a feel for the kinds of articles that will interest a publication's editors by reviewing back issues or archives and noting the topics that are typically covered. Most business outlets are highly segmented, with specific sections devoted to topics such as technology, career management, or health. Look for the sections that most closely relate to your field.

Remember, too, that if you want to maximize your chances of getting published, you need to provide some concrete take-away material for readers. The articles need to provide solid, action-oriented information that can help people improve their skills, earn more money, or advance in their careers.

The best way to develop editorial ideas is to consider your own experience. Think about problems you've encountered and overcome, and see if you can turn that knowledge into lessons from which others can benefit. You can also generate good ideas by reading journals and newspapers that report on new trends in your profession or that discuss problems that companies may be facing. Also, talk with your personal network to help generate ideas. Attend seminars and conferences. Speak with your peers. Find out what's on their minds and what type of information they want and need.

Tailoring your ideas and information

Successful writers pride themselves on their ability to tailor stories. This means that they're able to use the same raw information as the basis of several different articles, directed to different audiences and different outlets. There is nothing dishonest about this practice, but you need to know how to tailor each article you write to a specific audience. The style and level of technical detail you use when writing for a publication targeted to CEOs, for example, differs from the style and level you use for a publication read by recent college graduates. You have to be willing — and able — to make the adjustments.

Mollie Katzen

Although cooking was a lifelong love for Mollie Katzen, when she began her career, it was merely a way for Katzen, an aspiring artist, musician, and writer, to pay the bills. But her "day job" has become the source of her professional growth, allowing her to capitalize on all of her artistic talents. Acclaimed as one of the best-selling cookbook authors of all time, host of her own televised cooking show, and selected by *Health* magazine as one of the "Five Women Who Changed the Way We Eat," Katzen has developed her own recipe for personal fulfillment and career success.

A former student at the Eastman School of Music, Cornell University, and the San Francisco Art Institute — where she received her bachelor's degree in painting — Katzen never attended culinary school. Instead, she says she learned her skills on the job, by observing and doing.

At age 16, Katzen got her first cooking job and two years later began to develop a passion for preparing fresh vegetables. As she worked in various restaurants — and even opened one of

her own with several friends — she kept an illustrated recipe journal with her ideas for non-meat dishes. At the time, few widely known vegetarian cookbooks existed on the market. So when customers and friends began to request her recipes, Katzen produced a small, handlettered cookbook, the *Moosewood Cookbook,* funded by a local bookstore.

Since then, Katzen has continued to incorporate her artistry by illustrating her various cookbooks, including *The Enchanted Broccoli Forest, Still Life with Menu, Vegetable Heaven, Pretend Soup,* and *Honest Pretzels,* with close to four million books now in print. For her public television series, "Vegetable Heaven," she has served as executive producer, talent, writer, musician, and co-set designer. And she is now a featured writer and illustrator for Children's Television Workshop Online and *Sesame Street Parents* magazine, and is a charter member of the Harvard School of Public Health Nutrition Roundtable.

Making the pitch

Most outlets prefer (and sometimes insist) that you submit a pitch letter before submitting an article you've written. A *pitch letter* is nothing more than a brief proposal for the article you want to write. And it's rarely a formal letter — usually an e-mail message — but be sure to check with the outlet for each editor's preference. In the pitch, you describe the idea, explain why you think it appeals to the outlet's readers, and why you're qualified to write it. Here are the guidelines to keep in mind when writing pitch letters:

- ✔ **Keep it short.** Be brief — write no more than a paragraph or so.
- ✔ **Make it tailored.** Be familiar enough with the outlet to make sure that the idea you suggest is
  - Appropriate for its readership/visitors
  - Hasn't been covered extensively by that outlet in recent issues

✓ **Target the letter.** Address the letter to a specific individual, as opposed to simply "editor." If you're looking to be published in a specific section of the outlet (for example, the technology section), address the letter to the person in charge of that editorial department.

✓ **Be objective.** Be upbeat and positive but don't oversell. In other words, don't hit the editor over the head with how desperately she needs the article you're proposing. Make the case for your article crisply and concisely, and then let the editor decide.

✓ **Summarize.** Provide a brief but reasonably specific description of the content of your article. Summarize in a couple of sentences what the article is about and mention three or four of the key points that will be included.

Handling tricky issues of publishing

Dealing with the editors of publications and Web sites can be a bewildering and sometimes frustrating process. Here's some advice on three of the most tricky issues:

✓ **"Don't call us, we'll call you:"** Unless you're a regular contributor or a well-established writer, you may not learn for several weeks whether an article you've submitted has been accepted. Don't take it personally. Many publications and Web sites are woefully understaffed, and it sometimes takes that long before an editor can take a look at what you've written. If after two or three weeks the editor hasn't responded, it's okay to call or e-mail, but don't make a pest of yourself.

✓ **"It's for your own good:"** Most outlets consider it their right (and, in some instances, obligation) to edit your work in any way they feel will best serve the needs of their readers. If you're writing about a sensitive issue, you can usually arrange to see the edited version of your article before it goes to press. If you're not happy with the way the article has been edited, you can refuse to allow the publication to publish the article. Most outlets will comply with this wish, but that refusal will usually kill your relationship with the editor as well as future opportunities for publication with that organization.

✓ **"One at a time, please:"** However eager you may be to have your article appear in print, it's not usually a good idea to submit the same pitch letter to a variety of outlets at the same time. After all, how would you feel if you were an editor who receives a pitch letter, likes the idea, and then discovers that the author agreed to write the same article for a competing publication or Web site? That sort of practice isn't going to help your publishing career. As cumbersome and time-consuming as it is, send your pitch letter to one organization at a time and wait until the idea has been turned down before you send the same letter off to a different editor.

Cracking the Lecture Circuit

How would you like to be in the following situation? Every two weeks or so, you receive a phone call from a lecture bureau agent — the same person who handles Colin Powell, Suze Orman, or Tom Peters. The purpose of the call is to see if your schedule permits you to deliver a speech three or four months down the road. Your fee will be the usual — $25,000. And, as always, you'll fly first-class (at the client's expense) and stay in the best suite in the best hotel in town — Monte Carlo. And how, exactly, do you put yourself in a position to get these kinds of offers? Simple! Just do something extraordinary, like become the first person to climb Mt. Everest backwards.

Okay, back to reality. You undoubtedly understand the *lecture circuit,* as it is often called, is a whole lot easier to break into for some people. But even if you're not a well-known military professional, best-selling author, or famous management guru, you can still find any number of organizations in your area that would probably be delighted to have you come and speak to their groups, although probably not for $25,000 (you may have to settle for a souvenir mug or pen). Your compensation, however, may be that the audience includes people who are potential clients, customers, or associates. Best of all, the requirements for this particular corner of the lecture circuit, fortunately, are relatively minimal:

- ✔ **Value:** You need to be able to speak clearly and authoritatively about a topic or issue that's of interest or value to the people in the audience.

- ✔ **Expertise:** You need to be able to describe yourself (honestly) as an authority on the subject — someone who's actually done, written about, or studied the topic of the lecture.

- ✔ **Communication:** You need to be a reasonably accomplished public speaker — not a spellbinder, necessarily, but someone who isn't going to put audience members to sleep.

Finding your niche

Before you launch your speaking career, you need a focus. Naturally, the topic — or range of topics — you cover in your lectures should be related to your specialty or profession. But you have plenty of latitude here. If you earn your living as a Web designer, for example, you probably know a good deal about computers in general, which means that you could probably talk just as authoritatively on buying a computer as developing your own personal Web site — two topics that are likely to be of interest in many groups. If you're a human resource specialist, for example, you may well have a unique perspective on the importance of people skills that may be of interest to many industry associations.

Getting ready for prime time

After you've decided on a topic, the next step is to develop a presentation that will delight the audience. Give yourself plenty of time to develop your talk. Make sure that it's well organized and covers the key points that support your message. If you're going to use visuals, get some help (if you need it) from someone who has a good sense of graphic design. To play it safe, develop several versions of the talk so that you can adjust your presentation to the time specifications of different organizations. You may have one version that runs for 20 minutes and another version that runs for 45 minutes.

If you're not as confident in your ability to write the presentation as you are in your ability to deliver it, find people who can help you with the organization and scripting. And before you deliver your first lecture — regardless of where you present it — rehearse it numerous times, preferably before people who can provide honest feedback. If possible, use a video camera to tape your rehearsal and then take careful notes as you review the tape. Pay close attention to the pace and pitch of your voice as well as your body language. Make sure you project an image that's confident but also relaxed. If you have any doubts about your presentation skills, think about hiring a speaking coach for one or two sessions, or taking a one- or two-day seminar in public speaking. (For more information on presentation skills, see Chapter 14.)

Getting started

If, like most people in business, you don't intend to earn your living on the speaking circuit, you'll primarily rely on word-of-mouth to arrange speaking engagements. Consider developing a nice brochure, complete with photographs, a synopsis of the talk you want to give, a biography, and ringing endorsements from people who've hired you in the past. A tape recording of a recent lecture could also be helpful. At the very least, though, provide a potential client with the following material:

- A short outline of your speech
- Key points that will benefit the audience
- A one-page biography that summarizes your professional experience, educational background, lecture experience, and any other information that may enhance your attractiveness as a speaker
- References — names of organizations where you've previously lectured and the people to contact in those organizations

Making your mark in academia

Becoming affiliated as a part-time lecturer with a local university or professional school can be a good way not only to enhance your reputation but also to broaden your personal network. In addition, your affiliation with a school increases your credibility and offers you a competitive edge within your industry or field of work.

Of course, it's not easy to land a part-time teaching position in a reputable educational institution. The better known universities and business schools offer only a limited number of so-called *adjunct faculty positions* (you're hired as an independent contractor to teach a specific course), and are interested almost exclusively in professionals who have a proven track record in their specialty. Competition is also keen at community colleges and professional schools, where adjunct positions are widely sought by retired business professionals.

The best way to pursue teaching opportunities in any college is to review the course catalog and determine how many courses in your field are taught by full-time faculty members, as opposed to adjunct professors. After you've identified a local educational institution that offers courses in your specialty with apparent opportunities for adjunct professors, you have several options. The most direct approach is to find out the name of the person who heads the department related to your specialty. Write that person a letter that outlines your credentials and explains how you can offer your expertise to benefit the students.

You may also consider contacting individuals already teaching related courses and offer your services as either a guest lecturer or a substitute if, for some reason, the professor can't make a class. In either case, prepare for an interview (see Chapter 5) and work on a course outline that you can submit.

If you're unsuccessful in your first attempts to affiliate with a college or university as an adjunct professor, don't despair. You can also find teaching and lecturing opportunities in adult-education programs and in programs offered by many community and church groups. By establishing your reputation in these kinds of organizations, you enhance your chances of eventually securing a college or university position.

But here's a brief word of caution: If you're fortunate enough to teach or lecture at a local college or university, be certain that you're prepared to make the commitment. True, you may be teaching only once or twice a week for an hour or so, but you also need time to prepare the lectures, confer with students, and review papers. As interesting as they may be, part-time teaching positions aren't a viable option if you need to devote your time and energy to launching your business or securing jobs that just pay the rent.

Exploring opportunities

After you assemble this material, you're ready to launch your marketing campaign. Call upon your network of personal contacts to help arrange face-to-face meetings with the people responsible for booking speakers at their organizations. Many companies today, as part of their interest in employee education, hold lunch-time lectures. These sessions are fairly informal and, as such, offer an excellent opportunity to enhance your speaking skills and gain experience.

Here are some additional ideas for potential speaking engagements:

- **Community groups:** Your city or town probably has dozens of groups and clubs that welcome speakers. Examples may include your local Rotary Club, a PTA group, charitable organizations, groups affiliated with your YMCA, or church and temple groups.

- **Professional associations:** Professional associations are almost always looking for speakers to present at meetings and other special events. The larger and better-known organizations are, of course, more selective and tend to book speakers in advance. Start with regional organizations that may provide you with more immediate opportunities.

- **Conference and convention companies:** Most conventions, as part of their overall program, run conferences — seminars and workshops conducted by industry professionals. However, most of these groups put a premium on credentials, so you will likely need a solid track record to secure the engagement. Think of these options as the second phase of your marketing campaign. You may want to wait until you're an established lecturer before you aggressively pursue these opportunities.

Part V

The Part of Tens

The 5th Wave   **By Rich Tennant**

MIKE FELT HE'D PUT HIS CAREER IN HIGH GEAR WHEN HE BEGAN SPENDING HIS DAYS IN A BETTER SECTION OF THE MAGAZINE RACK

SPORTS

E-COMMERCE

Slacker...

In this part . . .

This part includes information about a variety of topics in lists of ten: Web sites to use as resources, questions and answers about common career quandaries, tips for career success, and more.

Chapter 18

Ten Key Principles of Career Success

Many of the traditional rules of getting ahead no longer apply in today's fast-paced, constantly changing, business environment. And the most important development by far is the role that you play in controlling your own career future. Simply put, you can't afford to stand back and let things happen in your career — you have to be the driving force that defines your goals and guides your progress. With this imperative in mind, this chapter gives you ten principles to adopt for career success.

Accept the New Reality

You can't assume that what's producing good results for you today will produce the same effects in the future. With changes taking place at warp speed in business today, it doesn't take very long for skills to lose market value or for jobs to require broader responsibilities. Accept the fact that the only constant you can count on is change. If you adopt a flexible attitude — rather than fearing or fighting change — you can stay ahead of the curve and take advantage of opportunities that will bring both career success and personal satisfaction.

Create a Strategic Vision for Yourself

Successful career management begins with a sense of personal vision — a clear idea of what you want to do with your life and how your aspirations support that goal. Your vision, of course, needs to be grounded in reality, which means that your career goals should be ambitious yet realistic. You don't need to have a detailed plan ready to implement by tomorrow. But at some point — and the sooner the better — take time to reflect on your interests, passions, skills, and attributes. Think about what you consider to be your ideal job, and then build a strategic plan that incorporates these elements and outlines specific goals and objectives.

Adopt a Value-Centered Approach

Your career goals should always be in sync with the values that define you as a person. Make sure you note your personal principles alongside your goals and objectives to remind you what's important. That way, as you handle inevitable challenges and surprises along your career path, you'll be better prepared to make smart choices. Adopting a value-centered approach to career decisions helps you nurture the passion that fuels career success and enables you to more rapidly overcome roadblocks.

Maintain a Long-Term Perspective

Make sure that every career decision you make supports — in part, at least — your ultimate career goals. Each assignment you accept and job you pursue needs to do more than add dollars to your paycheck. It should also move you a step closer to where you eventually want to be. It's possible, in fact, that some jobs or assignments you pursue will require short-term sacrifices. But these sacrifices may be well worth the price if they enable you to develop important skills or achieve objectives that help you reach your long-term goals.

Create Value Wherever You Go

In every job or assignment, your number-one priority should be creating value for the people and the company that hired you. This means going beyond the minimal requirements for job performance, striving in every way to make a difference that exceeds expectations. To put this principle to practical use, think of everyone with whom you work — clients, coworkers, supervisors, and employees — as customers to whom you provide an unparalleled level of service.

Develop Productive Work Habits

Regardless of your field, company, or level of experience, your career success is determined in large part by how effectively you manage yourself — adopting work habits and practices that allow you to maximize your skills and attributes. Be particularly aware of how efficiently you manage your time.

Conduct periodic time-management audits and try the following tips:

- ✔ Keep a log of what you do during a typical week and make sure that you create a logical correlation between the time you spend on a task and its priority.

- ✔ Pay attention to time bandits — tasks or situations that consume blocks of time that may otherwise be put to productive use.

- ✔ Stay organized and keep your desk free of clutter.

And always be on the lookout for new and creative ways to do your job better and more efficiently.

Seek a Balance

However committed you may be to your work and your career, don't lose sight of your personal priorities. Pay attention, in particular, to your health and the quality of your relationships. When you're relaxing at home or socializing with friends, keep work considerations from interfering with your ability to unwind and enjoy yourself. If you're having trouble doing so, you may want to explore ways to create a better work/life balance.

Never Stop Learning

Education doesn't cease the day you receive your diploma; it needs to be ongoing. Consider what you learned in school as the foundation of a continued learning process that will extend throughout your life. Among the options to explore for further education are certificate programs, professional seminars, training classes offered by your company, online courses, and private coaches (for certain skills).

Become an avid reader. Try to set aside a small amount of time each day (even if it's 30 minutes or so) to learn something new about your field, the world around you, and yourself. And be on the lookout for ways to expand your technical and interpersonal skills. Remember that you are the most valuable asset in your career strategy. Invest in yourself.

Expand Your Circle of Contacts

Many business people today credit their success to the support and guidance they received from their professional contacts. You can enhance your networking efforts in a variety of ways, such as joining professional associations, volunteering with community organizations, or pursuing special projects in your company. (See Chapter 15.)

The key is to make these activities a priority and be willing to devote the time and effort to initiate and sustain mutually beneficial relationships. In addition, seek out mentors — people you can turn to as confidants and advisors. Mentoring relationships take many forms and can benefit your career development in a number of ways, from advice on workplace politics to introducing new networking contacts. You may be surprised by how helpful people are if you simply ask for their assistance.

Take Setbacks in Stride

Virtually every success story in business is punctuated with so-called failures or setbacks. But you need to keep in mind that what's ultimately important is not how often you failed, but how you responded. Successful people know how to turn the disappointments they've experienced into learning experiences that propel them to greater heights. Emulate their example.

Chapter 19

Ten Ways to Enhance Your Communication Skills

*Y*ou may be hard-pressed to find any job in today's workplace in which your ability to communicate doesn't significantly impact your career advancement. Regardless of your ultimate career goals and strategies, it is to your advantage to develop effective written and oral communication skills. The advice in this chapter covers key principles relating to writing and speaking. (Check out Chapter 14 for further details on mastering the art of communication.)

Get Back to Basics

If, for whatever reason, you haven't yet mastered the basics of grammar and usage, chances are you're not as confident in your overall communication skills as you would like. As a result, you may be reluctant to express your views in certain situations for fear that you'll (gulp!) embarrass yourself. Fortunately, this is one communication shortcoming — critical though it may be — that is easily remedied.

Take some time to review the basics. (No groaning, please.) The essentials of grammar and usage aren't rocket science; some fourth-graders get A's in it. If you invest no more than 10 to 15 minutes a day reading through any one of the dozens of books on grammar and usage, you can master everything you need to know about proper English in a month or so. And after you nail down the basics, you can concentrate on your message.

Focus on Your Desired Outcome

In most business situations (coffee breaks excluded), you don't typically write to or speak with people simply for the sake of passing time or hearing yourself talk. You usually have a specific objective: You're responding to a request, asking for help, trying to solve a problem, or seeking to gain approval for an initiative. Communication in business, in other words, is always a means to an end, never the end itself. And the key to effective business communication is being aware at all times of your desired outcome — what you want your memo, letter, report, or presentation to accomplish. So before you begin writing or speaking, clearly define your ultimate goals. This helps you decide what information to include, the tone to use, and, in some situations, the most appropriate phrasing. Without this strategic focus, you may never know whether your efforts are successful.

Become a Better Listener

Because listening appears to be an innate ability, some people have a hard time accepting the notion that listening is a skill. But the fact is, effective communicators are invariably good listeners — and for an obvious reason: If you're not tuned in to the people with whom you're communicating, you're unlikely to convey your message in a meaningful way for your audience. And, therefore, you're not likely to achieve your desired outcome.

There's no trick, as such, to effective listening. It's primarily a matter of disciplining yourself to focus on what the other person is saying, rather than allowing your mind to drift or formulate a response. This advice sounds simple enough on the surface. The problem, however, is that effective listening isn't a skill that most people come by naturally; you have to work at it. For example, when you're talking on the phone, resist the temptation to check your e-mail, straighten your desk, or skim the financial section of the newspaper. Instead, provide your full attention to the other person. If you can train yourself to focus during a phone conversation, you'll find it much easier to do so in face-to-face interactions. And you'll also find that your communication skills improve as a result.

Pay Attention to Your Body Language

Whenever you're communicating with anyone in person, the words you use represent only one factor in the impression you ultimately convey. Equally, if not more important, is your body language — your eyes, posture, gestures, and overall demeanor. Eye contact, of course, is particularly key. Not only is it impolite to talk to people without looking them in the eye, but you'll also miss noticing how your message is being perceived. Maintaining good eye contact helps you gauge whether people understand what you're telling them and whether they're reacting the way you hoped they would.

Pay attention to your posture and gestures, especially when making a formal presentation. Be sensitive to any mannerisms that may be distracting to the audience, such as shifting your weight back and forth or constantly brushing back your hair. The best way to evaluate your overall body language is to review a videotape of a presentation you give.

Be a Good Tour Guide

Being a good tour guide when you communicate means making sure you're not losing your audience by wandering off your topic, using words and terms they don't understand, or throwing information at them too quickly. Whether you're writing a memo or giving a presentation, be sure to let people know — early on — its purpose and why it's relevant to them. Make sure, too, you're not so consumed by your own thoughts and information that you fail to notice how your audience is receiving your information. Finally, keep your priorities in mind when you communicate.

Whenever you're talking to someone who is angry or otherwise upset, for example, your first priority should be to calm the person down before you start to explain your point. And keep in mind that most people have notoriously short attention spans. If what you're saying isn't directly relevant to them, you could very well lose them — without even being aware of it.

Set Up a Disciplined Writing Routine

Writing is a challenge for many otherwise intelligent and competent business professionals. But more often than not, the reason so many people dislike writing isn't a lack of talent or skill. It's simply that most people don't manage their writing tasks very efficiently. To write clearly and concisely, you need to be able to think clearly, which means, in turn, that you need to be able to concentrate for sustained periods of time. And most business environments aren't conducive to sustained concentration. So if you're going to handle your writing tasks more effectively at work, you need to strategically minimize distractions. When you have a writing task to complete, set aside a block of time in your schedule during which you'll focus exclusively on that task. If your normal workspace is too noisy or distracting, find a more quiet place — an empty conference room, for example.

Write in a Natural Voice

If you're like most people, you probably find it easier to convey your message in person or over the phone than in any written communication. Sometimes it's because writing obliges you to make certain decisions — spelling and punctuation, for example — that you don't have to worry about when you're conversing. There's also a good chance, though, that the difficulties you encounter may be related to some misconceptions about writing style. You may feel that if you don't use 50-carat words in your documents, nobody will take you seriously or consider you intelligent. Don't allow yourself to believe this myth. You can probably convey most of the ideas you write in ways that mirror the way you speak. Here's a good rule to follow: If you wouldn't feel comfortable using a particular word or phrase when talking to someone, think twice before putting it in writing.

Use Strong Visuals

Americans live in a visual age, so as much as possible, in both your writing and your presenting, use visual devices to enhance the clarity and impact of your message. If you're writing a report and you find yourself struggling to describe an array of complex statistical or financial information, think about conveying that data in a chart or table. And whenever you're making a presentation in front of a small group, take advantage of the visual effects you can create with standard presentation software applications.

Here are three points to keep in mind when you're using this type of software:

- Minimize the amount of information you use on a slide (use bulleted text to support — not explain — your points).
- Make sure the typeface is large enough to be seen by people in the back of the room.
- Avoid the temptation to enhance a visual with a mixture of type sizes and styles. Simplicity is best.

Keep a Best-Practices File

One of the best ways to improve your communication skills — writing, in particular — is to emulate the practices of successful communicators. Whenever you find yourself reading a report, memo, or any form of communication that impresses you, make a copy of it and maintain it as part of a best-practices file. But before you file it away, set aside some quiet time to read the document over — not just once but several times — underlining or highlighting those portions that work particularly well. Try to determine what the writer is doing in a particular section and think about how that same approach or technique may work in your own writing. You can enhance your communication skills by modeling the excellence of others.

Look for Opportunities to Develop Your Skills

As with any skill, the more you practice, the more confident and effective you'll be. This principle is particularly true for presentation skills. If, like most people, you're a little shy about speaking in front of a group, consider registering for presentation seminars or becoming a member of your local Toastmasters International organization. These groups offer opportunities to hone your speaking skills in a friendly environment where most people in the audience share your same fears. When you're more comfortable in front of these friendly groups, you'll be ready to try out your new skills in real-world situations.

Be sure to ease your way into the process. Start by becoming a little more vocal in staff meetings, where the audience is familiar. Try to present your ideas clearly and concisely without being a bundle of nerves in the presence of the others, and then expand your reach. Volunteer to make presentations before senior management. After each presentation, critique yourself. Ask yourself whether you were sufficiently prepared and whether you handled questions smoothly. Don't get discouraged if you didn't do as well as you would have liked. Analyze what you may have done better and focus on that aspect of your presentation the next time around.

Chapter 20

Dealing with Ten Common Career-Management Quandaries

Career management is more art than science, and you're undoubtedly going to run into a great many situations in which the choices you face are anything but simple. Here, in a question-and-answer format, are ten questions that deal with some of the most vexing issues and common quandaries in career management. The answers should give you insights into how you can deal with these issues as they relate to your particular situation.

Should You Quit?

I just started a new position four months ago, and although I'm fairly good at it, the nature of the job is extremely stressful. Should I quit after only four months of employment?

Before you do anything, you need to figure out why you're feeling stressed. Is it because it's a new job, which is typically a bit stressful? Are your responsibilities high-pressure by nature, involving split-second decisions or complex financial reporting? Has your supervisor set unrealistic goals and expectations for you? Or do you simply not enjoy what you're doing, making it that much more difficult to handle pressures and challenges?

Adapting to a new job always takes time. Try to organize yourself as much as possible and be sure to devote your attention to the most strategic, high-level tasks and responsibilities. You may need to work a little harder and pull some longer hours at the beginning to make it through the transition period, but your investment will pay off. Be sure to allow for periodic breaks throughout the day so that you can recharge and refocus on your work.

If your responsibilities are intrinsically stressful, know that over time your perspective on them will improve. Most people are concerned about their performance at the beginning of a job, striving to make a good impression. But when you're involved in projects that don't allow for mistakes, the stress can seem overwhelming. As you gain more experience with these assignments, you'll feel more confident in your abilities and know what to do when challenges arise.

If you've tried all these approaches and still find that things aren't improving or that you simply dislike your job, you may want to move on. But remember: You still need to do the best possible job you can in your current position. Whether you stay with your present company or seek employment elsewhere, your hard work and determination will be reflected in your resume and references.

Should You Follow Your Manager to Another Company?

My manager, who has been a mentor to me, recently left our company to join another organization, and he asked me if I wanted to come work for him there. Do I leave my job to follow him or stay with my present company, which has been very good to me?

The first thing you need to ask yourself is, how will this decision affect your career? Although it can be very tempting to change jobs and continue to work with a manager you know and like, take a step back and look at the big picture. His departure could actually be good for your career because you may be next in line for a promotion. Remember that your former boss can still be your mentor even if you continue to stay with your present employer. In fact, sometimes it's more helpful to have a mentor who is outside of your organization so that you can more freely discuss issues and receive objective feedback.

To help you evaluate your options, make a list of all the factors that are important to you in a job and career. Then find out as much as you can about the other organization and your potential role in it. After you research the situation, ask yourself the following questions: What opportunities are available at your current firm? What's available at the other company? Which organization is more closely aligned with your values, interests, and career goals? Are there issues such as commute time, compensation, or family-friendly benefits that may affect your personal life? Base your decision on the things that can contribute to advancing your career.

Should You Ask for a Raise?

I found out that someone who has just been hired by my company is being paid more than I am — even though we have similar responsibilities and qualifications. Should I tell my manager that I know this information? Should I ask for a raise?

If you found out about the discrepancy because you inadvertently saw a confidential form or document listing his or her salary, you need to keep that discovery to yourself. Most likely, you shouldn't have been privy to that information anyway. But if someone — either the new employee or a coworker — is broadcasting the news without discretion, yes, you need to let your boss know. Your manager should be told when someone is indiscreetly discussing sensitive issues, such as compensation. Don't gossip or retell the story with all the sordid details — just plainly present the information, explaining that you thought he or she should be aware of the situation.

Before you ask for a raise, thoroughly review your accomplishments, credentials, and skills and research your market value. Don't automatically assume that you're just as qualified as the new hire and, therefore, should be paid the same, if not more. He or she may have hands-on experience in a particular field that's important to your company or advanced technical skills that you're not aware of. The best idea is to evaluate your own experience, skill sets, and contributions without comparing yourself to the other person.

Build a business case for why you deserve a raise. If you think it may present a clearer picture, revise your resume to reflect your recent accomplishments — pretend you're reapplying for your job. Consult salary surveys and research compensation trends. Is the labor market so competitive in your specialty or industry that your skills and abilities are more highly valued? Document this and gather information to back up your assertion. When you meet with your manager, discuss your findings and ask to reevaluate your compensation level. (See Chapter 14 for more information on asking for a raise.)

How Can You Get a Coworker to Do More Work?

I'm on a team with a coworker from my department who's not following through on responsibilities. Because we're in the same group with access to the same resources, I often end up doing his work as well as my own. How do I get him to do his own work so that I can do mine?

While teamwork is important, remember that your job isn't to make sure a coworker does his work. However, if his failures affect your ability to do your own job, you need to take action to remedy the situation.

Your first step is to sit down with him and discuss what's going on. Explain that you're experiencing an influx of work and — without complaining or casting judgments on your coworker — note that you've received certain requests that relate more to his area of authority. Stick to the facts, outlining specific instances and how they impacted your productivity. Remember that it's not your place to criticize his work style, competency, or diligence; your goal is to seek a resolution. And be sure to listen to his side of the story: He may be experiencing personal challenges that are temporarily affecting his job performance.

However, if the situation doesn't improve, meet with your supervisor. Let your manager know that you've tried to resolve the problem with your coworker. Express your desire to help the team succeed and your willingness to pitch in as needed, but indicate your concern in fulfilling your own responsibilities. Your supervisor will appreciate your initiative in trying to handle the situation one-on-one.

How Do You Admit That You're in Over Your Head?

How do I admit to my manager — without making myself look foolish — that I'm out of my league on a particular assignment that I originally thought I could handle?

The bigger question here is not *how* but *when*. And the answer is, as soon as possible. Good managers encourage their employees to set stretch goals but also recognize that staff members may need additional support or resources to achieve these objectives. It's up to you, however, to communicate your concerns and needs. And the sooner you do, the better your supervisor can help you come up to speed or reassign the project, if necessary.

Analyze the situation and determine the source of your difficulty. Are you unfamiliar with a particular software program? Are you unclear about the ultimate goal of a project? Do you need additional access to senior-level executives and decision-makers to answer key questions? If your difficulties can be solved with a short-term fix, such as a one-day training session or meeting with top-line executives, try to arrange these yourself.

But if you're placed in a position of authority without the proper experience or training, consult your supervisor. Identify the aspect of the project that you don't feel comfortable with — perhaps fielding media calls or making budgeting decisions. Ask your manager if someone can serve as your mentor or partner on this assignment, someone whose skills and experience would complement your own.

How Do You Own Up to a Mistake?

I inadvertently made a mistake in a recent report, which is now being shared with another department for use in an extremely important project. Do I tell the other department about the problem or hope that someone else discovers the mistake without my saying anything?

Honesty is truly the best policy, but be sure to tell those who most need to know. Let your manager know that you recently discovered the mistake. Apologize for the error. Mention that the report will be referenced by another department for an important project and offer to contact the project manager to point out the discrepancy.

Although you try your best to avoid them, everyone makes mistakes at one time or another. The important thing is that you minimize the impact of the error. And to ensure that you don't make the same mistake twice, spend a few moments thinking about what may have caused you to overlook the problem in the first place. Don't agonize over it, but try to grow from your mistakes so that you can be better prepared to avoid them in the future.

How Do You Get Better Assignments?

I'm a consultant working on a fairly high-level assignment with a company. My point person at this firm recently resigned and, because I've been receiving projects from various other employees, the tasks are somewhat below my experience level and don't relate to the original project objectives. What should I do?

If you're consulting through a staffing firm, contact your account manager. He or she can work directly with the firm to reevaluate the current project requirements and the level of support needed.

However, if you're working independently, you need to handle the matter yourself. Request a meeting with your former contact's manager to discuss the assignment and your future role. Provide a project report that notes key objectives and documents your achievements so that he or she can quickly review the situation. Be sure to include any recent requests that may or may not match the original project goals. Then ask for clarification on the assignment going forward. Has the objective evolved? Is there a new point person with whom you can work?

In most cases, the manager will need some time to gather more information before providing specific direction. In the meantime, fulfill your assignment to the best of your ability. If you don't hear back from the individual within a reasonable amount of time, follow up. And if the response you receive clearly indicates that the project goals no longer match your experience and qualifications, let him or her know. Unless you're okay with the new terms, indicate your willingness to continue consulting for the firm only on assignments that more directly relate to your skills and abilities. If you can, offer to stay on board until they can find a suitable replacement. You'll increase your chances of being rehired for future projects.

What's the Best Way to Work with the Boss's Daughter?

My boss's daughter has been assigned as a staff member in my department — what should I do?

Treat this situation as though you've been magically presented with a new employee whose strengths and qualifications have yet to be discovered. Schedule a one-on-one meeting on the first day and interview her as you would a first-time candidate. The hiring decision may be already made, but you still need to find out how she can complement your existing staff. What special skills and experience does she have? Is she a match for any projects within your department? If not, you'll have to get a little creative. Can she conduct research for a particularly large project in the works or be mentored to gain more experience? Look for ways that she can contribute to your team and treat her like any other staff member. Provide a thorough overview, set clear goals, and define responsibilities.

If she falls short of performance standards, have a talk with her just as you would any under-performing employee. And if the situation doesn't improve, meet with your boss to discuss the situation. Outline your steps to bring the individual up to speed and note the areas in which she failed to meet expectations.

Ask for suggestions of other methods to explore. But above all, don't go to your boss bearing a grudge against your new employee. Be objective and professional in your presentation of the situation and let your boss know that you want to find a way to work things out. If no solution is offered and you're counseled to keep her on board regardless, develop innovative ways to include her in your team without creating unnecessary problems for your staff.

How Can You Get Credit for Your Work?

What can I do about a coworker who is constantly taking credit for my accomplishments?

While you may be tempted to denounce your coworker and immediately reclaim the recognition that's rightly yours, think this through strategically. The important issue is that your supervisor is aware of your achievements. Although the opinions of your colleagues may seem important, your manager's assessment is most likely the deciding factor in your performance evaluations, promotions, and raises. Try not to worry too much about what others may think (although sometimes that's easier said than done).

First, have a face-to-face talk with your coworker to discover the source of miscommunication. Avoid a confrontation, but be specific about those times you noticed that he or she took credit for your work. Try to work things out between the two of you. If the behavior continues, you need to set the record straight with your supervisor. Mention your attempts to resolve the situation and let your manager know of your role in an important project for which your coworker is claiming credit. Don't make accusations, just lay out the facts and remain objective.

Be sure to pick your battles. If a coworker is seeking credit for a relatively minor accomplishment, let it go. Don't get so caught up in the competition for credit that you overlook the importance of teamwork. Your ultimate goal is to work together productively with all of your colleagues and share in both responsibilities and recognition.

How Do You Manage Former Coworkers?

How do I effectively manage people who used to be my coworkers?

As long as you've enjoyed a good, collaborative relationship with your former coworkers, you don't necessarily need to be concerned about being their manager. Remember that your primary responsibility as a manager is not so much to supervise or exert your authority but to inspire superior performance. In other words, you need to provide your staff members with the support they need to do their jobs well. And recognize that collaboration is the key to effective management. Rely on their expertise when making key decisions and keep the lines of communication open.

But even in the best of situations, you may run into some animosity from former coworkers who either have difficulty adjusting to the new relationship or may resent your leadership role. If you find yourself in this predicament, don't overreact — especially at the beginning. Meet individually with any staff members who cause problems or don't fulfill their responsibilities. Deal with situations case by case and allow for an open discussion of the issues. Of course, if a problem persists, you need to take some action — otherwise, the performance and morale of the entire group could suffer. But plan for the best and be sure that you and your staff work together as a team.

Chapter 21

Ten Questions to Ponder Before Becoming Self-Employed

In This Chapter
▶ Considering your goals and values
▶ Creating a plan
▶ Making a smooth transition
▶ Tracking your success

*N*o decision has more implications for both your career progress and personal life than leaving a full-time job to become an entrepreneur, independent contractor, or consultant. So whatever you do, make sure that you take time to think about your goals, interests, and values before you make the move. (Chapter 16 has further details.) This chapter shares ten key questions to ask yourself as you consider self-employment.

What Are Your Goals?

The decision to go out on your own should always be fueled by a fervent desire to work for yourself and be the master of your career future — as opposed to an escape route from a job you no longer enjoy. If you're unhappy in your current job, don't assume that working for yourself will, in and of itself, eliminate your dissatisfaction. Instead, look within yourself and determine whether you truly have a desire to go out on your own. Explore the possibility that if certain things were different in your current situation — a different boss, a shorter commute, a different kind of company — you could start to enjoy your work more without flying solo. In the end, the key question you need to ask yourself is how important is it for you, professionally and personally, to be independent.

Do You Have the Mindset for Independence?

Whether you succeed as a self-employed professional depends on more than simply your expertise and skills. Your mindset is also key.

Here are a few important questions to ask yourself:

- ✔ Are you by nature a self-starter?
- ✔ Do you easily adapt to new situations?
- ✔ Can you function efficiently when you're responsible for making all the decisions that affect both your business and career?

To gain insight into these questions, look back on your work experience and determine how effectively you've worked on independent projects in the past. For additional perspective, talk to people who know you well. See if their perceptions are consistent with your judgments. Above all, keep in mind that the issue here is whether your personality and work habits are well suited to the demands of self-employment.

What Path Will You Take?

Self-employment can take any number of forms, and you need to determine as early as possible what kind of a career path you want to take. Are you looking to develop and grow your own business or do you see yourself as a consultant or independent contractor? And assuming you're going to be a consultant or contractor, do you see yourself specializing in one area or working in a variety of fields? Each option has its own set of requirements, mindset, and approach. If you're eager to become an entrepreneur, for example, you need to map out a detailed growth plan that spells out how you'll fund and operate the company. If your goal is to become an independent contractor, think about whether you intend to market yourself or work with a staffing firm that will handle that aspect for you.

Is There a Market?

Before you go out on your own, spend as much time as possible researching the market for the service or product you'll be offering. Talk to as many people as you can who may be potential customers. Make sure your fee structure meets two fundamental criteria:

- ✔ It's competitive.
- ✔ You can make a living without working 100 hours per week.

Also make sure that the market isn't already saturated with people or companies offering the same product or service. If you're up against tough competition, be prepared to identify your unique selling proposition — something you're able to offer that differentiates you from your competitors.

How Much Will It Cost?

When estimating how much money you'll need to launch your practice or business, always overbudget. And don't be surprised if you still don't have enough. Be sure to account for additional expenses such as health benefits, life insurance, or increased auto use.

 If you've never been in business before (and haven't yet established credit), set aside extra money for establishing phone service or signing a lease for office space. Talk to people who've started businesses or practices similar to yours and find out what they've spent on start-up costs.

How Will It Affect Your Personal Life?

If you have a family, it's essential that everyone understands and supports your decision to go out on your own. Be honest. Don't try to sell them on the idea of how great things will be after you're professionally independent. Make sure they realize the pressures you may face and ask for their support. Also, let your friends know that you may be fairly busy for the first six months of operation. While you'll need to take time to relax and recharge occasionally, establishing your business will be your number-one priority for a while.

What Equipment and Staff Will You Need?

The basics for most self-employment ventures couldn't be more simple: a workspace, computer, fax machine, phone, and a filing cabinet. Anything else you may need will vary according to your practice or business and the goals you've set. Try to keep your initial overhead as low as possible and hold back on any major purchases until you've established a steady cash flow. Investigate opportunities to rent equipment or hire staff support on a project basis. Even if you're a consultant, you may find it helpful to occasionally employ an accountant to help you with your budget and billing.

How Will You Generate Business?

Assuming you don't already have groups of people already begging to pay for your product or service, how will you acquire clients and customers? Will you rely on your professional network for recommendations? Will you send e-mail or brochures and follow up with phone calls? Will you work with an outside agency to promote your talents? You have many options, some of which will be more appropriate to your market than others. Of course, some situations require more money while others depend on outside expertise. Carefully consider how much time and effort you need to devote to building a clientele.

How Do You Make the Transition?

For most people making the transition from regular employment to independence, the key issue is money. You want to make the move to self-employment without subjecting yourself or your family to severe financial pressure. The best way to meet this challenge, if possible, is to accumulate your own nest egg (enough money to spend on basic business and living expenses for six months). This allows you to focus your initial efforts on acquiring new business and building a reputation without being preoccupied by personal bills. If you don't already have this money in reserve, find out if you can work part-time with your current employer while you launch your new business. Of course, you always have the option of borrowing money from a bank or looking for outside investors. But before you do, sit down with your accountant or financial advisor to work out the most prudent strategy.

How Will You Track Your Progress?

You may not want to think about this when you're first getting started, but you can't ignore the possibility that you may decide, within a few months, that self-employment isn't for you. The fact that you're addressing this possibility doesn't mean that you're being negative — just realistic. Even if you're going into an entirely different field, maintain contact with former colleagues and try to keep pace with events in the industry you're leaving behind. Do your best, too, to part with your current employer on a positive note. Try to leave the door at least partly open.

Chapter 22

Ten Useful Books for Your Career-Management Library

• •

In This Chapter

▶ Figuring out your future

▶ Developing better habits

▶ Understanding the way management works

• •

ere's a brief summary of ten helpful books that relate to career management. Some of these resources are targeted to helping you find your next dream job, while others offer in-depth advice for becoming more effective in the job you already have.

Do What You Are: Discover the Perfect Career for You through the Secrets of Personality Type

by Paul D. Tieger and Barbara Barron-Tieger (Little Brown & Co., 1995)

This is one of a growing number of self-assessment books designed to help you identify your personality type or temperament as it relates to your career. The authors' system of categorizing personality types is similar to the groupings used by the Myers-Briggs Type Indicator (MBTI). But in contrast to many self-assessment books, the authors link this psychological data to potential jobs, offering suggestions for career choices and success. Of course, it takes more than an understanding of your personality type to find the perfect career, but this book is a useful tool for getting to know yourself a little better.

What Color Is Your Parachute? 2000: A Practical Manual for Job-Hunters & Career-Changers

by Richard Nelson Bolles (Ten Speed Press, 2000)

The periodic revisions of this classic best-selling career management book are probably not significant enough to warrant the purchase of a new copy every year. But if you've never read this book and you're looking for some fundamental career guidance, this is certainly a solid place to start.

Be warned, though: The strength of Bolles' book may also be one of its weaknesses. When Bolles originally wrote this book, he did so for fellow theologians and had no idea that the book would become a commercial success. As a result, the insights here are somewhat complex.

Discovering Your Career in Business

by Timothy Butler and James Waldroop (Perseus Press, 1997)

This is not so much a book as it is a series of navigation guides for today's workplace. The down-to-earth tone is reminiscent of *What Color Is Your Parachute,* but the advice is more career-specific. The authors intended this book to serve as the next best thing to a career-counseling session. And to the extent that any book can substitute for a one-on-one meeting with an experienced career counselor, it succeeds. The key feature is the Business Career Interest Inventory (included in disk format), with exercises to help you clarify your objectives. And case histories abound, lending both life and color to the explanations.

The 7 Habits of Highly Effective People: Powerful Lessons in Personal Change

by Steven R. Covey (Fireside, 1990)

Steven R. Covey wasn't the first person to advocate a values- and ethics-oriented approach to career success, but few business books in recent memory have had as much impact on so many people. Unlike a multitude of other how-to books, Covey's approach to achieving more balance in life can't be boiled down to a glib list of do's and don'ts. His observations on developing a personal vision, managing time, cooperation, and listening are meant to be pondered, not simply read. And the insights you gain are well worth the effort.

Working with Emotional Intelligence

by Daniel Goleman (Bantam, 1998)

Working with Emotional Intelligence is the sequel to Goleman's first book, *Emotional Intelligence,* which helped to popularize the notion that career success in today's workplace is determined by your emotional smarts — how you handle yourself and other people. Goleman defines emotional intelligence in terms of five general attributes:

- Self-awareness (how you manage yourself)
- Self-regulation (how you manage your internal states, impulses, and resources)
- Motivation (the emotional tendencies that guide you to certain goals)
- Empathy (how aware you are of other people's feelings and perspectives)
- Social skills (how adept you are at inducing desirable responses in others)

Rather than telling you what you should be doing, Goleman cites research and examples that demonstrate the validity of his concepts. And because he's such a skilled journalist — working as a reporter for *The New York Times* for 12 years — the book is easy to read.

The Fifth Discipline: The Art and Practice of the Learning Organization

by Peter Senge (Doubleday/Currency, 1990)

Although this book doesn't focus on career management per se, it offers an excellent introduction to the business concept known as *systems thinking.* As such, the information in this book will keep you in good stead if you find yourself working for the growing number of organizations that have begun to adopt some of Senge's key principles, such as continuous learning. What's particularly noteworthy about this book is that most of his observations about organizations can also be applied to an individual's approach to career management.

Career Intelligence: The 12 Rules for Work and Life Success

by Barbara Moses, Ph.D. (Berrett-Koehler Inc. 1998)

This is a solid, no-nonsense, career-guidance handbook that offers a basic game plan for becoming a career activist. Moses defines career activists as people who succeed by defining themselves apart from their organization, who widen their career choices through self-knowledge, and who practice the art of self-promotion. She writes in an upbeat, encouraging style and offers concrete advice on how to adapt and thrive in an uncertain world.

First, Break All the Rules: What the World's Greatest Managers Do Differently

by Marcus Buckingham and Curt Coffman (Simon & Schuster, 1999)

This book summarizes the work of two Gallup Organization consultants who analyzed the findings of a survey that involved more than 80,000 interviews with successful business managers. Easy-to-read and well-organized, this book offers concise, best-practice advice on most of the basic challenges you face in business, such as hiring the right people, assessing and managing employee performance, and maximizing productivity. Interview subjects include front-line supervisors; *Fortune* 500 managers; and key players in small, entrepreneurial companies. The book provides useful career lessons for managers at every level.

Management Challenges of the 21st Century

by Peter F. Drucker (HarperBusiness, New York, 1999)

Peter Drucker is universally regarded as the single most influential management thinker of this century, and his goal in this highly readable and insightful book — his first since 1993 — is twofold:

> ✔ To provide a clear picture of the monumental changes taking place in the world economy
>
> ✔ To offer guidance to business people who want to adapt to the new realities of the marketplace.

He's successful on both counts. Although this book isn't a career-management guide, as such, Drucker's views and insights are compelling and well worth incorporating into your career planning strategies. Drucker writes in a direct and incisive style and deals head-on with what he considers the ultimate challenge facing career-minded professionals in the 21st century: balancing work and life issues. If you've never read any of Peter Drucker's books before, this is a good place to start. If you're already familiar with Drucker's work, this book will be a good addition to your collection.

Project 50

by Tom Peters (Knopf, New York, 1999)

Not everyone relates comfortably to Tom Peters's gung-ho, punchy, and often UPPERCASE writing style. But Peters, unlike many business writers, has always felt compelled to do more than inform his readers — he wants to inspire them, as well. The underlying theme of this book is this: You can't expect to be highly successful in today's economy unless you're excited and enthusiastic about your work, and you have more power than you may think to generate this excitement and enthusiasm on your own. Peters urges you (when you have a choice) to be as selective as you can about the projects you undertake. But he also offers plenty of advice on how to put the WOW into projects that you didn't volunteer for and that you may not be terribly excited about. All things considered, this book may be more applicable to managers who want to inspire superior performance in their employees than it is for individuals. But it's an easy, enjoyable read, and it's laced throughout with little gems of advice.

Chapter 23

Ten Career-Related Web Sites

*T*he Internet, as you undoubtedly know, is an incredibly bountiful source of career-related resources and information. In fact, you may have trouble deciding which of the literally thousands of career-related sites to visit. Staffing firms such as Robert Half International (www.rhii.com) have job listings as well as valuable career content. This chapter highlights a few other sites to help get you started.

American Management Association (AMA)

The AMA (www.amanet.org) is the world's largest management-development organization, with branches and affiliate offices located throughout the world. Its Web site represents the most convenient way to get the latest information about all the various AMA seminars and online courses. After you identify a subject area that interests you, you can get a detailed description of the course, along with other particulars, and quickly view a list of where and when the course is going to be offered. You can also enroll online. In addition, the Web site allows access to AMA's research reports, which cover a broad range of business issues and provides the results of the AMA's worldwide surveys.

America Online

Nearly all the major Internet portals are solid sources of career management information. What's notable about America Online (AOL), located at www.aol.com, is the way this information is arranged. If you're a member, you have access to numerous categories, such as job search, career resources, executive information, profiles of professions, and workplace hints and tools. But even if you don't subscribe to AOL's services, you can take advantage of job search tools and services, chats, and career advice, including an online, condensed version of the Myers Briggs Type Indicator test.

Bureau of Labor Statistics

This Web site (www.bls.gov), which was created and is run by the federal government's Bureau of Labor Statistics, offers two great resources. The first is a downloadable version of the *Occupational Outlook Handbook,* the biennial publication that tells you nearly everything you could possibly want to know about a wide range of occupations. You can read about job specifics, such as responsibilities on the job, working conditions, training and education needed, earnings, and expected job prospects.

The other valuable resource is a companion publication called *Career Guide to Industries,* which offers similar insight into industries. The latest edition of this handbook profiles 42 industries, accounting for more than seven out of every ten wage and salary jobs in 1998.

Both books are excellent information sources for people who are either just beginning their professional careers and aren't sure what they want to do, or people who are considering a midcareer change. Other resources on the site include workplace studies and detailed analyses of the U.S. economy.

CareerPath.com

CareerPath.com (www.careerpath.com) is primarily a job-hunting resource that draws much of its content from daily newspaper classifieds throughout the United States, but it also offers one of the Internet's most extensive and varied collections of career-management advice. The Manage Your Career section of the site, which is updated weekly, consists of eight different departments, including a resource provided by Brainbench that lets you test yourself in more than 50 different technical proficiencies. In addition, the company research feature allows you to base your search on location or occupational specialty. And if you're itching to find out what it's like to be a floor trader, stunt coordinator, or child-care center director (to name just a few of specialties profiled), you can find out by accessing the site's Pro-files section.

Hoover's Online: The Business Network

Hoover's Online (www.hoovers.com) is known primarily for the quality, accuracy, and readability of its company and industry directories. The opening menu gives you a choice of categories of information and services. After you're inside Career Development, a job search tool links you to nearly 40 different Internet job sites, including those at hotjobs.com and BestJobsUSA.com.

You can also tap the resources of the Training Center, which links you directly to one of the Internet's largest directory of online courses for business professionals. Take advantage of the resources on this site as both a nonmember (free) or a member ($14.95 per month). The primary difference is the depth of detail you get when you start to research individual companies. All in all, this is a handsomely designed and easy-to-navigate Web site that can make you more career savvy.

Monster.com

As its name implies, Monster.com (www.monster.com) likes to do things in a big way. Apart from the fact that it lists hundreds of thousands of jobs, the distinguishing feature here is the all-encompassing array of career-management services and advice. The Career Center section of the Web site offers, among other things, help with resumes, cover letters, company research, networking, and advice targeted to individuals whose careers are in transition. You can also get involved in daily chats with career-management advisors. The site is well organized and easy to navigate.

Small Business Administration

This U.S. government-run Web site (www.sba.gov) offers anything and everything you could possibly want to know about starting and running your own business. The best place to start your tour of this site is the online library where you can download the most common business forms and government regulations, and access more than 2,500 shareware software packages covering virtually every aspect of business — from accounting to database management to inventory control. The site also provides you with detailed information on applying for an SBA loan and taking advantage of the SBA resources in your own community.

Smart Planet

SmartPlanet (www.smartplanet.com) describes itself as a "personal and professional learning community where people pursue goals and lifelong interests through online courses and human interaction." Logging on to this site gives you access to a voluminous number of courses (most self-study, but some instructor-led) along with an opportunity to share your responses with other members. SmartPlanet provides several ways to participate. If you want the free membership, you have access to complimentary information in a wide range of topic areas. You can also purchase fee-based courses à la carte. Membership options range in price, depending on the number of courses in which you're interested.

WetFeet.com

Wetfeet.com (www.wetfeet.com) is arguably the best place to go on the Internet to look for information about specific firms. Company information comes in three different forms. The first category consists of more than 1,000 one-page company overviews that describe what each company does, where it's located, what sorts of jobs it offers, and where to go on the Net to contact the company about getting a job. If you want more organizational insight, you can read interviews with senior managers of nearly 75 major companies. And if you want even more information — and are willing to pay for it — you can order or download WetFeet's Insider Guides, which provide a firsthand look at what it's really like to work in a particular company and what these firms seek in new employees.

Other features that make this Web site worthwhile are real-people profiles (first-person descriptions of what people in various jobs actually do day to day), a complimentary newsletter that keeps you up to date on what's happening in specific industries of career niches, and an extensive network of career-management information links.

WomenCONNECT.com

WomenCONNECT.com (www.womenconnect.com) gears its information and resources to professional women and women business owners. It divides its informational offerings into several different channels, with each channel broken down into a multitude of smaller categories. After you navigate to the Careers channel, you can access how-to articles covering more than two dozen different aspects of career management. You can explore topics such as office politics, mentoring, work/family balance, salary negotiations, business travel, networking, and mentoring.

Index

● *S* ●

Notes

Notes

Notes

Notes

WWW.DUMMIES.COM

Discover Dummies Online!

The Dummies Web Site is your fun and friendly online resource for the latest information about *For Dummies®* books and your favorite topics. The Web site is the place to communicate with us, exchange ideas with other *For Dummies* readers, chat with authors, and have fun!

Ten Fun and Useful Things You Can Do at www.dummies.com

1. Win free *For Dummies* books and more!
2. Register your book and be entered in a prize drawing.
3. Meet your favorite authors through the IDG Books Worldwide Author Chat Series.
4. Exchange helpful information with other *For Dummies* readers.
5. Discover other great *For Dummies* books you must have!
6. Purchase Dummieswear® exclusively from our Web site.
7. Buy *For Dummies* books online.
8. Talk to us. Make comments, ask questions, get answers!
9. Download free software.
10. Find additional useful resources from authors.

Link directly to these ten fun and useful things at **http://www.dummies.com/10useful**

For other technology titles from IDG Books Worldwide, go to
www.idgbooks.com

Not on the Web yet? It's easy to get started with *Dummies 101®: The Internet For Windows® 98* or *The Internet For Dummies®* at local retailers everywhere.

Find other *For Dummies* books on these topics:
Business • Career • Databases • Food & Beverage • Games • Gardening • Graphics • Hardware
Health & Fitness • Internet and the World Wide Web • Networking • Office Suites
Operating Systems • Personal Finance • Pets • Programming • Recreation • Sports
Spreadsheets • Teacher Resources • Test Prep • Word Processing

IDG BOOKS WORLDWIDE BOOK REGISTRATION

Register This Book and Win!

We want to hear from you!

Visit **http://my2cents.dummies.com** to register this book and tell us how you liked it!

✔ Get entered in our monthly prize giveaway.

✔ Give us feedback about this book — tell us what you like best, what you like least, or maybe what you'd like to ask the author and us to change!

✔ Let us know any other *For Dummies*® topics that interest you.

Your feedback helps us determine what books to publish, tells us what coverage to add as we revise our books, and lets us know whether we're meeting your needs as a *For Dummies* reader. You're our most valuable resource, and what you have to say is important to us!

Not on the Web yet? It's easy to get started with *Dummies 101*®: *The Internet For Windows*® *98* or *The Internet For Dummies*® at local retailers everywhere.

Or let us know what you think by sending us a letter at the following address:

For Dummies Book Registration
Dummies Press
10475 Crosspoint Blvd.
Indianapolis, IN 46256

™

BESTSELLING
BOOK SERIES